A Russian Factory Enters the Market Economy

This book charts the experiences of a textile enterprise in Russia during the 1990s, analysing post-Soviet management and managerial practices in order to illuminate the content, nature and direction of industrial restructuring in the Russian privatised sector during the years of economic transition. Based on extensive factory-level fieldwork, it focuses upon changes in ownership, management and labour organisation, unveiling the complex texture of social, communal and gender relations in the workplace over an extended period of time, including through crisis and bankruptcy, acquisition by new capitalist owners and attempted restructuring. It argues, contrary to dominant Western managerial theories which blame the failure of transition on the irrationality of Russian managerial strategies, that the rationale for the continued reliance on Soviet era managerial practices lay in the peculiar form of social relations in the workplace which were characteristic of the Soviet system. It engages with key issues, often neglected in the literature, such as social domination, power and conflict, that capture the problematic and open-ended character of social and economic transformation in post-Soviet production. It demonstrates that far from a simple transition to a market economy, the post-Soviet transition has reproduced most of the features of the old Soviet system, including its patterns of labour relations.

Claudio Morrison is a British Academy Postdoctoral Fellow in the Department of Sociology, at the University of Warwick, where he completed his PhD. His research interests include labour relations, organisational change and enterprise management. He has published articles on these issues in leading journals, including *Europe-Asia Studies*, *Post-Communist Economies* and *Research in Economic Anthropology*.

Routledge contemporary Russia and Eastern Europe series

Liberal Nationalism in Central Europe
Stefan Auer

Civil-Military Relations in Russia and Eastern Europe
David J. Betz

The Extreme Nationalist Threat in Russia
The growing influence of Western rightist ideas
Thomas Parland

Economic Development in Tatarstan
Global markets and a Russian region
Leo McCann

Adapting to Russia's New Labour Market
Gender and employment strategy
Edited by Sarah Ashwin

Building Democracy and Civil Society East of the Elbe
Essays in honour of Edmund Mokrzycki
Edited by Sven Eliaeson

The Telengits of Southern Siberia
Landscape, religion and knowledge in motion
Agnieszka Halemba

The Development of Capitalism in Russia
Simon Clarke

Russian Television Today
Primetime drama and comedy
David MacFadyen

The Rebuilding of Greater Russia
Putin's foreign policy towards the CIS countries
Bertil Nygren

A Russian Factory Enters the Market Economy
Claudio Morrison

A Russian Factory Enters the Market Economy

Claudio Morrison

LONDON AND NEW YORK

First published 2008
by Routledge
2 Park Square, Milton Park, Abingdon, Oxon OX14 4RN

Simultaneously published in the USA and Canada
by Routledge
711 Third Avenue Avenue, New York, NY 10017

Routledge is an imprint of the Taylor & Francis Group, an informa business

First issued in paperback 2012

Typeset in Times New Roman

British Library Cataloguing in Publication Data
A catalogue record for this book is available from the British Library

Library of Congress Cataloging in Publication Data
Morrison, Claudio, 1970-
   A Russian factory enters the market economy / Claudio Morrison.
   p. cm. -- (Routledge contemporary Russia and Eastern Europe series ; 11)
   Includes bibliographical references and index.
   1. Industrial management--Russia (Federation)--Case studies. 2. Industrial relations--Russia
   (Federation)--Case studies. 3. Free enterprise--Russia (Federation)--Case studies. I. Title.
   HD70.R8M67 2007
   338.60947--dc22
   2007018013

ISBN13: 978-0-415-41878-2 (hbk)
ISBN13: 978-0-415-54211-1 (pbk)

Contents

List of tables

Preface

Since the fall of the Soviet Union the endless Russian transition has mostly been presented as a swinging succession of alleged triumphs and equally dramatic failures. The liberal right has celebrated the installation of 'the market' and 'democracy' but has critically reviewed its mismanagement, culminating in the 1998 crash, while looking with increasing concern at the emergence of an assertive regime thereafter. On the left, the weakness of civil society, the apparently infinite patience of the workers and the population at large in the face of abusive authorities have painted a bleak picture in which continuity outgrows change, lending transition the character of an involution or degeneration rather than of reform or development.

As a result the debate has revolved, with few exceptions, around the polarised opposition of change and continuity, the former often identified with the inevitable accession to higher degrees of Westernisation, the latter more or less reduced to conservative 'resistance to change' or institutional inertia. The surprising lack of insight of such an approach, apart from the self-evident weakness of its predictive force, is represented by the spasmodic search for heroes, the champions of reform, and villains, the invariable conservatives or communist hardliners, regularly followed by delusions.

There is a host of reasons for that. It is a common argument among critics of transition that the thin line between prediction and prescription has been abundantly breached by those who claimed to explain transition while being very busy producing it, and in fact profiting from it, too. This argument cannot be generalised, though. In reality, the reading of the transformation in the former socialist bloc has much to do with the social and ideological climate in the capitalist West. While there is clearly a link between the crises and developments in the two systems, the dominant ideologies prevailing in capitalist countries once again have acted as a screen preventing a deeper investigation and a more balanced interpretation of recent events in the East.

The last two decades of the past century have seen the capitalist enterprise emerging as a dominant institution and its inspiring principals and operative practices becoming the reference model in organisational change. Managerialist ideologies have not only imposed neo-liberal recipes as a universal panacea but by the same token they have disguised the real nature of the enterprise as a

1

social institution shaped by power and riddled with conflicts and contradictions and ignored its crucial role in forging social relations in the society at large. Russia in turn has been one of the experimental grounds for neo-liberal ideologues and practitioners. Social sciences have not fared much better, uncovering and denouncing the social disasters produced by transition, its unfounded claims of change, yet relying on a soft pluralist approach that blurred rather than clarified the picture, with the popular reference to complexity, variability and plurality of discourses and cases. My growing discomfort with the way social transformation in Russia has been depicted has been one of the motivational and theoretical drives behind this work.

The research leading to this publication has been informed by an initial interest in power and command in the 'worker's state' and the desire to take a 'closer look' at factory life, trying to uncover its specificities *vis-à-vis* those of capitalist countries. In practice it has resulted in almost a decade spent in and around a company town, its textile mill, a privatised state company, and the industrial region, Ivanovo, containing them. The enterprise is viewed and analysed as a social, economic and technological organisation whose dynamics are shaped by social relations in production as well as by its reflexive interaction with other external institutions, political and well as economic.

My fieldwork has detailed the daily struggle of workers and managers to bring in the plan, the practices and reflections that the need for co-operation generates and reproduces as well as the different responses to mounting outside pressures. The focus has been on worker–manager relations and the labour process, on the one side, and the functions and articulation of powers within the managerial structure, on the other. Analysis has been aimed at identifying the forms in which work is organised, consent achieved and conflict defused. Research has revealed the extent to which managerial control achieved it by tolerating individual forms of insubordination and workers' awareness of the limited room for overt action in the face of feared reprisal and actual coercion.

The appearance of outside capitalist owners and the progress in organisational and technological restructuring have opened a new ground for looking into the managerial black box to identify constraints and contradictions in the manager–owner relationship. Without anticipating any of the specific substantive or theoretical conclusions of this work, I would like to underline that social relations and their outcomes have not been merely deduced from a general and abstract capital–labour relation. The division of labour, specific to the Soviet system and textile industry in particular has, mostly implicitly, been recognised as a driving force and key terrain for the contours and dynamics of these relations. Management has received full recognition in terms of both its agency and the constraints to it.

Viewing the capitalist form of management as just a particular form of management, and a particular system of social domination, allows us to cast a new light on the struggle between owners, managers and workers over the direction and outcome of transition in Russia – neither as the inevitable choice between marching towards progress and democracy or falling back into some variation of an authoritarian past, nor as a mere bargaining between stakeholders, but as a social struggle informed by historically specific ideological and material conditions. In taking this approach, we hope to put an end, among others, to the idea of an alleged 'resistance to change' of managers and workers, not only Russian, where instead a legitimate articulation of interests takes place, in fact in very unequal circumstances. Not so paradoxically, this study has uncovered much more change than have orthodox views.

This book would have not been possible without the continuous support of a large number of people and institutions. First and foremost, I would like to thank Simon Clarke, for without his continuous guidance and research assistance, and serene tolerance towards my many idiosyncrasies, this research might not have taken place. His work has been a source of constant inspiration in researching and interpreting social transformation in post-Soviet Russia. The Sociology Department at Warwick has provided me for many years now with a morally supportive and intellectually challenging environment. In particular, I would like to mention Tony Elger and Andrew Parker for their accurate comments on portions of the manuscript. Donald Filtzer has also contributed to this work in many ways with constructive and supportive criticism as external examiner and later as an enthusiastic referee. I owe him the understanding of crucial aspects of the Soviet social edifice.

On the Russian side, participation in the Russian project seminars with colleagues from the Institute for Comparative Labour Relations Research (ISITO) gave me an invaluable opportunity to share ideas and broaden my perspective. The welcoming warmth and rigorous work of such an unconventional community of scholars has provided an invaluable moral and intellectual contribution to my work.

This research is dedicated to the women and men of the Ivanovo textile region to whom I owe the understanding of the Russian world of work. I am especially indebted to the workers and managers of the company town where I conducted most of my research for welcoming me in their town and workplace and sharing with me their knowledge of the 'tools of the trade'. For allowing me into their lives, providing material support and continuous intellectual engagement, I should thank my gatekeepers, and now long-term friends, Nikolaj, Anatolij and Vitya. I am particularly grateful to Nadya and her daughter Tanya for teaching me what it is like to be a woman in Russia.

The ESRC and the University of Warwick, respectively with fees-only funding and a University Graduate Award, have provided financial support for my PhD research years. Funding by the British Academy in the form of a Postdoctoral Fellowship and a Small Research Grant allowed me to extend my fieldwork and work on the final manuscript. The Sociology Department, again with the crucial contribution of Simon Clarke, provided me with office space, technical resources and departmental research funds as well as with continued support in funding application bids. Reasserting the great contribution of colleagues and friends in substantially improving this work, I would like to state that its flaws and limitations are solely my responsibility.

Last, but not least, I am grateful for the love and support of my family and my partner, Olga.

1   Introduction

This study analyses post-Soviet management and managerial informal practices in order to understand the content, nature and direction of industrial restructuring in the Russian privatised sector. The main purpose of the research on which this volume is based has been to evaluate the rationality of the continued use of Soviet management practices in post-Soviet manufacturing enterprises a decade after the 'transition to a market economy' and in the face of claims that Russian managerial strategies are irrational (cf. Hendley, 1998).

This work developed out of a comprehensive case-study at a textile firm in the Ivanovo region and is based on extensive fieldwork (Bell and Newby, 1977; Parker, 1998). The research has focused on changes in ownership, management and labour organisation, and problems of reform experienced by the researched enterprise after privatisation, and continued well after the emergence of outside ownership. Fieldwork research was initially carried out between 2000 and 2003 at a large integrated cotton mill located in a company town. The research, intended for my PhD, has generated a detailed case-study illustrating managerial structures and strategies, incentive systems and informal bargaining as well as shop-floor dynamics and workers' forms of resistance. A second stage of the research has taken place from 2005 to 2007 as part of an ongoing postdoctoral fellowship. Following substantial changes in industry structures, involving the original case-study enterprise, the research focus has extended to holding companies and the relationship between the new owners and their corporate structures on the one side and managers on the other.

Theoretically, the research relies on a 'comparative and historical analysis' of Russian socio-economic transformation (Clarke, 2004, pp. 406–9), providing a full appreciation of Soviet social legacies. The current phase is understood as the movement from one set of contradictions, inherent in the Soviet mode of production, to another, characteristic of capitalism, rather than as a transition from the irrationality of the command economy to the rationality of the market.

Conversely, the transformation of the Russian economy in the 1990s has been presented by mainstream economists as a relatively simple transition from one system, the planned economy, to another, the capitalist market economy (cf. Sachs, 1993; Aslund, 1995; Blasi et al., 1997). Enterprise behaviour has mostly been examined to establish the degree to which it conformed to, or departed from, a pre-established Western capitalist model (see Ericson, 1998). Institutional legacies have been largely neglected or regarded as remnants of the past order. However, comparative and historical studies make it clear that differences between managerial practices and structures are determined by the environment in which they developed (Clark, R., 1979; Sapelli, 1990; Lazonick, 1991; Dore, 1973). Accordingly, changes in Russian management practices under transition can be better-considered as pragmatic adaptations to a changing environment (Grabher and Stark, 1998; Clarke, 1993; Di Leo, 1993). I maintain that the continuity in managerial practices can only be understood in relation to the peculiar nature of the past Soviet social order.

Drawing on the studies of Marxist authors such as Bob Arnot (1988), Simon Clarke (1993), Rita Di Leo (1973), Donald Filtzer (1986) and Hillel Ticktin (1992), I contend that the Soviet system was founded, as a form of domination, on the limited control over production by the ruling elite. These scholars found that, while Soviet workers were never allowed to decide what (and how much) to produce, they retained considerable autonomy in the workplace. In practice, they were left alone to sort out the vagaries of Soviet planning. It is to this condition that the concept of 'negative control' is applied.[1] The ruling elite is torn between deciding to assume direct control over production through managers and the need to preserve the social foundations of its power. A central argument of this study is that the existence in the former Soviet Union of '(negative) workers' control over production' continues to hinder the full transition to capitalism (Arnot, 1988; Clarke, 1993; Di Leo, 1973; Filtzer, 1986; Ticktin, 1992).

Within this framework, managerial strategies are analysed as informed and constrained by 'meaning and power' (Clark, E., 2004, pp. 610–12) rather than by an 'ahistorical, functionalist and technicist' rationality (Willmott, 1997, p. 1330). In particular, critical agency theory is relied upon in problematising the ownership–management relationship (Armstrong, 1991), now taking centre stage with the growth of outside ownership. In the context of Western capitalist enterprises this approach highlights not only the social dimension of trust, and therefore the inherently contradictory character of this relationship, but also the crucial role of managers in designing new control strategies (Armstrong, 1984, 1989, 1991). If the peculiarity of the Soviet economic system rests in the limited control by the elites over the production process, this, in turn, translates into a conflictual and distrustful relationship between the enterprise managers and overarching bodies. Managerial practices represent a direct consequence of this relationship. The problem rests in that they are a powerful tool to discipline workers and elicit their efforts to achieve planned physical output but represent

[1] Interpretations differ about whether to consider the increasing control by workers as the result of worker resistance. Filtzer (1986) supports this view, while Clarke (1993) argues that it results from the retreat of management. Di Leo (1973) interprets managerial retreat as a result of a political compromise between management and workers. All of these scholars share the view that for the capitalist transition to succeed a change of social relations in production has to take place with the risk of igniting class conflict.

a formidable barrier to efficiency-oriented innovation (Arnot, 1988; Filtzer, 1992). The emergence of outside ownership in privatised enterprises introduces a new dimension to this set of contradictions as the new owners are torn between the need to rely on old-style management and managers to keep businesses afloat and the increasingly pressing need to subject production to the generation of profits. This requires new owners to entrust managers with the tasks of restructuring, something they are both reluctant to commit to – and quite rightfully so, while Soviet management and its vagaries remain the norm, poisoning their relations.

It has been observed that the break-up of the command economy did not at first yield the sudden appearance of capitalist practices and institutions but a 'marketisation' led by speculative elements transferring resources from production to circulation (Burowoy, 2001). This has left the Soviet enterprise and its mode of operation more or less intact. The direct involvement of financial industrial groups in production, with a wave of acquisitions following the 1998 crisis, has provided grounds for interpreting post-Soviet transformation in Russia in terms of 'capitalist development' as well as the possibility of identifying its current limitations and challenges (Clarke, 2004, 2007).

The textile industry suffered severely from market 'capture' by trade intermediaries which in turn have become the major players in setting up holding companies. The longitudinal study of these companies allows for a detailed and illuminating account of these historical processes. The textile industry also represents an extreme case in terms of adaptation to the post-Soviet market with the worst recovery trend and a low level of restructuring (Hanzl and Havlik, 2003). Much of the blame has been placed on managers and inside ownership (Kouznetsov, 2004a, 2004b; Kreuger, 2004, pp. 82–103). For mainstream commentators, managerial behaviour remains an unsolved 'puzzle' (Kreuger, 2004, p. 102). Relying on qualitative data from a wide range of sources, this research challenges the conventional view of an ailing industry crippled by conservative managers, failing to grasp market opportunities.

One of the main arguments of this work is that red directors – i.e. Soviet-era managers taking advantage of the so-called *nomenklatura* privatisation – took over enterprises, but market conditions and public policies forced them to design survival strategies in continuity with the Soviet past. The takeover by traders after 1998 has not substantially modified the situation as they face the same structural problems. Old Soviet managerial practices are the only condition for them to work at the present technological level without endangering the authority of managers and owners. Yet Soviet practices aimed at managing the labour process also reproduce the traditional evils of low productivity, waste and indiscipline. The labour-cost advantage derived from this system, relying heavily on the extensive exploitation of cheap female labour, has so far deprived owners of any immediate incentive to break this vicious circle.

Russian textiles have made a swift recovery after the 1998 crisis, retaining a significant share of manufacturing employment. The growing competition from

China and other emerging economies, though, as well as the imminent accession to the WTO by Russia, has yet again raised doubts about the survival capabilities of the industry and renewed pressures for state subsidies from local political and economic circles (Preobrazhenskaya, 2005). It has also raised the pressure on managers and owners to seek a mutually satisfactory solution to the continued problems posed by managers' and workers' resistance to 'modernisation', which threatens to foil investments aimed at reaching the level of product quality and cost efficiency imposed by competition.

Background to the research

My interest in Soviet management and post-Soviet transformation developed out of my previous academic background and subsequent working experience. I read for my first degree from 1988 to 1993 in the Faculty of Political Sciences of the Naples Institute of Oriental Studies (IUO), specialising in Economies of the Socialist Countries and in Economic History. My final thesis on 'Scientific Management at the Fiat Motor Company and in Russian Factories' combined my disciplinary interests.

The window of opportunity for the case-study research occurred later in 1997, after I joined a training programme sponsored by the Italian foreign trade ministry, which included a paid internship in private firms. Via personal connections I successfully sought a firm operating in the former socialist countries. This way, I managed to spend five months working for a consulting firm that was involved in an enterprise-restructuring project in the Ivanovo textile region of European Russian.

I spent most of this time on placement in one Russian enterprise, living and working closely with Russian managers. This gave me an invaluable insight into the problems and opportunities facing the textile sector in Russia and particularly the range of problems facing Russian managers, as well as into the communication gap between Russian managers and Western European consultants. Formal and informal contacts with a variety of agents involved in the restructuring process made me aware of a set of unresolved questions to which Western business tools and their theoretical underpinnings had no solutions, hence prompting my commitment to resume my academic studies in search of an answer.

For this reason I registered at Warwick, working within the Russian Research Programme directed by Simon Clarke. After two years at Warwick spent reading literature and working, among other things, on an EC report on the textile industry and employment, having been accepted for a PhD and obtained full funding for it, I set to return to my Russian site to conduct my fieldwork research.

Sources and methodology

This book is based on a wide range of primary and secondary sources. The research is based on case studies relying on the use of a range of qualitative and ethnographic methods. The bulk of the fieldwork for the PhD case-study' research was conducted in the 2000–2 period. During the first stage, I worked for four months in the factory. I lived in the town and visited production managers in the shops daily. My later fieldwork consisted of several visits, which together amounted to more than one year. During these visits, I spent most of my time in managers' offices so as to become a 'piece of furniture' in the shops (Parker, 1998). The research was conducted by means of in-depth, semi-structured interviews with workers, managers and industrial consultants. It included participant observation, and the examination of published and unpublished data about the enterprise and the town. Individuals were surveyed with the help of a questionnaire followed by interviews. Production managers were surveyed in this manner, including one chief of production, five shop chiefs, and altogether 20 foremen and leading technicians. Approximately 100 workers were collectively and individually interviewed by me.

The research is part of an ongoing project for my British Academy Fellowship (2004–7) at the Sociology department in the University of Warwick. I visited the company town twice in 2005 while staying in Ivanovo in 2006, carrying out interviews with local informants and key experts. The collection of case-study materials on holding companies has taken the form of: semi-structured interviews with managers and workers at the two largest holdings in the region and interviews with local experts, including journalists, political consultants and three high-ranking trade union officials; collection of published and unpublished local materials on corporate affairs; participant observation in enterprise settings and informal managerial meetings.

Given the considerable suspicions towards formal interviews, my existing position as a factory insider was important for the successful completion of my fieldwork. Fieldwork was made possible by unrestricted access to the research settings. This does not mean it was easy to achieve. Becoming an insider has been an essential part of my activity on the site, which implied cultivating friendship, participating in local life within and outside the factory, becoming as much as possible 'one of them'. The role of gatekeepers was essential in keeping continued access against the threat posed by continuous changes in management and their attitude towards an awkward foreign student. In turn they became my key informants on most issues I researched and the mediators with other sources in this and other factories.

I tried to offset the risk of biased findings derived from relying on key informants by triangulation, direct observation, consulting local documents, and comparisons with other cases researched in the department. Direct observation was an essential part of my work. Barriers to communication often made it impossible to achieve information by interviewees in a neutral context, irrespective of their willingness to co-operate. My constant presence in managers' offices allowed me to reformulate research questions on the basis of common observable experience.

> Then I became alert to the 'Russian ways' and undertook to explore them. In so doing I tried to combine the participants' view of the subject and their self-understanding, on the one hand, and the descriptive discourse which would make it clear for an outsider on the other. (Ledeneva, 1998, p. 4)

In general, my personal experience as an insider, with the risks it entails for objectivity, has been constantly taken into account by me, rather than concealed, in the data analysis (Bell and Newby, 1977).

The analysis of case-study material and parallel theoretical elaboration has developed in an iterative fashion (see Clark, E., 2004, p. 609). Constant contact with informants has allowed further accumulation and refinement of case material. Participation in the activities of the Russian Research Projects run by Professor Clarke,[1] including expert group discussions at their seminars,[2] has been paramount in establishing the generalisability of findings and to elaborate a theoretical framework. Case-study research has proved invaluable in a corporate environment characterised by extensive red tape, widespread concealment of corporate activities, translating into unreliability of official sources; so has the acquaintance with a number of key respondents working at different levels and with different functions in the industry and the region.

The need for a critical approach to, and a scrupulous interpretation of, even the most basic data and trends applies generally to an economy in which manipulation of statistics, concealment of revenues and responsibilities are common and widespread. This should be particularly the case with the textile industry in the Ivanovo region. While the poor performance of the industry and its structural distortions are difficult to deny, the role of different agents and factors, and therefore its future perspectives, are open to debate.

For example, one of the critical indicators of the industry's sharp decline is the loss-making status of most enterprises (which varied around 60 per cent to 40 per cent in the last decade). At the same time, if the abnormal prices of cotton, energy and components which squeezed profits out of enterprise coffers and into the hands of traders (including payoffs for political intermediaries and factory directors) are taken into consideration, the picture might be somewhat different. So the trends in bankruptcies and employment should not be taken at face value considering that 'supply schemes' (*davalcheskaya skema*) were used for artificially bankrupting enterprises, while more recently inefficient establishments and 'dead souls' are kept on payrolls as part of artificial loss-creation schemes. In such cases the application of traditional assumptions about managerial behaviour and industry dynamics derived from mainstream

[1] 'Trade unions in post-socialist society: overcoming the state socialist legacy?', INTAS 03-51-6318; 'Management structures, employment relations and class formation in Russia', ESRC R000 23 9631.

[2] 3–10 April 2005, Sharm-el-Sheikh; 3–10 December 2005, Sharm-el-Sheikh; 3–5 April 2006, Moscow.

economics and managerial literature can lead to overlooking these phenomena. Failing to take them into account has produced serious misunderstandings about the state of the industry and the type of policies fostering its betterment (Hanzl and Havlik, 2003).

2 The struggle for access: exposing the centrality of personal relationships

All the efforts of an artist should be directed towards two forces: man and nature. On one side physical weakness, nervousness, a precocious sexual maturity, a passionate thirst for life and truth, insufficient knowledge alongside the wide trajectory of thought; on the other the immense flatland, the rigorous climate, the grey, sullen people, with its cold history of pain, the misgovernment po-tatarskyi, the bureaucracy, poverty, ignorance, the misery of capital cities, et cetera. Russian life crushes a man until nothing of him is left not even a stain of damp, it grinds him as it could do a one thousand pood rock

Anton Chekhov in Ryszard Kapuscinski, *Imperium*, 1994

The objective of this section is to chart the difficulty of access; to uncover the obstacles, practical, relational and cultural, which surrounded my life and research work at the enterprise and its surrounding community for more than three years, and the ways I tried to overcome them. One conviction stands at the centre of this experience: the centrality of personal relationships. Writing on doing research I feel that, other than narrative and methodological concerns, this endeavour is constrained and inspired by the need to walk back through the memory of the whole of these years' struggle to recover the essential passages of becoming an insider.

In this chapter I shall explain how becoming an insider was an intrinsic necessity of my research work and inextricably tied to the command of my topic: managerial practices and behaviour. The question, which I shall try to answer here, is why I was led to think and operate in this direction and how I actually managed to achieve such a level of intimacy with this working and social environment, with those areas of it that I found useful or simply accessible to my intervention. The questions at the forefront, both chronologically and methodologically, relate to the experience of access beginning in 1997: the need to escape isolation and rejection, breaking out of my association with consultants; the gradual integration into the social structure of the company town; last but not least, the development of strong ties with a gatekeeping figure.

Out of neutrality, taking the Russian side

What is the kind of approach one should take towards one's investigative environments? Should one assume it possible to carry out fieldwork in a sort of uncompromising self-sufficiency or rather incorporate into one's working style and interpretative framework those inputs emerging from respondents and their community? If so, where is the point at which compromise endangers our pledge to 'neutrality'? All these questions, the answers to which could make up a good deal of our research strategy, were not actually on my mind once I was dispatched to the field to support the research work of our consultants.

My position at the enterprise was immediately defined by the conflictual nature of the relationship between 'Western' consultants and Russian managers. Aside from substantive issues, it was primarily their working style that put them at odds with the Russians.

First, their psychological attitude was generally formal, assertive and inflexible. Even those who demonstrated sympathy for Russian reasons could not manage to modify the Western research approach and interpretative framework.

Second, consultants were subject to a high turnover, justified by the need to provide specific expertise. Furthermore, they travelled back and forth, keeping their working time with Russians within a tight schedule. They could communicate only through an interpreter and did not venture outside the luxury hotel where they were confined in their spare time. It is noticeable that Russians openly lamented the limits that this working style imposed on the development of personal relationships, which they clearly deemed a precondition for any further co-operation.

Third, they limited their contacts to senior management, which, with the exception of the director and his cronies, was a series of dull figures unprepared, as I learned, to provide any useful insight into enterprise issues.

The outcome not surprisingly was that on both sides a sense of discomfort reigned, which bred suspicion and non-co-operation, and hopelessness at understanding each other. No less important, this was followed by continuous questioning on the side of the Russians concerning our right to conduct research and use enterprise resources.

My reaction was to open debate with the Russians on all those matters that were objects of controversy. I also made myself available to accept their guidance and advice in conducting my work, eventually identifying room for co-operation between my personal research agenda and their need to cope with Italians.

Practically, I accommodated myself modestly in the town and moved to conduct my research with production managers in the shops on a permanent basis. This in turn allowed me to open serious discussions with them about the analytical tools we normally used for data collection, meeting their interest and consideration for my willingness to take into account their opinion. The outcome was very positive: I was not only granted the right to conduct research on an individual basis, overruling previous decisions to evict me from the city, but I was also invited to accompany their delegation abroad. This, when neither my skills nor my status alone could justify these decisions, says something of the premium paid by Russians for trust and friendship.

My moves, far from being a strategic or ideological option, were at first dictated by the immediate need to secure my presence in the research settings but were also motivated by sympathy and a desire to understand the reasons on the other side. Taking sides was limited neither to a manifestation of sympathy nor to a mere surrender to others' expectations. Breaking out of a supposedly neutral professionalism, which was in fact seen by respondents as a constant discrimination, was a precondition to gaining their trust and accessing the research field.

The role of gatekeepers: gaining access

A preliminary and fundamental task for a researcher on fieldwork is to secure continued and safe access to investigative settings. In the case of a Russian industrial enterprise the role of gatekeepers is played necessarily by the director or anyone able to influence his decisions. Through the process described above I became acquainted with key managers who were determinant in deciding my fate on this ground. In particular, I established a trustful and long-standing relationship with a young shop chief whose help was paramount in securing my position at the enterprise and supporting the practical and intellectual challenges my fieldwork entailed. Here I try to unveil the determinant role of personal relationship in deciding, and delimiting, access.

Kolya was first presented to me by the consultants as a young, intelligent and ambitious shop chief who worked as a contact man for any practical and formal concerns at the enterprise. Not surprisingly for a Soviet enterprise, a man from production was selected to act as reference point rather than a PR person, as he had the appropriate knowledge, the language skills and the interest to interact with foreign specialists. More importantly for the matter discussed here, he was a protégé of the then director and a good friend of the chief engineer.

As mentioned in the previous section, the director's reservations about the presence of consultants at the enterprise were strong enough when I arrived, and relationships deteriorated markedly over time. His irritation reached a climax when he openly refused to send a car to fetch one of our specialists after he had been deployed to a far-flung factory. I was the next 'victim'.

After a twelve-hour journey from Moscow, I presented myself at the factory gates where, to my bewilderment, I was told that the director wanted me to leave and a car was waiting to take me back to the regional capital. The most curious aspect of this decision was that he implicitly extended his authority outside the factory premises. In fact, as a feudal chief or police authority, he was practically expelling me from the city radius. As I had familiarity with the militiamen at the gates, they allowed me to contact Kolya who, in turn, arranged to conduct a negotiation. The meeting itself was a piece of theatre of Soviet times: my friend asked me to assume a humble posture, keep silent and assent to any remark on their side. In the presence of the director he explained that I was going to conduct research independently, severing connections with the consultants, putting myself at their disposal for any further need. Consent was achieved.

For the rest of the time my co-operation with the enterprise, in practice the mutual exchange of ideas and favours with Kolya and less often with the CE, further contributed to consolidate my position.

In the following years friendship and support, including invitations, were confirmed. Yet when PhD fieldwork proper was to be initiated in the autumn of 2000 the situation changed abruptly. New owners were taking over the administration, changing names at the top and jumbling established networks. Let's look at how previous connections operated in the new context and the attitude of outside ownership.

A new director, with whom I was told I had to renegotiate my right to access and work at the factory, was sitting now in the command room. The fact was repeated twice as the situation was constantly evolving, under bankruptcy proceedings, between the end of 2000 and early months of 2001. My friend once again volunteered to open the gate but this time he muttered that there was no guarantee of success. The new director was quite suspicious because of my attachment to the old management but primarily for the intrinsic weakness of his position in between two combatants, insiders and outsiders. I had to complement the efforts of managers by introducing myself as a researcher from a 'prestigious' academic institution. The accent in any case was on long-term ties with the enterprise, where I was universally taken as a trusted collaborator. I also had to present formal statements and a work plan, promising to report regularly on my activity. It was clear, though, that what we were seeking was merely his tolerance. In fact, once the goal was achieved he did not bother inquiring as to my dealings.

The split within managerial ranks, under greater external pressure to subordinate, further complicated the situation. The relationship between Kolya and the chief engineer deteriorated, weakening my position. The chief engineer at one point remarked 'You do not need credentials; we know you very well', but later he admitted his hopelessness with the new authority. Again we were able to sort it out, but only because of the cooling of insiders–outsiders infighting combined with the *fait accompli* of my continued presence. The entanglements produced by takeovers, quite frequent in the area, were replicated in another enterprise where we were seeking access. Here, despite the usual presentation, presents and internal lobbying, our efforts were nullified by direct orders from above.

These events call for some comments. First, in traditional enterprises there is no middleman, secretary or PR dealing with non-business visitors. (But new ones did not differ: all my interviews for a trade report in Moscow with new entrepreneurs were held with the director.) One has to go through the internal hierarchy, moving right to the top.

Second, it is clear that a direct appeal to the top management (*Vyschee Rukovodstvo*) implies their handling the matter personally. What does a personal relationship mean in this context? The dynamics reported above suggest: the idea of absolute discretion, in spite of any reciprocal recognition of respective functions and deployment of a set of procedures; therefore, the strictly individual character of the relationship with authorities, depending on their political agenda, authority, at worst caprice or personal interest (presents are always welcome up-front!); the centrality, to the contrary, of status and connections.

Third, when anyone from the former Soviet Union (FSU) heard my tale, they would almost automatically remind me that 'in Russia you start to build the house from the roof (*krysha*)' or 'you don't start anything there without protection'. Still, this point has to be handled carefully: long-term acquaintance does not always produce trust, and the conflictual, and ever changing, political and economic status of an enterprise weighs heavily on this point. The difference can be made by agreement with gatekeepers rooted in the personal and social experience at the factory, which creates a lasting commonality of interests.

Integrating into the social texture of the enterprise

The initial biographical experience of a researcher in an alien and unfamiliar context, as a tiny provincial town of Russia can appear at first glance, is dominated by loneliness and fear of rejection, and by a natural tendency to seek acceptance.

Building connections is obviously functional to qualitative research, providing opportunities to find respondents and collect information informally. Here I would like to stress that this process took place as a response to the primary need to overcome insecurity and feel socially and morally in accord with the researched community.

The questions were how and where to socialise with people and possibly open ground to find reliable respondents. As I have noted, access was not formally bound to specific guidelines, nor did it offer some hint or support concerning whom I should work with and how.

My contacts with those I could first get in touch with, from militiamen to canteen workers, revealed how easy it was to get about in the factory and make friends with people. The impetus was offered by my desire to prove my adaptability, living in a poor area, showing up regularly in the factory, taking on their eating, and especially drinking, customs. Discussions were no less important, as one can imagine the curiosity of people who had hardly ever seen foreigners. Here empathy played a major role in securing confidence.

On the other side, office (non-production) managers, who were in turn my main target, demonstrated themselves, even when superficially amicable, less open to any sort of complicity.

The climate was altogether different in production. My friend Kolya, every time I travelled there, felt it natural that I would stay with him in his office; alternatively he selected among other shop chiefs a 'quiet' and 'reliable' place where I could stay. Though I tended at first to accept with reservations, I had gradually to admit that it was both a pleasant and a useful solution. These offices, adjacent to production shops, were constantly stormed by personnel of every sort. Workers, clerks and other managers popped in or congregated to complain, for talks over personal or work matters, or simply for a chat. It seemed that people were quite free to move around, this obviously more in the case of managers and technicians than mere (female) workers.

Kolya was of the view that nowhere else could I find support and that an approach from outside was senseless: 'People have their talks and chats at the factory; they cannot dedicate their spare time to you,' he used to say. Not only was social life flourishing in these managerial corners, but also social life outside the factory was organised along the same lines. To my surprise, parties were often organised on a brigade or shop level; and even partners, whichever their sex, would hardly participate. Outside managerial circles, both male and female workers were equally committed to sticking to their comrades both inside and outside the factory. I therefore spent more and more time there, becoming almost 'a piece of furniture' in managerial offices.

Though people of every status and profession visited the offices, and my friends had acquaintances also in the central offices, I established a closer relationship with their colleagues in production. It was among these managers that I tended to look for help and support, not only to find respondents or information, but also to satisfy some basic needs like transport, accommodation, food etc. . . . Since my availability of resources was, as one would expect, much larger than the majority could afford, this was a controversial point in any relationship. I had the perception that this large divide would rather keep people at bay. To the contrary, with these managers exchange of favours would tend to offset this material and psychological gap, turning my knowledge and financial resources into an asset to spend in a relationship. Eventually I became accustomed to the idea that asking a friend was always the first option, and a recommendation could do better than a formal impersonal request.

While my inquiry into managerial structures was registering the malfunctioning of formal command lines and horizontal co-operation, creating abysses between employees and offices, my experience was telling me about personal relations based on friendship and mutuality, a network of connections and obligations, which I gradually joined.

Kolya and his friends more than once made reference to their group as a 'Mafia' or *komanda*, as opposed to other groups within the enterprise, and to the fact that I was now 'one of us'.

My gradual integration into Kolya's *komanda* reverberated in the rest of the labour collective. In my country, in Italy, a traditional form of asking a stranger about his identity, his name, is the question 'To whom do you belong?' I realised that during casual encounters with people from outside our circle, to relieve the awkwardness of mutual unfamiliarity, continuous references were made on both sides to my friends and whereabouts in production. Ideally, they represented a response to such a question. My status and the corresponding prerogatives were being defined by the set of relationships I was able to maintain.

Negotiating identities, establishing communication: nationality, class and gender in the field

As we saw, settling down in the research settings was about finding contacts and exploiting connections resulting in the construction of a network. The next logical step was to put it to use; employing a now popular analogy, it might be said that the first stage resembled the physical connection of hardware while the subsequent phase concerned the establishing of communication, which notably requires reciprocal identification via a common protocol. The analogy ends when, as one would easily recognise, human relations are considered with all their richness and variety. The implication, as I came to discover, is that identities have to be negotiated, and their content and boundaries can be constantly redefined through dialogue and communal experience, yet they have definite limits and their tolerance is subject to variation and reversal.

In reality, as hinted earlier in my account, identity politics was a crucial ingredient in gaining access to the researched community from the very beginning. As emerges from my initial experience, it was the immediate identification of local views and practices, corroborated by manifest sympathy for their claims and acceptance of their lifestyle, sustained by familiarity with Soviet traditions and command of the Russian language, that lent me the status of insider. Yet engagement and proximity bring forward the problems of being an outsider, growing in depth and scope as social events yield more ground for engagement in conversations.[1] Continuous engagements in such negotiations can enhance knowledge and acquaintance with the researched community as much as sharpening awareness of one's own identity.

Being a Westerner and a man, having connections with managers and a certain social status, have all proved significant in influencing my relationship

---

[1] It is important to observe how simple actions contributed to overcome them. What I ate, where I could afford to shop, where I lived and what I wore, and so forth, as well as the speechless manners which regulated the encounter with others were often more significant in deciding the possibility and the terms of such occurrences than any formal introduction.

with respondents either by determining their reaction or by generating a certain bias on my side. They represented potential barriers to communication that the dynamic interaction between those two processes helped to overcome.

A foreigner: empathy and the discovery of cultural differences

This small town is located in a historically marginal area lacking proximity to either thriving urban centres or main traffic routes, resulting in very little relation with outsiders, even from within Russia. The town was ethnically homogeneous to the point that one of the 'girls' in the finishing brigade born in Ukraine was normally referred to as 'the Ukrainian'. Except for accounts from migrants and television programmes, there was little engagement with changes in the country. This meant that outsiders might be greeted at first with suspicion but were generally not yet perceived as an immediate threat; for some I became an invaluable source for satisfying their curiosity about the outside world.

Among top managers suspicion was inevitably related to the secretive atmosphere concerning enterprise matters inherited from the Cold War. The chief engineer reminded me that until the early 1990s the KGB had objected to the presence of foreigners at the enterprise and watched them closely, most likely because of a once-strategic military installation located in the immediate vicinity. He also warned that, the chaotic state of law and order notwithstanding, they had retained most of their powers, only now they would focus on economic matters – something of a foresight in 1997. Thereafter my closest acquaintances, providing me with allegedly sensitive information, nicknamed me the 'angliskij spion', the English spy.

The potentials of empathy became evident when I became acquainted with the inner circle of cadre workers linked to my gatekeeper. Particularly touching memories are those of a meeting with a 'veteran' worker – something of a rarity owing to the sudden decline in life expectancy among Russian males. The chief of his shop thought quite correctly that he would make us happy by arranging such a meeting. Later we celebrated the event at his house, where he enthusiastically announced me to his wife as a trophy, the first foreigner making their acquaintance. He confessed that he had never had a chance to see one but for Germans, only in that case, he remarked, they were normally dead by the time he approached them. Such encounters might yield little in terms of actual data but produced a poignant sense of bonding with the respondents and the set of values and beliefs that informed their life.

A different and rather baffling realisation came instead on occasions when people would fail to accept my origins, i.e. Westerner and Italian, on the grounds that I did not look like one. Here a specific understanding of nationality was at work, used in the USSR to classify the peoples of the Union, which basically was another name for race or ethnic group. In practice, I was identified with what Russians normally refer to as 'litso yuzhnoj natsional'nosti' (a southern face), normally applied to people from the Caucasus, often with a derogatory meaning.[1] The virulent increase in racism in the last two years in Russia is for everybody to see. While there is certainly a line of continuity between this and the more naïve and mild form of xenophobia I first encountered in the early 2000s, in my case it never turned to abuse – at least, in dealing with the local population.

My nationality, i.e. Italian, was the one point I insisted on for acceptance, which proved in most cases to be positively welcomed. In the first place, nationality, one's association with the history and culture of a supposedly homogeneous nation-state community, was part of Soviet official policy and was an important identity marker – at least, among educated adults. Italy, as I discovered, called for numerous and disparate associations such as: the country which built Togliattigrad and the popular 'zhiguli' cars, had the largest partisan movement and communist party in the West; the country of neorealist cinema and (much more dubious) melodic music; more recently becoming more obviously attractive as a holiday destination and quality consumer goods manufacturer. Overall, despite disliking association with such commonsensical stereotypes, I felt that there was something to gain from it if it helped locals feel at ease, projecting a more familiar and less threatening imagery than one of a Western consultant or researcher. At the same time, I felt almost instinctively the need constantly to challenge them to avoid respondents and myself finding comfort in a pre-emptive narrative which prevented a real engagement with one's own experience of reality.

It was much more difficult to convey such an idea of national, and in fact social or political, specificities to acquaintances among youth of urban extraction who saw the West as a homogenous whole, as exemplified by the media representation of the USA. In these cases, appreciation of its technological and cultural marvels was coupled with criticism founded on the idea of a Western world dominated by calculative rationality opposed to the ingenuousness and deep spirituality of the Russian soul.

Class in the field: just a poor student?

My main concern when I began to work at the factory was to distance myself from the commonsensical imagery of the Westerner, rich businessman and invariably predatory male of some sort which prevailed in the country at that time, not without reason. Indicatively, as word first spread of an Italian settling in town with some working connections to the factory, rumours began to circulate that I was a rich man ready to buy the enterprise. Such a perception

---

[1] Once my landlady's fifteen-year-old daughter mentioned that she had heard her school teacher saying that HIV was spreading in the country because of African students; an argument then broke out with her mother about the racist nature of these unsubstantiated claims. Unfortunately, this was not the only occasion on which I had to fend off similar beliefs concerning, let us say, the role of Jews in the economic crisis or the natural inclination of 'gypsies' to crime and so forth. In some cases, my unusual, for an Italian, surname prompted the question whether I myself had Jewish origins.

was certainly influenced by the fact that, for a short period, I had been granted the privileges usually reserved to top-ranking officials; this included accommodation in a two-storey dacha, meals specially prepared by the director's chef, and a black Volga with a driver.

It was a cultural shock to many to learn that shortly afterwards I had moved to a block of post-war flats housing mostly impoverished pensioners and drunkards. Except for my gatekeeper and best friend, the idea of a bohemian student lifestyle, which made such living conditions both bearable and exciting, was beyond their understanding. Yet such extravagance modified my perceived status, from Western specialist to 'poor student', making it more acceptable for acquaintances to frequent me.

This was only partly true, though: it would be an act of naïve romanticism to hide the fact of being a privileged individual possessing substantially higher economic and cultural capital. Downplaying my status was welcomed by most managers and their acquaintances, but on occasions my social status was put under scrutiny, providing me with a stark reminder that: after all, such a close-knit community of co-workers was socially stratified, and subordinates – not only workers but cadres, too – had a strong awareness of it; the only way to fit into it was carefully to regulate my 'generosity' so as to avoid embarrassment to others or compromise my position.[1] The overall idea, quite simply, was that I should recognise existing hierarchies while at the same time gratifying friends. Keeping the balance between the two determined my reputation and defined the social and personal limits to interaction with different groups of respondents as well as the overall level of acceptance in the community.

One would not expect Russian factory workers to discuss class issues – at least, not in academic terms – yet for those who began to spend time with me and grew sufficiently confident the question arose as to who I actually was in social terms just as it did in terms of ethnic identity.

Boris Anatolievich is a man with a liking for erudition as well as being a distinguished mechanical engineer. It will not come as a surprise, then, if he sought to establish whether I was truly an intellectual. What he had in mind was the pre-revolutionary understanding of the word's meaning, of a clearly literary ascendance, but none the less bearing a strong class characterisation. Practically, this is how he put it: a member of the intelligentsia would be someone whose family has not been involved in productive work, which I understood roughly as manual work or business, for at least three generations. Boris might be fascinated by having such a kind of individual for companionship as I suspect there would be few in the town really keen to waste time on empty intellectual speculations as we often did.

The shop chief Vitya provided an altogether different experience. For him there were no doubts that I was a *burzhuj*, a bourgeois, as he used to mock me.

---

[1] So Kolya would see that I gave the appropriate presents to factory bosses or anyone else who was helpful, but would not like to be seen himself taking anything from me. With my second-best informant, a cadre worker and shop chief, the point would be rather to resist his pressures to exceed in liberalities.

The best friend and long-term ally of my gatekeeper Kolya, Vitya used to be a senior foreman, promoted to lead an entire shop when Kolya moved up to top management in the early 2000s. Highly appreciated for his technical skills, his ability to deal with workers at 'getting things done' and his loyalty, he represented the ideal candidate for Kolya's team. Yet he has never become a manager, never felt he was one in any case, retaining the attitude, habits and working style of the Soviet cadre worker. He relates to me the way he is used to with his 'masters': like someone who has no practical skills and needs to be shown around, provided for and bargained with for something in return. Recently, asking me for a substantial present, he supported his request in these terms: 'I'm your only real friend; I am the one who makes things happen; they [the managers, CM] only talk'.

For all the 'Vityas' here at the factory – and very much elsewhere, I suspect – the world is clearly divided between those who literally make and remake the world with their bare hands and those above simply sitting back and talking people round. I suspect that my association with their superior and my status as intellectual represented a clear barrier, which translated into a form of suspicion. It is most remarkable, then, that my determination to associate myself with them in their everyday life and take their concerns seriously yielded on some occasions a suspension of their judgement and the possibility of a more open dialogue.

The gender of research, or 'A man is a man and a woman is a woman'

The division of labour and the resulting social status and spending power might separate men in clearly demarcated hierarchies, but there is a terrain where they can confidently put social hatred and suspicion aside, giving way to an otherwise unimaginable intimacy, the common experience of manhood. It is a well-known story that Russian society is imbued with a strong patriarchal culture; whose common manifestation, and symbolic celebration, consists in the display of an exploitative approach in most aspects of gender relations. Here the supposed cultural and social divide between the working class and educated managers, apparently present in many Western European countries, is much less pronounced.[1]

To become an insider means expecting pressure by male and female acquaintances alike at showing compliance with such behaviour, aimed at proving one's 'real man' status. On the other side, a foreigner faces constant public scrutiny concerning the morality of his behaviour. Such a challenge translated for me into a number of risks and dilemmas.

On one side stood the need to create a trustful and friendly relationship as well as the strong sympathy I often felt for people who led a difficult life and

[1] Here we refer to the adherence to principles of gender equality widely accepted, at least formally, in Western Europe and the Anglo-Saxon world. This is not to imply in any way that patriarchy has been dealt with in any substantial way in such countries, as widely proved by the persistence of a gendered pay gap, systematic discrimination and job segregation, and the continued existence of sexual harassment.

showed sincere support for my work. On the other stood my personal inclination to assert my own views, not betraying the pledge to sincerity and, more importantly, the determination to avoid abusive actions towards anyone. At the level of discourse, this was only one of the many issues I might argue about with my respondents, putting me in the difficult position of compromising over sensitive issues such as politics, religion and gender equality. I had to accept that ideas such as peace, democracy and gender equality might be kept in disregard and reference to it taken as provocative towards one's national and cultural identity. In particular, as for gender equality, I found that some women, too, while lamenting their subordinate condition to man and complaining of their abusive attitude, might find a different male approach to male–female relationships difficult to understand.

On practical grounds I faced a twofold challange: to avoid association and practical involvement in sexist behaviour without entirely losing the favour of my male associates, and to overcome the suspicion of female respondents and helpers. As for the relationship with the latter, the fact of being a foreigner generally alarmed them regarding my possible conduct and intentions, and a more trustful and relaxed relationship could not be established before I turned out to be 'harmless'. This should be understood as part of a context in which women are held as 'free currency' (Bowers, 1996) and sexual harassment is frequent.[1]

The dominant view of gender relations is well summarised by the statement that 'above all, a man is a man and a woman is a woman'. To clarify such an essentialist, yet obscure in its abstraction, proposition, it might be helpful to give an account of the circumstances in which it emerged.

It was one afternoon in Vitya's office when the phone rang and the imminent visit of the newly appointed designer was announced: she was coming down from the main offices to discuss the use of new fabric patterns. This was a long-overdue event in the painfully slow adjustment of production to market requirements, and I was only too eager to witness such a meeting. Vitya, though, had other plans in his mind; he summarily asked me to vacate the premises, something that never happened even when he had a serious argument with the chief engineer. So what was it all about? He smiled and, to clarify his intentions, he pulled out a new bottle of vodka from his cabinet. The hint was sufficient to suggest what he had in mind. An argument followed as to the appropriateness of his behaviour. It should be pointed out that Vitya was used, like many male cadre workers, to indulge in drinking and harassing female employees at work; the former habit being stigmatised by his colleagues and superiors.

So, paradoxically, if I had at first been assigned to his office for him to support my activities, I had taken up almost naturally a guardianship function consisting basically in preventing the worst of his occasional outbursts of recklessness. And this seemed to be very much the moment for me to step in, so

[1] The generalised impoverishment, of which women workers were the primary victims, and the presence of a large female workforce – Ivanovo was, after all, the 'city of brides' – increased the likelihood of such occurrences.

I protested that the designer was a mature woman and a serious professional and that he had to bear in mind that there were roles at work which should be above private concerns. He replied that her age, status or profession did not matter as long as she was a woman, implying both that he felt entitled to maintain such conduct and that the expectations on the other side would not be different.

The systematic observation of male–female interaction in the factory and the town confirmed that what he contended was in fact a generalised belief, though obviously men and women had very different interpretations and expectations as to what it really meant in practice.

This is obviously not to suggest that elements of traditional morality were not present and in fact upheld in those circumstances when the contradictory and fundamentally male-biased nature of such tolerance became apparent, as my own position well exemplifies. My gatekeeper, unlike others always very discreet and cautious when talking about the private sphere, informed me right from the beginning about the conduct of other foreign guests. In practice, one of them, an Italian businessman, had left bitter memories as he deceived a number of girls into relationships with the promise of marriage; a second, again Italian, working on the setup of newly purchased machinery, simply asked his Russian partners to provide him with company, which they actually did. In Kolya's words there was no hint of a judgement; he was simply trying to sound out my intentions, I suppose. It was enough for him to know that my position in these matters was altogether different and that, having a stable partner, I fitted into his idea of normality. I also suspect that such warnings led me initially to be overcautious about interaction with female respondents. When I did, problems inevitably came to the surface.

Vitya's office is regularly visited by three trainees, young girls who work as supervisors in the shop. Vitya's attitude to them is ambiguous: he is amicable but barely hides his intentions towards them. As would often be the case in such circumstances, he tends to bully them, asking for help with refreshments and, worst of all, making embarrassing innuendoes. The girls have different reactions ranging from open verbal challenges to the more modest shy-away tactic. They are not, however, in a position either to denounce his behaviour or to reject his advances as their position is fully dependent on him, which in turn has the unconditional support of the, mostly male, shop management. These people might seriously stigmatise the precarious state of his marital relations, but there seems to be little concern for the girls. In such a context they seem to adopt a tactic of minimal resistance, maintaining a complacent attitude, accepting the flirting and the partying.

Among others, he asks them to help me out when I am bound for town. This has given me the chance to begin talking with them outside the evident constraints posed by his presence and the stifling atmosphere it generates for all of us. The youngest, already married, has so far been spared by Vitya and offers keenly to spend a morning out of work in town, where I treat her to a decent meal in a small restaurant targeting mostly the new rich in town. This would be a way to reciprocate but also to exploit conviviality to put a respondent at ease and favour a less formal relationship, something I would normally do with male respondents. This time, though, the consequences of what appeared to me a minor occurrence after all were altogether different. It turned out that she had never been to a restaurant – like anyone below the rank of shop chief who was unfortunate enough to have been born too late to catch such an opportunity in Soviet times. As I later learned from other female respondents of similar age and status, an invitation of this kind might generate only one type of deduction or, as one of them put it explicitly: 'What you do is very unusual. Here they won't buy you a pizza without asking for *it*'.

A few days later, therefore, the husband showed up at the gate waiting for the end of the shift to settle things personally. Only the providential intervention of managers who testified to my reputation prevented an unpleasant confrontation, and ultimately all ended with an exchange of apologies and a conclusive handshake.[1] Further on, the girls became very fond of me and on occasions they were quite frank in talking about their condition, especially relative to Vitya, and proved quite enthusiastic to speak out about male–female relations. Yet the circumstances under which we operated, my own friendship with Vitya and more generally the association with managerial ranks in the company undeniably limited the possibility for interactions and to develop any friendship.

Gender differences present a formidable barrier to communication, in that they appear much less amenable to manipulation than other aspects of one's own identity. At the mill the gender divide was interwoven with a particular division of labour which characterised the scope and specific manifestations of male power. For the fieldworker interested precisely in unveiling these phenomena, it is particularly difficult to ignore or elude the operation of such a mechanism. Yet, while this barrier can not be suppressed, and so limits the type and amount of ethnographic records collected (something that extends to all other types of bias), to recognise the problematic character of gender relations and bring them into discussion with the respondents allows them to speak more openly about what would otherwise be overlooked or simply reduced to a stereotypical representation.

Fieldwork in the shop: method and meaning in Soviet factory research

The factory is a remarkable example of nineteenth-century industrial architecture, with its multi-floor red-brick workshops, the gothic towers and high chimneys lying along the river banks surrounded by an almost unspoiled environment; remnants of a time when Ivanovo was known as the Russian Manchester, literally a green field for the cotton magnates of incipient Russian

---

[1] An altogether different kind of reaction my anomalous to behaviour was instead voiced on another occasion by Boris: 'You see, I could not quite understand what you were up to and began to have doubts because, I mean, it is very strange that with your money and your age you do not take advantage of it. But now I think I understand and respect you: you are a true Stalinist.' Boris of course intended it as a compliment.

capitalism. The scene on the inside is equally dramatic – this time, though, because of the squalor and derelict state of the premises and the almost unbearable working conditions. The shop-floor landscape represents a typical outcome of the Soviet habit of repairing rather than replacing items such as buildings, equipment, interiors and the like, because of poor maintenance and complete disregard for any safety rules, have turned into the perfect background for a Dickensian novel. The smoke, the cotton dust, the noise of the looms, and the extreme climatic conditions complete such an unenviable workplace – one that I came to accept as normality, like everyone else around.[1]

While the main body of the workshops is occupied by large shops with hundreds of weaving machines, hidden in corridors or stair gangways are the offices of line managers: the small, usually messy office of the shop chief, his desk filled with papers, metal details and spare parts scattered around or the larger, more comfortable office of the factory chief.[2] During my stay in Russia, I spent most of my time in these offices (*kabinet*) and made them my base to organise data collection. The office of a production manager in such factories used to be a strategic point for observing factory life, not only at shop-floor level.[3] Line managers bargain assiduously with central offices and are responsible for implementing not only production plans and technological options but also employment policies. They deal personally with issues of wages, vacancies, holidays and so forth with a high level of discretion. Equally, issues of production flow, quality and maintenance force them to engage with other production and staff managers. During my stay I could fill up my notebooks simply recording the daily procession of workers, managers, and occasionally higher-ups popping in for complaints, meetings or simply for a chat.

Yet, at the beginning of my research work, I still believed that the bulk of my data should be sourced in a more traditional formalised fashion. I therefore set out to conduct questionnaire interviews with managers and later with women workers. This was also intended to avoid strong bias in favour of production managers, who made up the bulk of my key informants. An account of the difficulties, encountered with interviewing staff management on the one side and women workers on the other, provides for the specific features of these groups and their relationships with male production managers. Second, the

---

[1] This is not to say that workers, especially women machine operators as the most affected ones, were not critical or concerned about the continuous deterioration of their working environment, as routinely reported at meetings and in the local paper. And helplessly so, since, I suspect, the very extremity of the situation itself suggested no immediate fix being in prospect other than individual walkouts.

[2] It is remarkable that where the occupant is a woman manager – a rare occurrence until recently – order and cleanliness predominate, and the display of tools and metal parts is replaced by plants and other decorative elements. A Western-like anonymous office style was a privilege only top executives in the main offices had begun to appreciate.

[3] It is important to point out that the role of shop chiefs has been waning and recently in many factories this position has been obliterated as part of a rationalisation drive, its functions assigned to foremen and top production managers, without modifying substantially the scene in terms of problems and practices.

problems of establishing a fruitful dialogue with respondents highlight the barriers to communication I encountered, such as being a man, being associated with male production personnel, and the techniques deployed to overcome them: empathy, dialogical interaction, observation and triangulation.

Interviewing staff managers: a tale of red tape

The administration of the enterprise is extremely bureaucratic, so that staff personnel such as accountants, technicians, and pay and personnel clerks are present at every level of the hierarchy. Top functional managers, though, are, as expected, located away from production in the 'main offices' – actually a modest building on one side of the main gate. Here in order of importance are the director and the chief engineer, sharing a separate section of the second floor with a waiting room, secretaries and the usual double padded doors, alongside the accounting, pay and personnel offices, while the commercial and procurement departments shared the first floor.

The separation was not merely physical, as I soon came to realise: these office workers appeared relative to production managers both reluctant to co-operate and lacking confidence in their own field. Failing at first to obtain sufficient information, I turned to the director himself, asking him to authorise them in written form to fill in my questionnaires. His reply was positive, but his sarcastic comments about their attitude were even more indicative of the state of affairs in these quarters of the enterprise. Hearing my complaints at their obstructive and fearful attitude, he burst out: 'Ah, they are afraid to speak. I do not see the point. They know nothing!' For all my knowledge of the peculiarity of Russian bureaucracy, these circumstances were in defiance of my initial expectations, built, I suppose, around the commonsensical views of what top managers should look like in a 'Western' corporate environment.

In the Western world, marketing, public auditing, the pressure of the public and not least internal informational needs have all led enterprises to produce extensive informational material and adequate structures to process and circulate it. On the contrary, Soviet tradition is particularly notorious for resisting any external scrutiny. Enterprises in the past were quite cautious about disclosing any information which could jeopardise relations with overarching state institutions, particularly because they systematically concealed resources so as to avoid tightening of plan targets. Their offices would routinely fabricate financial and output data and were badly staffed and equipped. Transition does not seem to have provided them with any incentive for change: the new Russian business world is based on secrecy to avoid the taxman, the claims of creditors and unpaid workers. Not least the fact that security agencies are suspicious of foreign intrusion influences managerial attitudes. And managers in central offices, such as accountants and salesmen, are extremely reluctant to disclose information as traditionally they are judged less by merit than by loyalty to the administration. In my case, I suspect, their silence might as well represent a display of loyalty to the new owners, at the time looking for cuts among unproductive workers.

Methodologically, such an experience indicates how apparent failure can still contribute to a better understanding of an institution; in terms of the subject matter it indicates the greater relevance of production managers in the day-to-day running of the factory and therefore as respondents.

Interviewing women workers: struggling with gender and class barriers

Since mid-2001, after a year or so of fieldwork, I had come to know quite a lot about shop-floor bargaining. Yet again, male shop leaders were the primary source of my knowledge. The bulk of the workforce instead is made up of female machine operators and office workers. Observation and respondents' accounts of bargaining pointed to a systematic, though piecemeal, confrontation along gender lines. I therefore felt that interviewing women workers was essential to grasp the nature of social relations in the enterprise.

The arrangement of interviews with this category of employees proved the most problematic of all. I intended to carry out interviews outside the factory; in fact more than one among my female acquaintances had routinely expressed distrust towards male managers, and I felt that such a location might be intimidating. This proved impossible because, as my friend and shop chief pointed out, 'women are too busy to spend their spare time talking to you and would find it awkward to meet a foreign man in private'. He therefore offered to summon a brigade of weavers and asked them to fill in my questionnaire. At first, workers reacted with fear and distrust towards my activities and put up a defensive attitude. For a start, they responded to my questionnaire collectively. My landlady later, so as to mitigate my disappointment at the matter, observed that women workers fear exposing themselves and would not stand up individually in an open context. Such a reaction was not universal; a number of women from the shops volunteered for interview. This was the case with women that for a number of reasons, such as a different professional or ethnic background, seemed not to fit entirely into the social and cultural framework of the shop. In such cases, their longing for a listening ear outside the usual circles, and the determination to display their difference and greater intellectual understanding of the situation, provided a common ground of mutual interest and curiosity.

One should not get the impression that such reluctance was merely prejudicial, some kind of automatic rejection of men and managers. And, to the extent that it did, there were some well-grounded justifications for it. My early disappointment at questionnaire responses was indeed produced by the fact that workers seemed quite insincere in their description of work and bargaining practices and had produced what appeared to me a prefabricated discourse made up of the usual complaints about low pay and bad working conditions and professed ignorance of the functioning of the payment system. Shop managers had all reported how determined women workers were to make their plan and bargain informally, and I was equally determined to see the issue through with them.

When a number of workers came into the shop chief's office, I had the opportunity to confront them in his absence, seeking clarification about their answers to the questionnaire. Initially, they replied defensively, asking 'What do you want to know?' or 'What are we supposed to say?', revealing that the problem was less of misunderstanding than of the political sensitivity of the subject matter. Then a worker eventually brought the issue into the open, declaring: 'We will not tell you [how we manage to make the plan, CM] otherwise they will further cut down our wages.' Further, it emerged that overall they did not actually know how wages were calculated and felt it unfair that there seemed not to be any clear relation between effort and reward, something that managers formally maintained as the tenet of the piece-rate system. As far as they were concerned, stress on quality rather than on quantity was just a trick for lowering wages as they rejected managerial claims that it was their responsibility if the yarn they manufactured was of such poor quality; in the end they had a plan to make and barely managed to do so.

Tough questioning and a lot of patience were as important to achieve a full and, relatively, honest account as was previous knowledge of the matter learned in months spent in production – and specifically command of the technical and colloquial jargon necessary to convey and manipulate it. Such a breakthrough, I suspect, was only possible because workers felt challenged to provide their own account and found that our argument was a safe ground to this end. My open discussion of problems and responsibilities challenged and punctured, at least for a moment, the ritualised discourse that they normally put up in their defence.

Unveiling managerial practices: beyond the Western managerial bias

When Westerners approach a post-Soviet enterprise their first perception is usually declined in negative terms: management is *dis*organised, workers are *un*willing and *un*prepared to do their job, different departments are *un*cooperative, technology is *backward*, and, therefore, their product is *not* suitable for the market. The conventional explanation for the chaotic state of production pointed to the irrationality of the planned economy. Why, then, years after its dismantling, do these conditions continue unabated? Mainstream views throughout the 1990s have blamed conservative managers pursuing 'traditional' Soviet practices. Unsatisfied with the superficiality of this approach, this research has rested on the attempt to uncover the social determinants of these practices, by investigating the relational aspect of the above-mentioned issues. The task has proved much more difficult to achieve than originally planned, despite the apparent willingness of production managers to co-operate, because a strong Western bias continued to inform research questions proving intractable to respondents. As a result, the latter were induced, no less than the above-mentioned categories, to resort to a formal script hindering their actual practices and the underlying motives inspiring them. The following example will clarify this point, showing how initial difficulties were overcome through iteration and triangulation.

The hiring and firing system and its practical application are essential to understand changes in the post-Soviet enterprise. In Soviet times, firing was formally and practically very difficult to achieve by management, and there were more incentives to keep extra workers than to release the less productive. At a time when massive lay-offs are apparently on every enterprise agenda, and cost efficiency has made its way into assessment of managerial jobs, this has become a very sensitive issue. I asked Kolya directly about the subject. His early reply, though, was quite disappointing. At first he simply argued that he acted according to the procedure and offered to explain it. My attempt to explain my interest in real circumstances and criteria influencing his decisions was met with bafflement; he simply replied: 'I cannot understand what you want to know.' Further, he protested that managers were not considering firing people; in fact they were suffering a serious outflow of specialised personnel, and they therefore struggled to keep as many workers as possible.

I drew my first conclusion that my search for a rapid swing to Western practices had been impossible in the factory and therefore my question had been ill conceived. Yet workers were afraid of being fired or relocated within the factory, and the actual workforce had been reduced by one-third since privatisation. The occasion to clarify this point emerged after I noticed how on several occasions workers, employees or applicants came to *our* office to negotiate their employment conditions at the factory. If workers did not find the proposed position acceptable, or the manager had nothing to offer in his shop/department, they were invited to apply directly to the shop chief or foreman. In case of internal relocation, the manager searched for consensual agreement, but when there was evidence of misbehaviour he was quite resolute in forcing people to face their failures. After one of these arguments, I asked Kolya about how he decided these issues. He explained to me, first, the formal framework within which these negotiations took place, the obligation of the factory to offer alternative jobs to workers whose job was obliterated. Then he candidly admitted that they generally offered good jobs to the best workers while he could easily get rid of unwanted ones by denying them a suitable post.

Further evidence emerged from the equally frequent cases of alcoholism on the job. Security had found one of *our* workers *v netrezvom vide*, i.e. in a state of alcoholic intoxication, and according to new disciplinary practices he should be fired. The discussion between shop chief and foreman over the most appropriate punishment ended with an illuminating outcome. Kolya said he was not going to take an unpopular decision. It was the foreman's responsibility to decide whether she wanted to keep this worker or not; in the end it was her fault if this man had been caught in such a state. Observation of workers' behaviour, followed by in-depth interviews, was employed to build a counterpoint to managerial views. Workers, manifesting their fear as well as appreciation and even devotion to their immediate superiors, revealed the extent of managerial authority as well as its particularly paternalistic form.

Let's try to understand the main passages of this research process. I asked why management is in no condition, free from 'socialist' rules and obligation, to impose discipline over workers and improve operational management of the production process. Reacting to their claim of unchanged work practices and relative justifications, I challenged them over the impossibility of change, something which I in fact presupposed before being explained. My insistence on an idea of efficiency drawing on Western management textbooks put me at odds with respondents' attempts to satisfy my curiosity. In particular, my emphasis on the exertion of managerial authority obscures how the search for a new organisational mechanism cannot avoid the problem of consent. On the receiving end, the prevailing script in managerial narratives features a harmonious collective threatened by the irresponsibility of a handful of careerists and troublemakers. The dialogue with my key informants which seemed blessed by the best auspices and had proceeded apparently unhindered for several months had reached a deadlock.

I suspect that most research on the subject tends to follow this path in that it fails to recognise that: there is a profound gap between formal policies and procedures and informal practices; this gap owes less to a mere unpredictability of human action than to the power-laden nature of these contexts and the ensuing conflictual character of the relations developing therein; correspondingly, one has to expect to encounter narratives that are aimed at justifying one's own behaviour and sustain claims in terms defined by the dominant group and therefore in apparent contradiction to actual practices. The likely outcome, in such a case, is a partial and distorted account of these practices and an explanatory mechanism centred on the idea of resistance to change and cultural barriers.

Soviet factory, Russian factory: observations about the typicality and relevance of the case-study

How should issues of validity and generalisability be dealt with in the case of research based on ethnographic work at one single study-case? It is important to point out that qualitative research *per se* has gained sufficient recognition within the social sciences that such a concern should not be interpreted as tending towards some sort of justification for the use of such a methodology. The same could be said for the use of the case-study method, which has long and successfully been employed in studying managerial restructuring and social relations in Russia.

What has troubled me over the years spent on this research has been, more specifically, the relevance and typicality of the object of my study. In fact, as my picture of the region and the sector became clearer, and the situation in the country as a whole unfolded, it became clear that textiles and Ivanovo had become a synonym for backwardness and helplessness at reform. In short, I began to wonder whether the study was not focusing on marginal subjects in a marginal context. A second question concerned the generalisability of the findings or what could be learned from the study of a specific site such as a single factory. Such questions have obviously been asked before; hereafter we shall review the arguments put forward in fieldwork-based pioneering works which appealed to me for a certain similarity of circumstances with the present research.

Economic marginality and social relevance: what can Ivanovo textiles teach us?

Most research on Russian industry has focused on strategic objects such as the Soviet 'crown jewels' in the aerospace or military–industrial complex, the powerful energy sector or the emerging private sector. The textile industry is far from attracting such attention both nationally and internationally. A Russian researcher I happened to contact in Ivanovo in 2002 confided that she was quite surprised by my interest in the region: 'You hardly see any foreigners around here,' she observed. There might be good reasons for it: Ivanovo is the poorest region in European Russia; it owes its living to an industry that has lost out since the 1930s and that many believe to be without an economically meaningful future. Moreover, my research setting proper, a company town, is universally considered a relic of the industrial age with no prospects other than inevitable decline (which by all means is quite observable in my case).

It is not just the sector or the locality performing badly, as this reverberates on the people, too: as one respondent so colourfully, and dramatically, put it, reacting to my display of interest in the women workers from the poorly paid and marginal finishing shop: 'They are scum, a bunch of alcoholics . . . Let me explain it – Ivanovo is the most socially degenerated place in Russia, our province the worst in the region, seemingly the enterprise within it and the finishing shop is the worst human environment in the factory.'

Following James Scott in *Weapons of the Weak*, one might therefore ask:

> 'Why are we here, in a village of no particular significance, examining the struggle of a handful of history's losers? . . . a class over whom the wave of progress is about to roll. And the big battalions of the state, of capitalist relations . . . and of demography itself are arrayed against them.' But also quite rightfully observe that: 'The justification for such an enterprise must lie precisely in its banality – in the fact that these circumstances are the normal context in which class conflict has historically occurred.' (Scott, 1985, p. 27)

The workers, cadres and line managers of the company town, with their apparently passive and naïve acceptance of privatisation, with their stubborn attachment to Soviet values but also with their individual forms of resistance, represent the reality of the world of production in contemporary Russia, the apparently inexplicable 'patience of the working class' and the 'resistance to change' of factory management, which have dominated the debate about the alleged post-Soviet transition.

The paternalistic and authoritarian forms of management encountered here, with the corollary of a pervasive chauvinistic culture, epitomise power as it is understood and exercised in every organisational quarter of Putin's Russia. So much for the coryphaei of democratisation. Equally, the enterprise, despite its technological backwardness and acute financial crisis, or maybe because of these negative records, provides a clear example of the economic disaster produced by liberalisation and the strategies and adjustments 'red directors' and Soviet managers put forward in the 1990s to weather it.

Finally, decline notwithstanding, since 1998 this industry has experienced a recovery linked to the emergence of a new form of corporate management, the holding company, proving to be in line with current trends in the national economy. Its slow and uncertain path towards capitalist forms of management, marked by a strong continuity with the Soviet past, might appear in our case more vividly while, precisely for this reason, making it a better case for highlighting and explaining the profound contradictions of this process, which are often blurred in apparently successful cases of adaptation.

A Russian factory

Once we have decided that this enterprise is typical, in that it well represents for us Russian industry as a whole, it remains to be seen what should be the standard for comparison. For most transitologists it makes perfect sense to measure Russian practices and performance against 'Western' standards. In our case, too, the consultants operating at the factory identified Western management and technology as their benchmarks and at the same time the goal Russians should achieve, facilitated to an extent by the latter still looking, however critically, at Western European enterprises for clues as to how to turn their business around. Yet, as Granick pointed out in the 1960s, there is no such thing as a typical American, let alone, Western enterprise (Granick, 1960, p. 242). They vary considerably in size, organisation and technological level. Today's world of production is even more complicated as – to stay within textiles – national systems have given way to long and complex production chains stretching across such diverse places as North Africa, Central Asia and the Far East.

The answer to such a puzzle should move from the consideration that 'Russian factories are different from American [i.e. 'Western', CM] ones. Each individual plant might have its American counterpart, *but in the mass they are of a different breed* [my italics, CM]. How do we know this? From the Russian statistics and from their account of average performance' (Granick, 1960, p. 243).

Only this work is based on the assumption that such a different breed is one fundamentally social in kind. That is to say that the Soviet enterprise can be studied as a socio-economic institution of its own kind, contrasting it with capitalist ones. The Russian enterprise, its features and mode of operation, are largely dependent on the system of social relations which the Soviet system rested upon. And, to the present time, the findings from our observation of its activities are consistent with such an interpretation in that they reveal meanings and constraints informing managers and workers alike in line with such a system, providing a useful explanatory framework to an otherwise inexplicable trajectory of development. It follows that differences in performance and statistical variations, to the extent that official data might be assumed reliable, are epiphenomenal, something that needs itself to be proved and made sense of rather than the basis for constructing an explanatory framework.

The problem with mainstream interpretations consists in that liberal economists, and area-studies scholars who adhere to their precepts, assume that the economic laws they have designed operate universally in economic systems, perceivable differences in structures and behaviour being accounted for by historical accidents, institutional or cultural barriers which are in any case assumed as exogenous factors. Therefore, once the Soviet institutional architecture disappears, they more or less implicitly treat the Russian enterprise as a normal, i.e. capitalist, firm. Observable differences, in fact the catastrophic failure of their predictions and the reform process on which they rested, are blamed, rather than actually explained, on Russian or Soviet cultural differences and institutional legacies. The penetration of capital into the pre-existing socio-economic texture of Russian enterprises is, instead, precisely what this research is aimed at investigating so as to verify the extent and the ways in which it is actually occurring.

The next task in introducing our case-study will consist in making such assumptions about the nature of the Soviet system and the Russian enterprise explicit, providing the research with a comparative historical interpretative framework.

3 Transition and the Soviet legacy: Western ideology and Soviet reality

The organisation of productive forces . . . the planning of the national economy do not constitute the object of the political economy of socialism but of the economic policy of its cadres.

J. Stalin

This chapter provides our research into post-Soviet management of industrial firms with an analytical and historical background. We shall discuss how Soviet economic institutions functioned, and indicate the scope and limits of reforms attempted by the Soviet leadership in the 1970s and 1980s, leading to the present attempt at capitalist restoration. This will serve a twofold purpose:

To test the explanatory potential of the orthodox theory of the firm and of mainstream approaches to managerial behaviour, as applied to the Soviet context. This will shed light on the limits of, and to such an extent refute, those interpretations of the Soviet system, and transition theories based on them, which, by considering Soviet management as a distorted version of its Western equivalent, fail to grasp its peculiarities and fundamental contradictions.

To present an alternative account of the functioning and evolution of Soviet economic institutions, which draws on critical approaches focusing on the labour process as the determinant of managerial practices and enterprise behaviour. This will allow us to identify the social–economic structures and processes that resisted reforms under Soviet rule and survived institutional change following its demise, allowing the Soviet legacy to be fully accounted for in shaping transition and constraining restructuring.

Hence we shall first try to understand the position that the enterprise assumed and the role management played in the wider framework of the Soviet economy. Here the focus is on long-term structural features as they emerged from the debate among Western and Soviet scholars when unsuccessful reforms from the 1960s onward produced growing awareness of both the specificity of the Soviet economic system and the critical state in which it then existed. Although the organisation of the Soviet economy had its roots in Stalinist industrialisation in the 1930s and in the period of post-war reconstruction, we shall be primarily concerned in this chapter with the essential features of the 'mature' Soviet system as it became bureaucratised after Stalin's death and persisted, without fundamental changes, until Gorbachev dismantled it in the late 1980s. Although we shall review the failure of various attempts to reform the system to highlight the persistence of its fundamental inadequacies, we shall not look in detail at the important, though not fundamental, changes that took place over this period.

The Soviet economy has been universally recognised as a specific economic system; but, depending on the theoretical approach, different pictures have been given of its nature, characteristics and evolution. We shall first look at those studies that view the Soviet enterprise as an irrational variant of its Western counterpart and explain its features as a result of its subordination to the command administrative structure. These studies have provided an invaluable insight into Soviet managerial practices but for the most part have failed to address the main contradictions of the system. The failure of reforms before and after the demise of the USSR demonstrates that the removal of the institutional structure of the Soviet system did not automatically imply the development of market forces and transition to capitalism.

We shall therefore turn to the comparative contributions of a group of scholars who have developed their analysis on the basis of Marxist attention to relations in production. They all assume that the Soviet system was characterised by a form of social domination in which the dominant stratum controlled the production surplus but not the production process. This explains the chaotic nature of the production process and the ambiguous position of management. Enterprise managers were torn between the pressure from above to achieve growing production targets and the need to secure the co-operation of workers in pursuing plan fulfilment. Managerial practices were therefore a rational response not simply to an institutional framework but to the constraints of a social process.

We maintain that, historically, the Soviet system was not the result of the installation either of economic planning or of a systematic bureaucratic direction of the economy. It emerged from the dramatic social conflict around the management of the economy initiated by the political drive of the Stalin-led Party to make the direction of the economy its permanent base of power. The social outcomes of the Soviet system, namely the atomisation of society and workers' negative control over the production process, were to remain fundamentally untouched by successive attempts at reforms in the post-war years, ultimately accounting for its long-term decline. These are the issues we should turn to, first when briefly considering the theoretical arguments about the nature of the system, subsequently when we shall discuss the functioning of the enterprise.

On the other side, economic growth and organisational changes introduced by reforms from Khrushchev to Gorbachev modified significantly both the material and institutional contexts in which managers operated. No less important, it is in the context of the late Soviet period that growing expectations met with increasing disillusion about the possibility of modifying even slightly the status quo in the management of factories. This appears to have affected significantly managers' and workers' attitudes, including those featured in our case-study, during transition. For these reasons our account of the features and problems in the Soviet enterprise focuses on the late Soviet period, followed by a discussion of the reforms up to the latest attempt at capitalist restoration.

Managerial control and its limits in the Soviet economy

What were the position of the enterprise and the role of its management in the Soviet economy? In formal terms the Soviet enterprise was the last link in the chain of a command system characterised by strict uniformity and a stress on fixed hierarchical relations of authority and standardised tables of organisation. Managers were mainly engineers or accountants, selected and trained by the Party to carry out instructions from above. Western scholars of economics saw this as a deviation from the experience of free entrepreneurship and organisational diversity of the West (Berliner, 1957, 1988; Granick, 1960; Gregory, 1989; Linz and Moskoff, 1989; Schroeder, 1989). The replacement of a horizontal market relationship with a vertical administrative hierarchy impeded rational decision-making based on market prices and the discipline imposed by profit-seeking in a competitive environment. Even admitting the growing scope of conscious management in resource allocation, they pointed a finger at organisational rigidity and over-centralisation as a limit to efficiency and economic development.

It was soon realised, though, that the real practice of planning and plan fulfilment defied the description of a simple top-down command system. Starting from the post-war period, Soviet authorities and Western analysts recognised that managers had larger autonomy than formerly stated and that their decisions could be detrimental to economic performance. Managers were able to meet plan targets only at the cost of systematically violating instructions and regulations, defying any attempt at imposing effective use of resources. Command levers were unable to achieve more than gross quantitative targets, and the control system failed to detect infractions effectively.

The Soviet system: a centralised command economy?

The shortcomings of the planning mechanism, its inability to synthesise and convey in an operational form the objectives of the centre to operative units are radical and undeniable. Since ultimate decisions about what and how much to produce lay in the hands of top-level political bodies, they incorporated the preferences of an elite rather than the needs of the population or the capacity of the productive system. Nevertheless, orthodox analysis has focused on the technical ability of the system to ascertain its allocative efficiency.

The planning mechanism was plagued by the separation of power and information. In order to design viable plans, the centre had to base its decisions on information concerning productive capacity and resources, which was available only at enterprise level. Second, it had to set targets consistently with this information, making sure that balances between supply and demand be guaranteed at every level of the production–distribution chains. The plan was in fact drafted for the whole economy simultaneously and left no formal channel for adjustments. Several assumptions should be met in order for this mechanism to work smoothly: unambiguousness of target indicators, willingness and ability of subordinates and control bodies to disclose information.

The ability of the centre to convey its quantitative priorities to enterprises in an operative and unambiguous form has been much debated. Planners used synthetic indicators and normative coefficients in physical terms, and since they were defined at aggregate level they corresponded only approximately to what had originally been required by users. Descending the bureaucratic hierarchy they were disaggregated, becoming amenable to manipulation. Other than clarity of targets, another problem was the priority scale among them, which emerged every time targets conflicted. Administrative transmission of targets did not provide quantitative elements for decision-making. Attempts at introducing normative (technically validated) planning and economic (price-based) indicators proved ineffective because they extended rather than reduced the scope for independent decisions by managers.

The failure of planning was twofold: it was unable directly to manage the operation of enterprises because of inconsistency of targets but it was also unable to regulate them by providing incentives to efficient decision-making. Managers were deprived of direct control over resources and their use but were not guaranteed that targets imposed from above would match inputs assigned to them. The uncertainty over supply was the cause of well-known managerial practices aimed at building a safety factor. Managerial performance was assessed primarily on the achievement of gross product in physical terms, so managers manipulated information about capacity and input availability in order to achieve easy plans. In this way they further undermined the rationality of planning; in particular they inflated demand for labour and supplies. More importantly, the pressure on production targets led to indifference towards costs and quality with consequences of generalised scarcity and poor quality of goods. The response at the level of the individual enterprise was hoarding of labour and supply, production autarky, modified product mix and so on. A vicious circle was established, in which managerial practices tended to limit uncertainty and avoid risk of plan failure, which generated disruptions along production chains, reproducing the conditions which were the very cause of these practices. These analyses led to the conclusion that: the planning mechanism did not provide an effective framework to regulate the Soviet economy; managerial behaviour was a rational response to the set of constraints and opportunities in which they operated.

The inconsistencies of planning favoured the idea that the Soviet economy could be better-described as an administrative–command system rather than as a planned one. Administrative methods were the actual means by which resources were allocated. Ministries, the bureaucratic machinery that functioned as a mediator between political decision-makers and the production units, played a dominant role in the running of the economy. In the day-to-day experience of managers, most of the blame for vagaries of planning was in fact referred to the reality of ministerial rule, and both Soviet and Western analysts came to concentrate on ministry–enterprise relations as the actual source of economic malfunctioning.

The Soviet bureaucracy was affected by monopolisation, a high level of concentration of power and autarkic tendencies. A study of the behaviour of line managers in the ministries concluded that the logic of ministerial rule reflected the same rationale as enterprise management since they responded to the same set of constraints (Gregory, 1989).

In relation to enterprises, ministries exercised petty tutelage, a practice of direct intervention to question current management and production, which was a further source of insecurity and instability of factory life. Ministerial intrusive attitudes stifled managerial autonomy and stimulated their resistance to the disclosure of information. At the same time, such attitudes were justified by the need to guarantee co-ordination between enterprises and among branches. The bureaucracy managed supply insecurity, and the perpetual deficit of supply was therefore the condition to justify its existence and the base of its enormous power.

From an orthodox point of view, the analysis of Soviet economic organisation proved that the practices of the agents were a rational response to the irrationality of the system. The absence of the naturally equilibrating forces of the market left agents to pursue their interests in an environment characterised by unequal distribution of information leading to the establishment of a seller's market with all its negative consequences. Western economic orthodoxy concluded that the historical experience of planning had generated an over-centralised administrative hierarchy that kept the economy in a monopolistic grip and resisted any attempt at partial reform to avoid relinquishing its power.

The restoration of economic rationality should pass through the dismantling of the ministerial system and the resurgence of market relationships.

In so far as this approach can be related to the expectations raised by the reform programme of transition started in 1992, it did not find confirmation in the experience of its implementation. Evidence shows that managerial practices intensified or evolved in new forms rather than being supplanted by Western managerial styles.

The Soviet economic system: an imperfect system of social domination

The limits of the orthodox understanding of the firm in the capitalist economy account for mainstream transition theories failing to grasp the specific socio-economic dynamics in post-Soviet societies. In the first place we have the idea that economic problems have a universal character enshrined in the rationality of economic man. This has led Western analysts to apply to the Soviet economy and its agents the same methods of assessment developed in a capitalist context, despite their recognition of the absence of market relations.

Second, the idea that market relations allow co-operation on an equal basis and that the market clears any position of advantage based on unequal distribution of information led them to consider, when recognised, the dominant position of the economic elite in the Soviet context as an extraordinary case.

Organisations, though, are more than simply technical devices or social functions; they are always social constructs in which power relations materialise. Organisations in the economic realm are the formalised product of social relations of production that decide how wealth is produced and distributed.

As a *sui generis* social formation, the Soviet system, like the capitalist one, was a form of domination with its own specific rationality. The specific cause of its instability, manifested in poor economic performance, was that the ruling stratum depended for the reproduction of its position on the control of surplus product but did not achieve the control of surplus production.

Money could not play its regulatory role, imposing its universal and impersonal discipline on producers (both managers and workers) and guaranteeing distribution of rewards consistently with the position occupied in the production process. Without the medium of the commodity, social authority had to manifest itself in a direct way in the form of personal relations of dependency and surplus extracted in kind (a feature many suggest has rather strengthened in the 1990s, despite capitalist penetration in the economy).

Such a system was intrinsically unstable and required hyper-centralisation to counter centripetal tendencies coming from different layers of the elite, all competing for the appropriation of surplus.[1] This explains, among other things, why the strictly hierarchical administrative structures centred on branch ministries remained the only viable mechanism to manage the economy in the Soviet system. Any attempt to decentralise the system and grant greater autonomy to production units, aimed at gaining efficiency, resulted in loss of co-ordination and greater shortages, threatening to bring chaos to the economy.[2]

A corollary of highly personalised and hierarchical management is the separation of power and information.[3] Hyper-centralisation in industrial management brings as a consequence a de-facto decentralisation. This results from the inability of the centre to handle all the decisions it is formally entitled

---

[1] This is the central argument made by Ticktin (1992).

[2] Naishul' observes that reforms based on the 'introduction of "economic methods" damaged the entire economy' (Naishul', 1991, p. 33). *Perestroika*, by loosening control over enterprises, 'has resulted in the disruption of co-ordination through vertical links' (ibid., p. 34). In a system in which producers respond to higher bodies rather than to customers, granting freedom to individual economic units means permitting the arbitrary alteration of production programmes.

[3] As Filtzer argued, 'the elite could only maintain control through hyper-centralisation'. This engendered such a contradiction that the elite also needed managers to provide perfect information and loyally execute its plans. Yet both managers and workers had every reason to collude in circumventing instructions (Filtzer, 1994, p. 2).

to, producing disorganisation and waste of resources in production. Such a problem became common in large enterprises of the then developing heavy industry in the West at the turn of the last century. It can be added that the sheer size of waste and the evident disorganisation of Soviet production were the inevitable outcome of extending such a form of management, with the ensuing problems, to an entire economy. The response in the West was the managerial revolution, which meant, on the one hand, transferring decision-making over specific functions and areas down to professional managers and, on the other hand, introducing scientific management in production, revolutionising the labour process.

To understand why the Soviets were unable or unwilling to make such a move we have to look at the other side of the spectrum of society to see what form was assumed by the labour process in the Soviet system.[1] The establishment of such a form of control implied that society was extremely atomised. This meant that workers were deprived of any collective form to express their interests and raise grievances, reacting instead with individualised forms of resistance, including slack work, deceit, a high level of turnover and disregard for quality. This exacerbated the level of disruption already resulting from the disorganisation of the economy. Managers, differently from what one would expect in capitalist economies, showed a lenient attitude towards discipline violations. They tolerated low productivity and sometimes colluded with workers in circumventing instructions, especially concerning the observance of safety rules, maintenance and quality standards, in order to bring in the plan and protect customary earnings.

Managers entered into this pattern of informal bargaining and resisted any attempt by the Party-State to modify its terms as they needed workers' co-operation to overcome the numerous bottlenecks and uncertainties that plagued production at enterprise level. That is to say that workers, while deprived of any effective power, were forced to sort out for themselves the vagaries of the system, being granted in such a way a form of 'negative' control over the design and execution of their jobs. Managers had to do so partly because of the shortage of labour and partly because they had neither better means to discipline workers – in the first place the power to hire and fire – nor incentives to elicit their efforts. It is apparent that this was a self-reinforcing process in which workers' and managers' practices furthered disruption while trying to overcome their immediate consequences with the intention of preserving their interests. Despite the fact that most disruptions derived from these very practices, the behaviour of workers and managers retains its rationale in the fact that they confronted the reality of Soviet production as an external given environment. The a-conflictual nature of industrial relations, which is at the same time a cause and a consequence of alienation and demotivation in society, was the founding pillar of the political domination of the elite. At the same time, it was also the major barrier to economic development, therefore an obstacle to the long-term material reproduction of the system (Filtzer, 1994, pp. 6–7).

[1]   See a brief but extremely clear statement of this argument in Filtzer (1994, pp. 2–6).

Without anticipating our conclusions, this brief theoretical overview allows some considerations about the features of Soviet industrial management, which in turn help sharpen our focus. In the 1960s scholars seemed to recognise a common trend in industrial societies reaching across the Iron Curtain, imagining a converging trend dominated by the technological imperatives of mass production and bureaucratic forms of administration. Though abandoned in its original formulation, this 'convergence' approach has surfaced again in the interpretation of the Soviet economic decline as the failure to replace a 'Fordist' rigid framework with the flexible and decentralised environment required by digital technologies. Rita Di Leo, opening a discussion about future perspectives in post-Soviet Russia, significantly warned about the recurrent tendency 'to fall into the error of seeing convergence between the communist world, post-communism and our own world' (Di Leo, 1993, p. 3).

The discussion of the Soviet economic system outlined above should suffice for outlining the centrality of social relations in production to the definition of economic problems and, to this extent, for highlighting the peculiar character of the Soviet experience as compared to capitalist countries.

In this perspective it emerges how the Soviet system was not simply an imperfect system of economic administration, but more fundamentally a power mechanism of social control. The pattern of informal bargaining at shop-floor level that emerged within its framework amounted to no less than a specific form of labour process, therefore requiring more than simply new incentives or technology to be overcome.

Finally, it is important to stress that the informal nature of managerial practices, their emergence and continued survival indicate how the economic mechanism reflected no less pressures and autonomous, unforeseen reactions from below than the strategies of the elite and the analyses of scholars.

It is our task now to provide a historical account of enterprise structure and functioning in the late Soviet period. We shall present features and problems of the Soviet economy from Khrushchev onward, describe the organisation of the enterprise and managerial practices, and finally we shall see how unsuccessful reforms led to the decision by the elite to reintroduce capitalism.

The enterprise in the Soviet economy

In the previous section we stressed the fundamental continuity in the type of economic management that prevailed in the Soviet Union on the basis of its underlying system of social relations as they emerged from Stalinist industrialisation. This does not mean that growth did not take place, modifying both the material bases and the terms of the economic problems and therefore the solutions that were put forward by the elite.

Problems and perspectives of the Soviet enterprise from Khrushchev to Brezhnev

From the 1950s the Soviet economy saw the gradual erosion of the conditions which had permitted the high growth rates of the first five-year plans. The expansion of the industrial base had been achieved by an extensive growth of production capacity at the expense of productivity. The constant expansion of fixed capital led to the absorption of reserves of labour, ending the condition of labour surplus and calling for a switch in development strategy (see Di Leo, 1980, pp. 7–26; Naishul', 1991, pp. 15–17). The mobilisation of labour reserves in the countryside and among the female population required the expansion and modernisation of the low-productivity service and consumer sectors, including agriculture, which had so far been neglected by the planners.

Between the 1960s and the 1970s the Soviet economy assumed the structural features of mature industrialised countries (Di Leo, 1980, pp. 65–77). The comparison, though, stays at the level of statistical aggregates. The reality was more one of adapting old structures towards new uses. The production of consumer durables was assigned, for example, to heavy industry. Industrial enterprises could be required to provide materials and labour to modernise collective farms and bring in the harvest. These practices, while putting strain on the enterprises involved, brought few advantages to the recipient consumer sector. Equally problematic was the case of new plants in this sector.

New enterprises continued to be established following the model of the large integrated factory, which dominated heavy industry in the inter-war period, despite the fact that, especially for consumer goods, the Western experience was one of decentralisation. This option had less to do with bureaucratic inertia or myopia of the planners than with the peculiarities of Soviet planning and enterprise management at this stage. In the first place, concentrating the many production stages required for manufacturing a single good into a single factory, and under a single branch-ministry roof, meant reducing the economic links required to co-ordinate its production. This would simplify the job of the administrative system already strained to control resources (see Naishul', 1991, pp. 16, 17, 31). Second, the role of the enterprise as the sole provider of social services for its employees (housing, rest homes, child care, sometimes schooling, training, sport facilities), which had actually been expanding in those years, led to a preference for large, single-site establishments. This meant also that these enterprises were often oversized and under-capitalised.

The priority criteria discriminating between sectors A and B (heavy and light industry), productive and non-productive work, which had been set during Stalinist industrialisation, continued to affect the allocation of resources, reflecting the different bargaining power of various branches, ministries and individual enterprises.

The consumer sector was plagued by a relatively higher scarcity of resources with which to entice workers from other industries, while tighter plans meant heavier workloads and harsher working conditions. Under these circumstances this sector suffered a high turnover and a continued scarcity of qualified personnel (Di Leo, 1980, pp. 82–9). In general, the lack of collective means by which workers could raise their grievances and improve their conditions made changing job across regions, industries and enterprises the only available mechanism for mobility.

The continued preference for capital goods industries was justified by the need to provide additional resources for the expansion of the economy, in particular the consumer sector, but the under-funding in this area of the economy translated into low productivity and low quality of output. The low quality and scarcity of consumer goods were, in turn, causes of demotivation among workers and a reason for hoarding resources and engaging in unplanned or illicit activities on a worrying scale. These phenomena assumed the character of a vicious circle generalised to the whole economy.

The need to reverse this trend, raise living standards and so entice the workforce to support actively the efforts of the elite to restore efficiency in the system was first attempted with a spate of reforms by Khrushchev and Kosygin in the 1950s and 1960s.[1]

'Under Stalin the wages system had been dominated by a plethora of different rates and wage scales' (Filtzer, 1994, p. 65), so that the same job with the same skill content could be paid at different rates even within factories of the same industry. The result was to deprive wages of any incentive function, except stimulating turnover. The reform set to simplify and centralise the system, restoring a relation between effort and reward (see Filtzer, 1994, p. 58).

The centrepiece of the reform was in any case the attempt to force managers and workers into accepting 'scientific norms', i.e. centrally established output quotas. Under Stalin the policies of productivity had favoured individual norm over-fulfilment to break factory-level resistance to ambitious plan targets.[2] The lack of relation between individual output quotas and plan level, though, meant that managers kept norms low, allowing easy over-fulfilment by workers. In this way managers tolerated a low level of productivity and inflated the earnings of rate-busters, in exchange for their co-operation in overcoming production bottlenecks. Since the introduction of new norms was to achieve a generalised increase in output quotas with a corresponding loss in workers' earnings, the reform also proposed a corresponding increase in basic wages.

The reform was asking managers to rationalise production, strengthening their control over the production process. This notwithstanding, managers resisted new norms and systematically circumvented the wage system because the irregularity of supplies and the unevenness of the production process required continued reliance on workers' co-operation, which in turn could only be achieved by the flexible, discretionary use of the payment system.

The incentives introduced with the more organic 1965 enterprise reform were to suffer the same fate. The reform introduced specific funds for bonuses and

[1] Here we shall concentrate briefly on the effects on enterprise organisation and activity, looking in more depth at the aims of the 1965 enterprise reform in a separate section (see Di Leo, op. cit., pp. 105–12; Filtzer, 1994, pp. 56–60).

[2] For an insight into the politics of productivity at the height of workers' mobilisation under Stalin, see Siegelbaum (1988).

social welfare, which were to be financed by the enterprise directly out of its revenues. In this way, the amount available for rewards was made dependent on enterprise performance, i.e. overall plan fulfilment. Together with the provision of specific funds for welfare provision, this new incentive mechanism was intended to make the entire workforce benefit from better performance, stimulating collective responsibility.

As part of a larger scheme aimed at introducing greater managerial autonomy and accountability, the reform faltered, therefore failing to establish any relation between greater effort and larger funds. The fact that revenues depended on administrative pricing and technical evaluation meant that they did not necessarily bear any relation to actual economic activity. More simply, decisions to concede funds and grant actual supplies had a purely political character, as is well illustrated by the situation of the consumer sector, including textiles, which used to have its revenues systematically siphoned off to subsidise heavy industry (see Filtzer, 1994, pp. 168–70). More generally, size as well as branch and location had more significance for provision of social facilities than actual enterprise performance.

On the other hand, managers once again manipulated the system, turning welfare provision (priority access to housing, scarce goods and services) into a discretionary tool to reward the efforts of individual workers. In so doing they were thwarting the objective of the reform while, at the same time, acquiring a powerful means to assert their authority and elicit workers' efforts.

The combined effect of these processes was, at macroeconomic level, continuing low productivity, waste of capital resources and high wage expenditures. The planning system ended up strained by the need to co-ordinate a complex network of dispersed technological chains and by pressures to provide resources for wages and investment to all sectors (Naishul', 1991, pp. 16–17). The enterprise management, more contradictorily, acquired greater leverage over workers by the personalised use of bonuses and the large array of social benefits now available. This overall had a 'corrupting effect on workers and managers alike, has reinforced workers' atomisation, and thereby has strengthened the elite's political control over the system' (Filtzer, 1994, p. 58). These are the elements which ushered in the Brezhnev era, combining economic stagnation with a cautious attitude to changes nurtured both by political self-confidence and by a greater understanding of the limitations of the system.

The enterprise in the Brezhnev era: managers and the planning system

The overall result of the struggle over the functioning of the planning system in the thirties was, as is well known, the establishment of a rigidly centralised mechanism of production and distribution which formally limited the control by management over the factors of production and their utilisation. The job of managers consisted in the negotiation and fulfilment of the plan. Factors of production as well as fixed capital were provided by the State, and their characteristics and use defined in detail. The ultimate goal on which managerial work was assessed and rewarded was the achievement of the planned level of production in physical terms. The most pressing constraints to which management was subjected in its pursuit were the insecurity of supply, the shortage of wage funds and materials, and the irregular rhythm of the production process.

Though all these phenomena resulted ultimately from the action of managers themselves, they appeared to each enterprise as objective conditions. To overcome these constraints managers engaged in well-known informal practices. Despite the substantial changes in the political and economic environment, which we outlined above, they remained strikingly similar over time, constrained as they were by the contradictions of the Soviet system of social relations. In the following sections we shall see how managerial practices led to the definition of the relationship with both workers and the State, contributing to shape the dynamic of the system as well as the position they occupied in it.

The actual exercise of authority by the Party-State took place at two stages of the economic process: the negotiation of the plan and its actual implementation.[1]

The actual formulation of the plan itself, despite the formal involvement of all parties concerned, was fundamentally a top-down process, incorporating the preferences of the elite. Managers and workers *alike* had therefore no grounds to co-operate in its conception and no interest in providing honestly the information required for its correct formulation. The golden rules that presided over the formulation of plans, 'taut planning' and 'planning from the achieved level', meant that enterprises were obliged fully to utilise capacity and constantly to increase output.

The fact that managers were held responsible for the fulfilment of the plan, but were not guaranteed supplies nor had sufficient control over production, made their interest run against the elite's determination constantly to increase productivity and therefore surplus extraction. Managers would therefore try to negotiate an easy plan, understating their actual capacity and availability of resources and inflating their requests for supply, while planners would rather raise figures in the opposite direction. The plan itself was therefore a reflection of the relative bargaining power of the parties to the negotiation. Managers, particularly directors, despite being a section of the elite, acted as representatives of their community in trying to extract greater resources from the centre, and their popularity and prestige were also dependent on it. This resulted in continuous imbalances along technological chains, which again justified managerial resistance to disclosing information. This in turn called for higher bodies to overcome managerial resistance by putting enormous pressure on managers and control organs towards the achievement of output targets.

Within the enterprise the overwhelming stress on gross output targets led production managers to silence those officials who were responsible for the financial and economic aspects of the activity. In a planned economy these were necessarily secondary aspects of the economic system, but they were still essential to measure its effectiveness and guarantee a flow of information to the

---

[1] On the control mechanism put in place by the Party-State to check managerial work, and for a detailed description of deceptive practices by managers, we rely on the accounts of Berliner (1957; 1988) and Granick (1954; 1960).

centre. Their subordination to the production units cleared the way for manipulation of this means by managers so as to conceal information and cheat about actual performance. Outside the factory, enterprise management tried to establish a web of connections, providing them with additional resources to face shortages and with silent approval in case of outright failures, lubricated by the exchange of favours usually referred to as *blat* (see Berliner, 1957; Ledeneva, 1998).

The ministerial structures soon learned that their performance was to be judged by the same criteria applied to the enterprises they were supposed to control. They were quite eager to obtain a branch plan which could be safely attained by 'their' enterprises and help them to receive all they needed. Nevertheless, the interest of the individual enterprise could well contrast with that of the higher administration because the latter was just interested in the branch output regardless of the individual results of each enterprise.

Local authorities, too, were held responsible and made their careers out of the productive success of their enterprises, so they were all too interested to promote them at the expense of their control function. Furthermore, the social burdens imposed by the State on enterprises, as means to guarantee the loyalty and participation of the workforce, extended beyond the boundaries of the factory, strengthening the mutual involvement between economic and political bodies. Here, too, the ability of the top managers to exert their influence did not pass without consequences. Many functions performed by civil and political bodies relied in reality on the enterprise resources, and their officials were often on the enterprise payroll.[1]

Other bodies that performed a control function were the banking system and the state financial agencies. Unlike the former, they had no connection with the enterprises and were in a better position to perform their duties. The banking system was responsible for running the accounts of the enterprise, allowing wage payments and inter-firm clearings. The enterprise was usually successful in circumventing control over wage expenditures, which were decisive to continue production with bonus-driven storming.[2] The same could not be said of investment funds that, though made available by the law on profit in 1965, were usually held up or confiscated by ministries and fiscal agencies. In general, enterprises learned never to use capital funds or to ask for credits as this could involve intrusive actions by the banks.

The fiscal system was directly connected to the payments mechanism: as enterprises operated on a non-cash basis and their finances were forced into

---

[1] On the 'mutual involvement' between managers and political bodies, see Berliner (1957); for the non-economic burdens as a source of conflict and diseconomies, see Siegelbaum (1988).

[2] Before the late 1980s, when Gorbachev's wage reform forced enterprises into full self-financing, the wage fund – at least, for basic wages – was subsidised in full by the State. One way to inflate the wage fund was therefore to increase artificially the number of jobs. This exemplifies how formal controls were quite strict but had no regard to the economic viability of the operations involved.

compulsory holdings, tax collection was exerted on settlement. As a result, enterprises were always strapped for funds. This aspect of the economic belt between the centre and the enterprises was undoubtedly of secondary importance to the extent that the flow of goods was independent of financial balances, i.e. guaranteed at fixed prices by the planning bodies. They gained in relevance as soon as the reforms introduced self-financing[1] and enterprises themselves began claiming greater control over formal economic levers. The results were discouraging mainly because these bodies were quite effective at siphoning off financial resources from the most profitable enterprises. As a result, commodity currency remained for managers a safer means of exchange and they grew warier about reforms which left the last word about the allocation of resources in State hands.

The growth of the economy, as we said in the previous section, exacerbated the problem of co-ordination between branches. The ministerial system, though, proved irreplaceable after the ill-fated attempt at decentralisation under Khrushchev. As a result 'executive bodies proliferated' (Amodio, 1993, p. 228). This could not remain without consequences. Unlike in the case of basic industries erected during the first five-year plans, the new ones required a greater number of diverse input per type of output, calling for a considerable number of executive and technical bodies to be involved in decision-making. The nature of negotiation changed as a result, resembling less a simple command system, featuring a top-down relationship between a single administration and its subordinate enterprises, than an 'administrative market' based on an 'economy of getting approval'.[2] In reality, the complexities of plan negotiation and adjustment that this change entailed, and the greater uncertainty about supplies that it generated, led to a growth in the scale and scope of the informal practices put in place by enterprises and ministries.

Enterprises strove to reduce dependency on suppliers by engaging in autarkic production of goods and components. This required substantial investment, which in turn produced only sub-standard output at higher costs. In the case of new technologies imported from the West, for which spare parts might be unavailable, this practice undermined the improvements in quality and productivity they were meant to achieve. Another practice was to reduce the range of goods and the number of components necessary to manufacture them. Standardisation, though, was carried out without reference to the needs of users,

---

[1] A first attempt to introduce profit-and-loss accounting, or *khozraschet*, in practice enterprise self-financing, was made with the so-called 'law on profit' envisaged in the enterprise reform introduced by Kosygin in 1965 (see Di Leo, 1983). Partial and then full self-financing were respectively introduced in 1987 and 1990 (see Filtzer, 1994, pp. 129–47).

[2] It is the main argument of Naishul' (1991) that an entirely new system of administration emerged in the Brezhnev era, namely the 'administrative market' as opposed to an earlier command system. Actually all of the tendencies and problems that appeared at this stage had manifested themselves much earlier. He nevertheless provides a powerful description of this system and succeeds in pointing out both its conservative character and its extreme vulnerability.

generating more problems for recipient industries and dissatisfaction among consumers.

The growing inability of the planning organs to stay ahead of the pressure from below to provide a growing array of goods and services for collective and, increasingly, private consumption led to the expansion and consolidation of informal networks exchanging and producing goods outside the sphere of the plan. Economically this was again another blow to the system as it drove resources out of the planned sphere of production and distribution. Socially it was also problematic as it generated a visible disparity in privileges and consumption and undermined any official incentive policy (see Di Leo, 1985). Politically, it helped the entrenchment of the economic and party elite at the expense of central organs, providing a powerful base for centripetal forces.

As we observed, these tendencies were present at all times, stemming from the instability of the system and generating conflicts to appropriate surplus among different layers of the elite. In the late Brezhnev years, the inability of the centre to generate additional resources led to a stalemate.

Linz's research on bureaucracy, based on first-hand interviews, provides evidence for this thesis (see Linz, 1988). Her study concluded that: Soviet managers had less scope to win lower targets while facing increasing difficulties in procurement; the bureaucracy simply struggled to overcome economic stagnation by stretching further the extraction of output without offering additional resources either for current production or investments.

This critical point was reached as a result of the fundamental inability of the system to achieve significant increases in productivity, ultimately demanding greater efforts from workers. It is in the workplace that one has to search for an explanation of the failure to modernise the economy and switch to an intensive form of development.

The enterprise in the Brezhnev era: managers and workers

The position occupied by managers in the factory, their functions and relationship with the workforce, was very different indeed in the Soviet Union as compared with its Western counterparts. The struggle for power and industrialisation by the Soviet elite shaped in an absolutely novel fashion the economic system by establishing a particular relation of domination over the working masses. The technical–scientific intelligentsia in general was marginalised and excluded from decision-making to the advantage of the Party elite and a new administrative apparatus. Factory managers in particular saw their control and authority over workers seriously undermined. With Taylorism the capitalist enterprise had brought job conception into managerial hands, using continuous technological change to break workers' resistance and unity.[1] In

---

[1] It is a widespread belief in Western literature that Taylorism had been adopted by the Soviets in the 1920s. Evidence usually points to the experiments run by Gastev and the interest expressed by Lenin himself for scientific management (see Littler, 1984). While the formal adoption of organisational innovations immediately related to

Soviet factories, managerial authority, given the limited control over technology and allocation of resources, rested essentially on paternalistic relations.

The Soviet factory was primarily identified as a production unit; and production managers, mainly engineers, were the core of the managerial structure. Nevertheless, main enterprise departments exercised little control over workshops, to which most managerial functions were decentralised. The command line privileged vertical relations, with little care for co-ordination among different stages of production. Each shop acted like the enterprise with superior bodies, bargaining for its targets, price and supply. Even at shop level, line managers were not permanently involved in scheduling production and supervising workers, which was rather the job of foremen and shift leaders.

The apparent result for observers was a production process proceeding in an anarchic fashion, with workers left alone to cope with the well-known vagaries of the Soviet workplace. Workers' behaviour seemed to follow suit, with extraordinarily high rates of idleness, unjustified leave and turnover, and all the related consequences of low discipline. Why did managers flee from production and hand over their functions to workers? Why in the face of continuous campaigns was the state unable to stimulate managers to manage and workers to work?

This can be explained partly as a direct consequence of the peculiar nature of the planning system and the set of constraints and objectives it imposed on managers. The real goal on which managerial performance was assessed was the fulfilment of the plan target in physical terms, making secondary any consideration of costs and so reducing the incentive to verify how production was actually carried out at shop-floor level.

Second, the main problem managers had to face was the uneven flow of supply, the poor quality of materials and equipment which directly or indirectly jammed production flow and effectively impeded any tight scheduling. On the contrary, it required the constant co-operation of workers to overcome these disruptions.

Scarcity also applied to labour, which meant that workers were in a strong bargaining position, as managers were very keen to keep extra staff to meet peak-time work demands (the all-out efforts to meet plan targets) and extra-factory work.

Furthermore, taut planning meant that managers had an incentive to underestimate capacity and resist upgrading of norms and the introduction of centrally determined output quotas. This also represented essential grounds for collusion between the workforce and managers.

Managers therefore, unlike their Western counterparts, had little incentive to make their way into the production process constantly to increase productivity and cut manufacturing costs, while they had every reason to reach an accommodation with workers.

Taylor's methods were to become a lasting feature of Soviet work organisation, the broader substance of Taylorism as a vehicle of change in the social relations in production is nowhere to be found in the history of Soviet industrialisation.

This does not mean that managers had no authority over workers. Workers operated in an unhealthy and often very dangerous working environment and were forced to accept heavy workloads, especially when plan deadlines approached. Soviet workers had no right to strike or otherwise to act collectively to further their grievances. The Party and official trade unions acted formally in the interests of workers but only in so far as it coincided with the line of the enterprise direction and the higher bodies. Political atomisation meant that workers could resist managerial pressures only in an individual form, depending on their specific circumstances.

In Soviet factories, workers' performance still in the 1980s was controlled by the use of the piece-rate system. This system was amenable to manipulation from below in capitalist enterprises, usually in the form of output restriction, in so far as both managers and workers were keen to achieve stable standards of output and maintenance of appropriate earning patterns (see Granick, 1954). Managers were interested in constant production flow and stable wage costs, and bargained with workers over speed. It should be understood, though, that in the West it was central offices that set standards and upgraded them constantly thanks to continuous organisational and technological change. In any case, output restriction in a capitalist enterprise could not be maintained indefinitely, as low productivity immediately activated pressures from above on the side of rising costs.

In the Soviet environment, lacking this form of check, managers left output norms to be set on the shop floor by informal bargaining with workers, tolerating low standards and high rates of over-fulfilment. In this way they acquired an easy mechanism of incentive through bonuses for over-fulfilment, but at the cost of low productivity, abnormal differences in earnings and equally high disparities between tight and loose norms within and among workshops and factories. The State, worried about declining productivity growth and rising wage costs, tried to counteract this with campaigns, reforms and incentive schemes aimed at tightening up discipline, raising norms and inducing managers to greater organisational efforts. Managers, though, resisted any attempt to modify the status quo.

The main explanatory factor here is identified in the vicious circle between labour scarcity at the general level and workers' negative control in the workplace. The low discipline and the ensuing low productivity were tolerated in order to retain workers, but these phenomena only reproduced the conditions of poor economic performance and continuous disruptions that led managers to labour-hoarding. This argument has led to the consolatory conclusion that, once the distorting constraints of Soviet planning were lifted and mass unemployment reintroduced, managers could regain control of production and achieve rationalisation (see Clarke, 1993).

The labour process engendered by Stalinist industrialisation corresponded to a structuring of a hierarchy in the shops and a corresponding labour organisation that defied managerial rationalisation no less than genuine workers' autonomy.

The Soviet workforce was very far from being a homogeneous mass; it was in fact highly stratified, and this was the base on which fragmentation and alienation could be realised and control achieved.

Production was effectively organised around a restricted number of production and auxiliary workers who guaranteed the achievement of the plan. These shock workers enjoyed extensive privileges granted at personal level and usually disguised under the banners of socialist competition. They were the trouble-shooters and rate-busters on whom managers relied to bring in the plan.

As for the large mass of unskilled auxiliaries and clerks who filled the factory payrolls, Clarke correctly points out that they did play a different role, being otherwise of little help in carrying out the production process. They represented the pool from which reliable cadre workers could be recruited and against whom the working elite could reflect its privileged position, but also an internal reserve army that could counterbalance the claims of skilled production workers, labelled as careerist by the less fortunate or less ambitious others.

So the Soviet workshop resembled at first glance the organisational model prevailing in capitalist factories until the inter-war period, before the rationalisation exemplified by the introduction of the assembly line. Yet it did not stage the antagonistic confrontation found in the capitalist countries of highly organised skilled workers versus a managerial hierarchy determined to break workers' control and privileges.

This kind of organisation did not simply restrain output growth but represented a formidable barrier to technological innovation – at least, in the form in which it was taking place in the West. Still in the 1960s and 1970s the Soviet leadership continued to look at Western technology as a model and relied heavily on imports to fill the technological gap. To run production processes centred on assembly lines efficiently, at the same time extremely rigid and vulnerable to minimal disruption, required an absolute control over the workforce no less than over the flow of supply. If managers did not feel practically in a condition to assert it because of the practical limitations they encountered in organising production, for the elite it was essentially a political problem. As we shall see in more detail in the next section, the 1965 reform envisaged a revitalisation of managerial functions as a conscious response to the requirements imposed by the Western technologies.[1] It rapidly ran into the contradiction of assigning the task of introducing the assembly line to those very shop hierarchies which it would probably have supplanted.

Under the Brezhnev leadership the idea of introducing Western managerial practices was shelved, replaced with an appreciation of the specific forms of Soviet labour organisation. The more general relaxation towards informal practices reflected the new approach. These policies, though, did not address the problem of modernisation in a new fashion, as they continued to rely on

---

[1] This seems to recall the situation party leaders and planners faced earlier, in the 1930s, when trying to adapt Western technology, imported to start large-scale industrialisation, to the new social and political conditions produced by the revolution (see Bailes, 1978; Bertolissi, 1978; Sutton, 1968).

Western imports and models. They did even less to address the dramatic fall in productivity growth, now approaching stagnation levels.

Crisis and reforms: the Soviet system in question

The history of reforms attempted by the Party during the whole post-war period can be viewed in two different ways: they can be understood as a genuine effort to enable enterprises to accomplish their productive functions by easing pressure on targets and making planning more reliable.[1] The official political drive and the urge of planners and economists all pointed at reducing the petty tutelage of the ministries, allowing more freedom in the use of resources and even recognising the contribution of formerly illegal practices – use of resources for non-planned sales and services.

Consistently with the theoretical approach outlined in the first section, we appreciate the alternative interpretation that the perennial search for solutions was indeed driven by the elite's determination to restore control over the process of surplus extraction. The methods might differ, reflecting the different appreciation that the elite had of the contradictions of the system and the severity of the crisis that crippled it. But they all had to address the problem of labour productivity and foundered on the fundamental task of restructuring the labour process (see Filtzer, 1994, p. 4). We shall sketch them briefly, before considering the dilemmas posed by the decision to attempt the full transition to capitalism.

The new policy of productivity: reforming through incentives

Under Khrushchev, the early reformers gave themselves the task of overcoming the opposition of the producers to intensification of their efforts, looking at the large Western producers of consumer goods as a model.[2] They felt as a key determinant the need to guarantee to the enterprises a safer environment. The introduction of a generalised system of welfare in the enterprises together with higher wage equality was meant to establish a new social pact with the work-force to reduce labour turnover and elicit the production discipline of modern enterprises. At the same time, the burden of the coercive system was abandoned in favour of material incentives. Top managers aspired to enjoy greater dignity and more resources for themselves and their workers. In reality, the implementation of the reforms appeared more problematic. The higher administrations continued to retain the same prerogatives as in the past, and the

---

[1] Analysts became more aware of the contradictions of the system and increasingly sceptical about its ability to adjust itself over a long period of time (see Berliner, 1988; Di Leo, 1980, 1985). But it was not until the final collapse of the USSR that the dissatisfaction of the elite with the 'socialist system' fully unfolded. A role was probably played by self-interested considerations by Western scholars.

[2] On the social policy of the USSR from Khrushchev to Brezhnev, see Di Leo (1983); on the Khrushchev reforms, see Filtzer (1992).

most ambitious attempts to shift the economic levers in favour of other bodies failed to materialise (Filtzer, 1992).

The development of enterprise welfare gave managers a powerful lever to exert its authority, but also an economic burden, sustained at the expense of production. Managers saw it as a means to reduce turnover, increase co-operation and the productivity of their workforce. Managers used welfare as a new resource to pursue their usual strategy, making the consumption of these benefits dependent on the availability of resources and on the merit of workers.

With the command system unchanged, only the privileged sector had enough resources to afford significant improvements in enterprise welfare, and this ironically implied the continuation of the poor provision of consumer goods by a beleaguered light industry, which in turn undermined the effectiveness of incentives even for workers in heavy industry.[1]

The uneven increase in wages and welfare provision under the Khrushchev reforms, which bore little if any relation to increases in productivity, undermined the concomitant attempt to consider labour a factor of production whose productivity had to be increased 'scientifically' by managers. This led to the abandonment of the Khrushchev wage reforms in 1964, to be followed by a more focused experiment with Western managerial methods.

Reforming labour organisation: the Shchekino experiment and its consequences

The continued reforms of the economy never intervened in the fundamental contradictions of the system. In the 1960s, though, the idea of introducing Western technologies prompted a reorganisation of labour, which amounted to a serious attempt at rationalising the labour process. Its failure showed the impossibility of reforming the Soviet system.[2]

In 1968 the Soviet leadership resolved to attempt an experiment which contained many elements of novelty and seemed to indicate that the Soviet economy was eventually coming to terms with Western 'rationality' in industrial management.

The Soviet economy was experiencing a slow-down in productivity and low levels of resource utilisation that, coupled with the decline in natural population growth, would have made the model of extensive growth, with no further employable people, unviable. The underlying causes were identified as labour shortages, low labour discipline, high labour turnover and under-utilisation of capacity. While all of these elements were in fact familiar faults of the system as it had existed so far, they were now seen as an impediment to economic development. In those years in fact the country was trying to make consumer

---

[1] For the role played by enterprise welfare in strengthening the enterprise profile, see Di Leo (1980); and, for the divide between sectors A and B, and its poisonous consequences in terms of economic effectiveness and social balance, see Filtzer (1994).

[2] This section is based on accounts of the experiment in Arnot (1988), from page 106 onward, and Di Leo (1973, 1983).

goods a priority while maintaining the heavy burden of the military sector. The need to increase the productivity of the heavy industry servicing the secondary sector became a priority. In particular, the focus fell on the poor utilisation of the labour force in auxiliary jobs, which lowered productivity and hoarded labour.

The Shchekino experiment was carried out in a large chemical plant in Tula *oblast'* in central European Russia, not far from Moscow. The experiment, as in previous cases, was aimed at raising labour productivity by relating rewards more closely to results. In this case, though, the use of incentives was made dependent on the 'scientific' reorganisation of labour leading to the elimination of overstaffing. The economised wage fund would be redistributed among the remaining workforce while those made redundant would be made available to other production units. Reorganisation was achieved by: raising workers' qualifications; introducing multitasking; the introduction of 'technically substantiated norms'; the use of internal committees supported by outside specialists to identify surplus labour. The result was combination of jobs and amalgamation of facilities leading to the shedding of excess labour, tighter discipline and (to a lower extent) higher wages. Productivity grew enormously, and so did state revenues. This type of reform was extended, but initial successes did not replicate themselves elsewhere and lost their momentum at the original sites as well.

What were the causes of failure? They have to be partly ascribed to the planning mechanism. The experiment tightened control over labour but also increased managerial responsibilities. Managers at the original site agreed to participate on the basis that stable working conditions were provided, i.e. even flow of supplies, stable plan and wage fund; the impossibility of replicating this condition across the entire system made reformed enterprises more vulnerable against the caprices of ministerial planning and procurement. Managerial reluctance is only fully understandable against the difficulties they faced in the shops. The initial experiment had involved a great deal of studying and bargaining with workers but made clear their resistance to intensification of work and subsequent disappointment at the meagre economic rewards. Fear of dismissal was paramount in bending their resistance. Again, these conditions could not be replicated. As managers themselves would not jeopardise co-operation with workers against the uncertain outcomes of rationalisation, large-scale restructuring was bound to fail. Moreover, much of the reduction in the labour force had been achieved by dismissing workers in 'peripheral' areas, reducing the social and welfare benefits, most importantly housing, that the enterprise could provide for its workers. Finally, the experiment was strictly limited in its scope, since the removal of workers who could be sacrificed without jeopardising plan fulfilment could not be repeated (Arnot, 1988). The very same combine that staged the initial experiment was outperformed by other factories a year later, raising concerns about the long-term effects of this strategy. According to managers themselves, the problem lay in the adjustment of planning to the new conditions in the enterprise which deprived managers of the usual safety net necessary to face an uncertain environment.

More significantly, the experiment left unanswered the crucial question as to how further increases in productivity could be achieved. The Soviets always regarded new technology in a neutral way, lacking appreciation of the resistance to innovation displayed by management. Other than the risks of disruptions imposed by planning, the problem lay in the lack of self-generating innovation within the enterprises. The Fordist revolution put into managerial hands the ability constantly to revolutionise production techniques while workers' successful attempts at regaining partial control over their work (and over surplus distribution) through collective action provided an important incentive to pursue innovation as a means to increase surplus-extraction. The lack of this tool in Soviet managerial hands and the refusal of the elite to endanger its position through open confrontation with workers meant that these experiments, even when successful, were necessarily short-lived and gave only partial relief to the otherwise stagnating economy.

Reforms under Brezhnev

The quite different type of reforms introduced in the 1970s indicates that the Party leadership considered much safer the utilisation of traditional administrative means of surplus extraction coupled with the traditional appeal to workers' self-activation.

Instead of replacing the administrative command system with new bodies or with economic levers, as tried before, the Party set to improve the system itself by incorporating the informal practices which had so far emerged spontaneously to adjust and compensate for its deficiencies.

The most important measures were the 1979 decree 'on the improvement of the planning system', which envisaged the introduction of the enterprise 'passport' and the introduction of the 'counter plan', stipulated in 1983, to be presented by enterprises (Di Leo, 1985, 319–20).

The intention to fill the missing links in the planning system was also complemented by the introduction of an intermediate body, the *ob'edinenie*, or industrial association, which was supposed to co-ordinate innovation, sales and procurement policies of a group of enterprises in the same branch. Supposedly associations should have been able to manage enterprises more closely and effectively than distant bureaucratic ministerial bodies (Schroeder, 1989). The immediate reference in the West was large corporations. This institution, and in general the policy of re-centralisation, was also to characterise the initial stage of Gorbachev's reform of the ministerial system with equally disappointing results, other than the further entrenchment of the ministerial elite.

Labour organisation, away from Western rationalisation, saw the experiment of the work brigades introduced in 1979 and generalised thereafter until 1984. The system at the same time recognised the practice of informal adjustment of work organisation and corresponding wage payments and expected it to be formalised, providing incentives for improvements. The key element was the introduction of collective responsibility for results that should supplant the individualistic approach to norm fulfilment. In theory workers were asked to save on use of labour and materials, participating in savings (see Filtzer, 1994, 70–1). This system endangered the authority of the shop hierarchy, which could only exist in the grey area of informality; it became therefore prey, like other incentives, to manipulation by foremen and line managers. By the same token it raised workers' suspicion. In any case, general problems that affected production flow made it simply impossible for these groups, any more than enterprises as a whole, to cut production buffers without running the risk of failing to fulfil their contract.

From reforms to transition

This account provides us with all the contradictory elements on the ground at the time when the last attempt to reform the system took place under the Gorbachev leadership. These reforms can be interpreted as a genuine effort to introduce economic freedoms in the country; we shall rather argue that they represented the last attempt to regain control over the economy by replacing administrative with economic levers (Filtzer, 1994).

The failure of Gorbachev's economic reforms lies in the ensuing power struggle among sections of the elite, this time including elements of the emerging private sector. It is important to notice that they differed little from the previous experiments outlined earlier in this chapter. The substantial difference with past situations was the absolute lack of additional resources in the economy to foster change, and therefore the pressing need to increase surplus extraction. This led reforms 'too far', freeing enterprises from even the imperfect control which ministries exercised on them, generating an irreversible crisis. At that point the problem became essentially political, i.e. the socio-economic base, with all its problems, remained untouched.

Once the parties recognised their inability to pursue their goals within the old framework and the whole system became the object of reform, each of them tried at the same time to make the most of their previous assets and to reach a better position in the new spheres opened up by the shift to an unregulated economy. Conflicting interests, which were previously subjected to negotiations within the framework of the planned economy and involved a high level of co-operation, were to become the leading force of disintegration. Di Leo, reflecting in 1993 on the failure of Gorbachev, pointed out how the Soviet economic oligarchy first supported him, achieving independence from Gosplan and the Central Committee, and then switched its allegiance to the radicals, the so-called democratic faction, hoping to profit from the advancing process of economic and political disintegration. The two factions, though, split dramatically as reformers took a strong pro-market anti-industrial stance (Di Leo, 1993, p. 5).

Enterprise top management at first resisted Gorbachev's reforms and continued to operate in the traditional way, with directors subverting attempts to introduce workplace democracy and asserting their rights to 'one-man management'. Many directors did not even welcome the prospect of increasing independence, preferring the relative security that ministerial control provided. But, as it became clear in the late 1980s that the transition to a market economy was advancing, a growing number of directors interpreted the reforms as an opportunity eventually to assert a fully fledged control over the enterprise.[1] Their understanding of the functioning of the economy was nevertheless limited to their traditional sphere of control, production and procurement. Enterprise directors failed to detect the risks implicit in liberalisation, which left them completely powerless against foreign competition and internal trade speculation.

In the political sphere, the emergence of the radical leadership of Westerners utterly reversed their expectations: the double standard assumed by the new politicians between new entrepreneurs and old directors made it clear that a new set of interests had been established at the expense of the latter. We should, then, turn to investigate, on the one hand, the resetting of economic institutions, focusing on the privatisation process as part of a more general political and ideological "revolution", and, on the other hand, the adaptation of managerial strategies to the new economic environment.

The team of 'reformers' put together by A. Chubais at the end of 1991 inherited the task of reasserting control over the economy, i.e. the red directors; but this time both the means and the goals were to be, at least nominally, radically different. They engaged in a battle to lead the country on the road to capitalism and did so with ruthless determination. Compromise was still considered an actual necessity with both the new businessmen and the directorial elite, but they successfully imposed the introduction of capitalism in Russia as the only viable alternative to an already unlikely, and supposedly unpopular, restoration of the Soviet system. Their clear ideological stance gained the favour of leading academics and politicians, especially in the US, which provided them with the resources and the international political support to strike the balance of power in their favour.

At that point the discourse, if not the reality, of the struggle over the economy turned into a crusade to set the country on the road to capitalism. This ideological overtone has almost entirely characterised mainstream discourse on both sides of the former Iron Curtain, until the general collapse of the financial system in 1998 opened the way for criticism to gain ground and respectability. It was the market, the firm and economic man, which featured in the 'myth of the market economy', the cornerstones of the reform ideologues and practitioners. The ideological stance of the 'Westerners' fraction is well delineated in Lester's Gramscian account of the struggle for hegemony in the Russia of the early 1990s (Lester, 1995, p. 84–96): 'without doubt the dominant theme that lies at the core of the Westerners' hegemonic strategy is the emphasis on . . . the notion of *possessive* individualism . . . The cash nexus and private ownership, of course, are the ultimate rewards and the ultimate driving forces of the newly engendered acquisitive instincts' (ibid., p. 92).[2] For radical reformers, it was

---

[1] A debate about the position of directors in the age of transition is reported in Lester (1995).

[2] By the same token, the idea of a society dominated by large corporations concentrating national resources at the expense of the many, favoured by the right-wing nationalists

only after private property had been secured in the hands of genuine entrepreneurs that an effective check of property over management would have been possible, permitting thorough restructuring. They therefore concentrated their expectations and efforts on carrying out a rapid privatisation process rather than on restructuring enterprises[1] or reorganising the regulatory framework of the economy.

The privatised enterprise in post-Soviet Russia

Privatisation of state enterprises was a pillar of the 'transition' designed by reformers; it was also an utmost necessity once the gradual liberalisation of economic organisation under Gorbachev, on the one hand, and the collapse of the ministerial system, on the other, had left no option but to set enterprises free. But, while for reformers this was a means to prevent or reverse managerial bailouts, a *de facto* privatisation in favour of old management, for the latter it was a way to consolidate their autonomous existence. As for the specific scheme that should have been adopted for privatisation, the idea of open auctions allowing direct entry from outside/international investors was discarded in favour of 'people's' privatisation. This was a variant of the Czech privatisation programme based on the issuing of vouchers to the population with a certain nominal value to be used for share purchase at open auctions. It was expected that vouchers would mostly have been traded on the secondary market and pooled in management funds so as to allow the concentration of stocks in the hands of block-holders.

The major divide between the reformers and the directorial elite concentrated on whether the labour collective was to be conceded majority ownership, since in the second case, it was argued, insiders' control would have persisted through collusion between workers and management. In the programme designed by the government, the first option 'allocated 25% of the shares to the workers free in the form of non-voting stocks with the right to buy a further 10% with a 30% rebate' (Clarke, 1994, p. 6). The second option, strongly advocated by the Industrial Union of A. Vol'skii, represented the interests of industrial management. This 'allowed the workers to purchase a controlling interest in the enterprise directly, instead of having to bid at auctions . . . under the second option a full 51% of the shares were available (to the employees) at a purely nominal price' (Clarke, 1994, p. 6).

As observed by K. Hendley in her study of early managerial privatisation, the support for employee ownership (EO) by management should be viewed as more than a short-sighted attempt to grab state property to continue pursuing rent-seeking strategies. While designing a suitable form of corporate

and reported in this book bring some reminiscence of more recent trends in Russian political and economic life.

[1] A summary of the 'popular' arguments in favour of immediate mass privatisation and its alleged accomplishments can be found in the 1990s *Economist* (Cowley, 1995; Grimond, 1997).

governance, top management linked privatisation in the form of employee ownership to a strategy aimed at enhancing productivity and workers' loyalty. EO had been pursued since spontaneous privatisation and then became the main argument of the industrial lobby when the formal mass privatisation scheme was designed. The motives brought forward in favour of its adoption focused precisely on promoting 'the harmonisation of the interests of various social groups at the same time as . . . a rather high degree of economic effectiveness' (Hendley, 1998, p. 189).

According to Simon Clarke, a managerial strategy aimed at maintaining and strengthening the 'partnership' with the labour collective developed at different stages of the privatisation process and almost independently of the form it assumed. It was embedded in the paternalistic–authoritarian methods of rule typical of the Soviet system, which were accentuated by the circumstances of transition. In a situation in where control was not substantiated by clear property rights, workers' support and subordination was essential for preventing threats from outsiders which might use corporate bodies for hostile takeovers. To the contrary, the reformers were giving voice to the growing anti-worker feelings of the political and intellectual elite, and urged the reforms to 'put those who work and those who rule back in place' (Di Leo, 1993).

A more balanced, and certainly more honest, account of the situation made clear that there was little room for alternatives, if privatisation was to be implemented. As observed later by Frydman, though outside ownership is the standard in Western experience of corporate governance and should be viewed as the invariable outcome of a successful transition programme, this was hardly attainable with the first stage of privatisation (Frydman, Pistor and Rapaczynski, 1996). In the first place it was largely recognised that the magnitude of the nominal shares' value far exceeded the then available level of market capitalisation. Second, massive entry of foreign capital was discouraged by the 'externalities' related to the high social costs of restructuring (Frydman et al., op. cit., p. 23). Given the priority of introducing hard budget constraints into the economic system and the low desirability of continued state ownership, the only feasible option was allowing employee ownership.

Not surprisingly, the second wave of the privatisation process, 1992–94, 'marked an almost total capitulation to the demands of the industrial *nomenklatura*' (Clarke, 1994, p. 6). The implementation of the programme proceeded consistently with their requests. As many as 74 per cent of the privatised enterprises chose the second option (Gurkov, 1998), and later surveys estimated that at least 65 per cent represented all insiders' shareholding (Blasi et al., 1997). To stress even further the balance in this direction, it has been noted that the other option was favoured by managers when they feared that the workers' stake might end up in outsiders' hands. Managers furthermore pursued different strategies aimed at consolidating their position, from the purchase of shares from workers and on the secondary market to pooling and freezing the remaining shares under the direct control of the board (see Clarke, 1994).

These surveys confirm that the real working of the corporate institutions of privatised companies provides more reason to believe that managers remained firmly in control with little possibility for them to evolve into outsider-owned companies (Blasi et al., 1997, p. 49). This has been sufficient for advocates of reforms to blame on management the setback of the Russian transition programme, the lack of restructuring and the frailty of Russian recovery at the end of the decade.[1] Their main argument initially was that Russian managers were inherently incapable of understanding and practising Western management; then, as the crisis deepened, that it was their irrational strategies that produced the distortive effects, causing the derailment of an otherwise certain path to capitalism and prosperity. It is the task of our study to prove otherwise. We can briefly recall the literature which has countered these arguments on theoretical grounds as well as undertaking empirical research.

> As for the essential nature of the capitalist system that is actually being constructed in reality . . . according to Michael Burawoy and Pavel Krotov, the optimists of the Western orientation have grossly exaggerated . . . the depth of economic transition in post-communist Russia. [Because] what certainly has not changed is the old type of relations in production . . . where "monopolies retain their grip on the supply of crucial commodities, and workers continue to retain their hold on production". A similar line of argument has been taken by Simon Clarke. (Lester, 1995, pp. 118–19)

In order to understand why managers continued to rely on traditional institutional arrangements and practices we have to look into their strategies and the factors which influenced their formulation and implementation. Grancelli (1995) categorises the enterprise position and the corresponding strategies according to three types of approach: rent-seeking, short-term profit-oriented, market-oriented. While many mainstream analysts (see Gurkov, 1998; Polonsky and Edwards, 1998) place a high value on managers' culture and capabilities to explain the hazardous behaviour contained in the two earlier lines of action, empirical findings also refer to the difficulties managers have to face and the possible rationality of their choices (Hendley, 1998; Polonsky and Edwards, 1998). It is with the systematic case-study based programme directed by Simon Clarke that the aims, objectives and rationale of Russian enterprise management come to the fore.

His main findings about the strategy of Russian management in the early stages of the reform can be summarised in the following points:

> These three elements [rent-seeking, market-oriented strategy, paternalism, CM] are by no means mutually exclusive, differences between one enterprise

---

[1] The liberal politician Yavlinsky, in a public speech in Washington, noted how '82% of all enterprises in the Russian Federation no longer belong to the State. But he suggested that few of them were actually publicly owned. Instead, their owners are in fact the old communist-era managers. And these people view their new possessions more like the collective farms of the past than the private enterprises of the market economy' (Goble, 1997).

and another relate to the balance between them . . . Moreover, in conditions of extreme economic and political instability a conservative strategy may be the best way of securing the long-term profitability of the enterprise . . . However the substantive differences in strategy are often far less than the contrasting rhetorics might indicate, because the enterprise is severely constrained by both its internal relationships and external circumstances in what it can do . . . Therefore privatisation provides very little incentive to investment or even significant reorganisation. (Clarke, 1994, p.13)

The case-study will unveil in what these external and internal constraints consist, how management responded to them and to what extent outside ownership could bring changes to economic organisation and managerial practices.

4 A world of textiles: the market, the industry and the enterprise

In debates on international trade the assumption is often made that export goods are 'carried to the shore, put on a boat, and sold in second countries for what the market will bear' as if aggressive exporters were targeting developed markets. In fact, trade in clothing and textiles appears more to be masterminded by agents in the importing countries. However, it is hard to assess who are the agents involved in international trade in textiles – statistical information on this is not publicly available.

Scheffer, 1994, p. 11

Textiles is classified as Light Industry but only an idiot could believe that working in textiles is a light job.

Folk saying – Russian male textile workers

This chapter introduces the case-study research with background information about recent developments in the industry and the markets both in Russia and at world level.[1] This will help us locate the position of the case-study enterprise and the region in the economic geography of world textiles. This framework provides the set of threats and opportunities which constrain the industry and the enterprise. For, however far Russian management practices and problems might differ, as we shall see, from world standards, all the major actors encountered in our research have been increasingly forced to deal with the wider global context.

Transition and restructuring in fact has meant for Russian management the requirement not only in theory to confront Western models but also to face the reality of international competition. Yet, in Russia itself and particularly in the textile industry, privatisation and liberalisation have produced something very

---

[1] For sources about world and EU textiles, see reports from ILO (1995, 1996) and OETH (1994, 1999). For Russia and the Ivanovo, region data and information have been found in FAS [Foreign Agricultural Service/ US Department of Agriculture] Gain reports (Vassileva and Trachtenberg, 1998, 1999a, 1999b, 1999c,2000, 2001; Vassileva and Hager, 2002)

different from the textbook market and the entrepreneurial rational agents. This is evident from two very different accounts, offered in this chapter, of market and industry developments in Russian textiles in the 1990s. At the end of the section a background to the case-study enterprise provides a brief history of the company town, placed in the wider socio-economic context of the Ivanovo region, as well as its key co-ordinates in terms of production, organisation and corporate history.

Market and industry in textiles: the global context

The textile sector represents a mature industry with a relatively low level of investment and technological innovation and with low economies of scale. This industry exists in most developed and developing countries, and the growth in output and export from the former has fuelled fierce competition in the past thirty years. Its importance for employment in most countries prompted the introduction of a protectionist regime, the Multi-Fibre Agreement, which has not hampered trade growth but distorted it. Both developed and newly industrialised countries (NICs) have heavily restructured, introducing newer technologies, and have shifted to niche markets or delocalised production. This has created a new world division of labour, penalising the new entrants in developing countries (Russia among them). Workers have paid for it almost everywhere with the threat of unemployment, worsening working conditions and downward pressure on wages.

Basic features of the industry

It might be useful to commence by reporting some features of the industry which represent at the same time the common traits it has assumed in its historical evolution and the bases of its latest developments and contemporary problems (see Singleton, 1997). The textile industry, generally in association with clothing (TCI), is usually referred to in historical and economic contexts as one of the lesser or light industries. This is to imply one or more of the following characteristics:

(1) The TCI represented the leading sector in the first industrial revolution and has set itself in the first stages of industrial development in second-comer and developing countries.
(2) The industry rapidly became 'mature'; i.e. it presents a lower rate of investment, technological progress and rate of profitability relative to other industries. It also means that it lost its strategic character as soon as countries developed a robust industrial and service sector.
(3) The lower intensity of capital also means that: (1) TCI retained to various degrees labour-intensive stages of production. This has lent the industry a new strategic significance in employment policies; (2) in terms of enterprise structure, TCI firms are smaller in size and limited in scope.

(4) These features combine with a high percentage of low-paid, unskilled (often harshly exploited) female workers. ILO statistics place female employment at around 40–50 per cent in textiles and 70–80 per cent in clothing production (see ILO Reports, 1995, 1996).

(5) TCI is also a basic industry in the sense that it provides essential consumer goods and exists in almost all countries.

Trade and production in the TCI: major post-war trends

The combination of these historical factors (accessibility of mature technology, labour-cost advantages, availability of local skills, demand for basic goods) has made the TCI into a major source of income and employment for most developing countries (DCs). This has been raising concerns among industrialised countries (ICs) interested in retaining their dominant market position and employment levels. Since the Second World War there has been considerable growth in trading of TCI goods, characterised by fierce competition between the two blocs and among DCs. This has induced, in the last thirty years, substantial modifications in the world division of labour in the sector, in market quota distribution and in the structure of production. These changes can be summarised in the following points:

The EU (and the USA) as a whole is still a world-leading exporter of textiles and clothing, second only to PR China; extra-EU trade accounts for 14.6 per cent of world textile exports and 9 per cent of world clothing exports. All major European producers figure in the top ten of world exporters. EU countries are also major importers, and the EU as a whole is a net importer of textiles and clothing, despite a positive trade balance in textiles. The deficits in trade balance have been deteriorating over time to the advantage of developing countries, Asian and lately OPT[1] partners (see Spinanger, 1995).

A process of regional integration with neighbouring countries rapidly developed at the turn of the last decade, only partly captured by data on OPT. It complements sourcing policies in the Far East and has set the industry on the way to internationalisation of production. Mediterranean countries and former-socialist countries provide 21.4 per cent and 20 per cent respectively of EU imports. Both areas show a surplus in total textile and clothing trade with the EU but OPT partners are in deficit for textiles and they register stable import growth of clothing as well (see OETH, 1999).

The growing role of DCs in production and the competition by NICs, now principally from PR China, have induced: the establishment of considerable customs barriers (the MFA agreement imposing quotas on DCs); the

---

[1] Outward processing trade, a form of outsourcing consisting in the enterprise exporting temporarily a semi-finished good for processing abroad in order to save labour costs by taking the more labour-intensive stages of production abroad. OPT specifically referred to EU agreements with neighbouring countries, regulating these practices. While the OPT regime is being phased out, outsourcing trade similar in practice to OPT is growing.

restructuring of the industry in ICs. The 1970s saw a peak in imports as well as the heaviest losses in employment with closures of the largest production outlets. The response has been a combination of technological innovation to cut costs and specialisation in technical and high-quality goods. Clothing and most low-cost–low-quality commodities were outsourced or relocated abroad, boosting OPT trade in textiles. Later in the 1990s, textiles for clothing were threatened with being gradually outsourced, too.

The fundamental changes that trade and restructuring have promoted in the ICs can be summarised in the following points:

> Despite data that might indicate the emergence of an autonomous competitive edge by DCs, specific research on industry structures indicates that imports do not come as a result of aggressive export policies of developing countries but 80 per cent originate from EU-based manufacturers, distributors and designers.

> Distributors are assuming an increasing role in dealing with these functions, bypassing traditional manufacturers. They are responsible for the increasing contraction of manufacturing in the sector.

> There is an ongoing shift from production to service activities. These businesses focus on the last and most profitable part of the production–distribution chain, retaining logistics, marketing, design and finishing functions. All the rest is outsourced.

> Conversely DCs, while playing a growing role in production and export, suffer greatly from: the procrastination of the quota system and anti-dumping policies by ICs; an unfavourable division of labour which relegates them to providers of low-cost commodities or commission-based orders; an extreme competition, both political and economic, to gain a gateway in IC markets, which depresses revenues with heavy impact on salaries and working conditions in developing countries.

Market and industry in textiles: Russia and the Ivanovo region

The Russian textile industry, based in Ivanovo and the central region of European Russia, had seen a dramatic development at the beginning of the twentieth century but was badly neglected in Soviet times (Kouznetsov, 2004a, 2004b; Treivish, 2004). Unsurprisingly, privatisation and liberalisation dramatically accelerated its decline. The Russian TCI sector was badly equipped to confront integration into the international market. Apart from the typical distortions of a Soviet-type industry, it suffered from the marginality of consumer goods production under planning and a historical prevalence of textile commodities in its product assortment.

Trade liberalisation and the disruption of the command chain have resulted in the collapse of production with ensuing social dislocation and the absolute dominance of imports in the internal market. The Ivanovo region, dominated by the TCI sector, has suffered badly with the slump in production in the 1990s but has recovered most of its Soviet output thanks to the collapse of the industry elsewhere (Adams and Vassilieva, 2003a, 2003b, 2004, 2005) and is now undergoing restructuring under the lead of Central Asian and Moscow trade companies. The dominant activity has remained the processing and export of low-value cotton fabrics, light cloth for state procurement and other inexpensive low-quality commodities.

In turn, the dominance of the industry in the region is primarily responsible for Ivanovo presenting the worst social and economic indicators in European Russia, which makes its survival a dramatic social issue and the object of political controversy. The future of the region is clouded by the fact that its low level of economic diversification offers little perspective for alternative development paths (see Keune, 1996). The social and political situation offers an equally bleak picture. High levels of real unemployment, the lowest income in European Russia and high levels of criminal activity are simply indicators of a generalised social decline.

The problematic situation in the industry raises two fundamental sets of questions: one relates to causes and responsibilities which determined the present situation; the other concerns the actual possibility of, and conditions for, successful recovery. The former issue is dealt with by looking first at the figures of decline and then at the facts behind it, providing a historical account of enterprise strategies.

Russian textiles in figures: the industry performance from the 1990s to the present

In the 1990s the Russian textile industry was characterised by four intertwined developments: a dramatic fall in output; a shift in product assortment towards cotton fabrics; a geographical dislocation of production, assigning to Ivanovo the lion's share of cotton goods manufacturing; a rearrangement of the industry structure, with traders acquiring a dominant role in the value chain by controlling supply and distribution.

Production fell continuously during the 1990s; the decline being both sharper and more prolonged than in general manufacturing. By 1996 fabric output had fallen to 1,401 million square metres, down from around 2,000 million in 1994 (Vassileva and Hager, 2002). As a result, in 2000, while overall manufacturing output was at around 60 per cent of its 1990 level, the index for textiles was a mere 20 per cent (Hanzl and Havlik, 2003). A recovery began only after the 1998 crisis but has been short-lived, reaching its peak in 2002. Fabric production, cotton fabrics in particular, features less depressing results. In 2000 output was at 32 per cent of the initial 1990 levels, and the share of cotton had risen to above 80 per cent of overall Russian fabric production. The recovery, though, has not been equally shared among regions (and enterprises). If production of cotton fabrics had fallen from around five and a half million to less than two million square metres between 1990 and 2000, production in the Ivanovo region accounted for 1,200,000 at the end of the period, or 67 per cent of the 1990 level, raising its share of Russian cotton fabrics output from 33 per cent to 70 per cent (Adams and Vassilieva, 2003a, 2003b, 2004, 2005). Furthermore, production in the region is narrowly focused on these items. In the Soviet period cotton amounted to 80 per cent of all fabric production; the previous decade saw the almost complete disappearance of non-cotton and clothing production (at least from statistics). Attempts at diversifying the product range have been timid, and current plans to move into flax processing and home and bed linen are dependent on company strategies and industrial policy.

At the same time, reports from the same years indicate that most mills in the region, around 80 per cent, were still unprofitable, burdened with social costs and equipped with outdated machinery (Vassileva and Trachtenberg, 2000). A major obstacle to restructuring pointed towards the dominance of traders and intermediaries. It is calculated that 90 per cent of textile output was produced under 'tolling' or 'processing-only' agreements, which stifled manufacturers' revenues and decision-making powers. The termination of barter arrangements with Uzbekistan, which lasted into the late 1990s, resulted in the domination of imports based on these arrangements; whereas the raw cotton and the finished products remain the property of the raw- material suppliers, and mills are merely paid for processing. Although tolling lowers costs by allowing imports to enter free of duty and value-added tax, and removes the need for Russian mills to buy cotton with hard currency, it also removes a mill's decision-making power over production and marketing and blocks the development of a recovery strategy which could attract investment (ibid., pp. 3–4).

No less importantly, textiles' contribution to the regional economy is still significant. It accounted for 76 per cent of 'exports', or US$7,466 million, in 2003, more than half of industrial employment but only 30 per cent of manufacturing output value and 11 per cent of capital funds (Federal Service of State Statistics, 2004).

In terms of exports, the industry has failed to take advantage of global growth in sectoral trade, being a net importer particularly in the clothing component, and has been outperformed by other former socialist countries in Eastern Europe. The Russian share of the EU market is insignificant. Unlike Eastern European countries (CEECs), Russia was not a significant partner for outward processing trade (OPT) in the 1990s, and the lifting of quotas in 1998 has not brought significant changes. Correspondingly, foreign direct investments have not materialised. The export structure reflects the anomalous preponderance of textiles over clothing in production with 44 per cent of exports to the EU concentrated in this category. A significant price gap also indicates that the sector concentrates on low-quality–low-cost items (Hanzl and Havlick, 2003).

Overall, textiles do not play a significant role in the Russian economy, with less than 10 per cent of employment at the federal level and only a fraction of GDP (ibid.) and exports, but represent a critical resource for the Ivanovo region. Second, it appears that the industry has fundamentally failed to adapt to trends in the international markets, coming to rely on a narrow range of goods with the lowest value and growth potential. In order to understand what stands behind these trends, it is necessary to look at institutional arrangements within the industry and the power struggles that reshaped them.

The industry structure

In 1995–7 the management consultants' firm where I was employed conducted a thorough examination of the state of the TCI in Russia, the analysis focusing on enterprises in the Ivanovo region. The local industry output amounted to over 60 per cent of the Russian output of cotton fabrics, up to 50 per cent of linen output, while wool-made goods were only 5 per cent of total Russian output (GosKomStat data). The analysis outlines their main features, highlighting their organisational and operational dysfunctions as considered in comparison with standards of their Western and Asian competitors.

Their main features are: the dominant role of production among business areas; functional organisational structures, notwithstanding the scale of production and the product range; integrated production chain within individual enterprises; highly specialised dedicated machinery; prominent role of the welfare system.

The internal organisation was understood as functional to these structural features and appeared substantially in continuity with the Soviet past. Its key elements can be summarised in the following points: corporate management was bureaucratic; there was no relation between formally appointed positions and real jobs; sales and accounting functions were little taken into consideration; marketing was weak or non-existent, and commercial functions were mostly concerned with barter deals rather than being busy with market sales, pricing and analysis of competitors.

At the all-industry level, the lack of co-operation among individual enterprises was negatively stressed, particularly given the significantly high sectoral specialisation of this geographic area. Enterprises did not show any interest in or ability to develop a division of labour and persisted in manufacturing the same kind of goods, resulting in destructive competition. Still, they have not been able to set a common standing towards suppliers and final customers in order to strengthen their position in terms of price and quality. As a result their contractual power was low, and many of them had virtually become a mere productive unit under large financial–industrial groups or ambiguous intermediaries.

The market structure

It was admitted that the current enterprise organisation and its management were consistent with the situation in the industry and the 'market' in Russia. In fact, the collapse of the command economy has not delivered anything close to competitive open markets. On the supply side, the 'retreat' by the State had meant partly a mere change of the legal status under which former state agencies operated, partly the entry of new subjects like banks, investment funds and trade intermediaries. The lack of funds limits the choice of suppliers, strengthening the position of these subjects. These companies pursued a rent-seeking strategy aimed at maintaining their monopolistic position instead of fostering investments and business-oriented restructuring.

On the demand side, the positioning of the enterprises was equally weak. With shrinking orders from the State, textile industries were supposed, as any other consumer-oriented industry, to be led by mass consumption. But, more than any other consumer goods manufacturer, they found themselves overtaken by foreign competitors. Many industries were forced to look at exports of cheap commodities as the vital source of revenues, while their market share at home was at stake. As a result these enterprises were operated in survival mode with no chance of survival in the long term.

This analysis provides a useful insight into the economic and organisational structure of the industry, and yet by retaining the assumptions of rational agency and competitive markets, specific to capitalist mainstream economics, fails to explain the behaviour of the agents and to predict further developments in the industry. Its focus on the enterprise and its insistence on restructuring individual production units into capitalist companies fails to see that other forces are leading the regional economy in a different direction. By the same token, its lack of interest in industrial relations, power and conflict within the enterprise leads consultants to obscure the major social and cultural constraints to managerial action.

Red managers, the market and the State

Textile enterprises gained independence from ministerial rule with the first wave of privatisation in the early 1990s.[1] Formally, they were transformed into employee-owned joint-stock companies; in reality, it was top management or the director alone who took full control. Against initial expectations, though, from the outset, the opportunities ascribed to transition were more than outweighed by the effects of institutional disruptions and economic crisis. Structural features of the industry meant that textiles were particularly disadvantaged in facing these changes.[2] First, hyperinflation wiped out enterprises' working capital; the break-up of the Soviet Union left enterprises without their traditional sources of supply, forcing them to renegotiate cotton supplies on an individual basis under onerous conditions; the suspension of state orders and the collapse of the distribution network, combined with the ill-

---

[1] Privatisation, according to our respondents, did not imply a separation between public and private functions, rather their privatisation to the local ruling elite, which continued wrestling to secure control over public offices and enterprises alike as the only means to consolidate its power and wealth. For these reasons, privatisation was not perceived as such by the new 'owners', enterprise employees, who instead understood the whole process as managerial entrenchment. It is, in any case, difficult to maintain that it 'turned out relatively well' (see Kouznetsov, 2004b; Ivanov, S., 2001).

[2] These included, among others, outdated equipment, large scale and limited scope of product range and production facilities, lack of supply and sales capabilities.

considered liberalisation of foreign trade, led to foreign imports flooding the market before local manufacturers could even plan adjustment to competition.

Lack of funds, uneven production and decaying equipment worsened the situation in production, leading to increases in waste and indiscipline, reinforcing managerial reliance on workers. Furthermore, the industry was hit by a massive outflow of cadres, which prevented reform in employment strategies. To make things worse, as several top managers pointed out, 'an imprudent statement from the then prime minister Gaidar against the need for retaining a textile industry brought havoc among manufacturers' (Interview with manager, 2000; interview with factory director, 2005).

The response by directors was the adoption of survival strategies aimed at facing immediate threats; policies and outcomes varied greatly depending on the honesty and abilities of management as well as on the initial economic conditions of the enterprise. Overall, enterprises were faced with the following options.

A limited number of enterprises managed to access private financial services for purchases of raw materials and replacement of working capital, but these came at a cost of increasing indebtedness owing to soaring interest bills. A number of enterprises also enjoyed local government subsidies or guaranteed loans, which produced very much the same effect. These loans were dependent on personal ties and implied the retention of high employment levels and the enterprise social sphere. As for sales, most enterprises 'gave up the commercialisation of their output in favour of the "new Russian traders" in exchange for a rouble out of every five of sold output. Under this scheme the enterprise would receive 10 to 30 kopeks for each rouble depending on the honesty of the director. Many directors liked the scheme' (Interview with Ivanovo cotton mill director, 2005).

As financial sources began to dry up and profits failed to materialise, the shortage of cash led to an increasing role for barter. This further alienated managers from the final consumer and deepened their dependence on suppliers. Instead of downsizing and modernisation of products and production, management was to a lesser or greater extent forced to concentrate on production of the existing range as the only means to salvage the labour collective, feed supply lines and retain a satisfactory level of revenues. In the late 1990s a limited group of traders and financial intermediaries had concentrated the cotton business in their hands, while enterprises worked mostly on a 'processing only' basis. The terms of the deal leaned clearly in favour of traders, who squeezed any revenue out of production units while enterprises plunged into indebtedness.

On the eve of the 1998 crisis the situation was ripe for a change which saw trading companies forcing enterprises into bankruptcy 'by means of the controlling stake of debt liabilities' (Interview with Ivanovo cotton mill director, 2005).[1] The takeovers were, as rule, followed by the dismissal of the red

---

[1] Each holding has a different history, and among them not all enterprises were subjected to supply schemes (*davalcheskaya skhema*) before formal acquisition; still,

directors and top management loyal to them. This first wave of bankruptcies and acquisitions has led since 1999 to the formation of holding companies, which represent therefore a consolidation of private, often personal, businesses operating initially in the area of finance and commerce and primarily oriented to speculation.

As previous research has proved in the case of other industries (Clarke and Kabalina, 1994; Clarke, 1996), in textiles, too, managers were forced to design survival strategies which favoured the retention of Soviet managerial practices. Despite the new economic doctrine dictating otherwise, high production volumes, large labour collectives and political ties increased the chances to face the crisis in the short term. Bankruptcy, leaving aside structural inefficiencies and insiders' hazardous behaviour, often struck healthy businesses falling victim to trading houses' attempts fraudulently to appropriate production capacity and shut down competitors. This also explains the persistence of a high percentage of 'unprofitable' enterprises as the new owners exploited such status to avoid taxation and wage rises. Contrary to mainstream economists' expectations, market institutions and incentives failed to materialise, and what followed privatisation and liberalisation was rather a development in the conflict over resources by existing actors. More specifically, if managers did not develop a taste for innovation and customer orientation, this was very much the result of new traders and their political sponsors dominating supply and sales channels, orienting the business towards a narrow range of staple goods easy to place in barter deals, cheap exports and state procurement.

Managers and workers in production

It was said earlier that unfavourable conditions prevented enterprises from seriously intervening in production management, leaving traditional Soviet practices intact. This calls for an explanation of the nature and consequences of these practices and the causes of failure to change them, other than lack of investment.

Managers in the industry refer to this bundle of issues as 'the human factor': namely the resistance of top and middle management to the introduction of, and adherence to, standard procedures and control systems; the systematic failure of line managers to pay attention to quality and costs; and workers' lack of discipline, mostly exemplified by high levels of alcoholism and absenteeism. These phenomena were common currency in Soviet times and, according to industry practitioners and our own observation, have only worsened in the last decade. More importantly, change of ownership has apparently had little impact on their occurrence despite widespread claims pointing at Soviet directors as reasons for their endurance. The case is well exemplified by a complaint raised in an interview with the director of one of the best-equipped factories in a newly established Ivanovo-based textile trust. He reports that: 'No day ends without someone being fired for absenteeism or alcohol abuse. Before, it was understood

politically masterminded bankruptcy has been the standard procedure for takeover, according to a wide range of local industry and media sources.

that people drank out of despair. Nowadays, since they have a good wage, they can afford the extra drink' (Okhotnikova, V., 2006, p. 2).

This statement tells us a number of things about personnel management. First of all, such a statement highlights that the nature of the problem and its seriousness has not changed much from the late Brezhnev period, despite the dramatic fall in workers' bargaining power owing to privatisation and high unemployment. Second, methods to tackle it have not changed, either; the major control lever remains the wage and disciplinary system, with ensuing high wage-disparities. In this case an alleged average wage of 6,000 Rb, with skilled professions climbing up to 12,000 Rb (against an average of 3,500 Rb in the local industry) indicates a substantial failure of monetary incentives to attract and discipline 'dutiful' workers.

Significantly the interviewee refers to the usual argument of unfavourable labour-market conditions to justify this trend. Evidence of low productivity and high staffing levels from interviews and direct observation, though, suggests that the industry is crippled by a vicious circle of labour-hoarding and under-employment, on the one side, and labour scarcity, on the other. Overall, research findings point to the fact that production mismanagement is both widespread and systemic and its roots should be sought in work organisation and the underlying system of social relations regulating these work communities.

It is well known that Soviet managers had little control over the production process, which was the responsibility of workers (Arnot, 1988; Filtzer, 1992): foremen and workers' leaders would oversee work in the shops, and the piece-rate made sure workers did their best to earn their bonus. Yet the lack of managerial co-ordination made disruptions inevitable and discipline violations hard to detect. True, textiles, a women's industry, saw less of the latter, mostly among male specialists, but their prominent role has proved a major cause of conflicts and disruptions. One of the consequences of disregard for women's work is represented by the neglect of health and safety considerations reflected in the despicable state of work-places, the state of decay of equipment and facilities, and the use of a four-shift timetable (see Filtzer, 1992, pp. 177–208). These conditions have further depressed productivity and act as a barrier to attracting qualified workers. This 'sexual' division of labour allows the depreciation and exploitation of female work, which, in turn, has proved a powerful basis for managerial control (Bowers, 1996; Monousova, 1996). It also deprives owners of immediate economic incentives for technological and organisational innovation.

This brief account of the nature and causes of the crisis that has crippled the Russian textile industry allows us to challenge a number of commonsensical views regarding the decline of the industry. Our main conclusions are: that obstacles to restructuring lie deep in the social texture of labour collectives, something Russian managers (and in fact foreign experts) were not equipped to recognise early on and easily tackle later; that any transformation was halted by a hostile political and economic environment, whatever directors' political meddling and wealth-amassing hazards may have counted for; therefore, what outside owners have inherited is not the sole product of insiders' mismanagement but the very consequence of their strategy. The long stand-off between insiders and outsiders suggests that relations between management and ownership are not set to run smoothly but also provide grounds to justify managerial resistance and suspicion. The new holdings, emerging as the major players in the business in the early 2000s, are entangled in the same contradictions, and are therefore bound to face the challenges existing before takeover.

Case-study background: the Upper Volga Textile Combine

When I was first assigned to this enterprise, in 1997, under an internship scheme with a consulting firm, I wondered why the employer had felt that precisely this one, among the twelve enterprises falling into our project, was a safe and interesting place for me to work. The chief of our Russian-based team argued that the company was still in good shape relative to others, i.e. it was neither bankrupt nor suffering from dramatic social or economic turns, and was therefore a stable and safe environment. He added, though, that by no means should I interpret this as an indicator of business success: in his view the factory lived only because, as a company town with a large workforce, it enjoyed a political dividend in the form of public support; in practice he meant that this was a dinosaur doomed to extinction. Those better-placed to win the race were smaller enterprises led by entrepreneurial directors. Events, as we shall see, have instead taken a quite different turn that none of us would have envisaged at the time. The enterprise outlived what then appeared its competitors but only to become a third-rank sweatshop under a trading house.[1] This indicates the difficulty of introducing a case-study as a typical, successful or otherwise neatly classifiable example. Here are just some basic historical, social and economic specificities of this case-study site; the best way to familiarise with it rests in the reading of the history of this organisation as it unfolds in time and unveils its complexity in the next substantive chapters.

Rise and fall of a company town: a brief socio-economic history of Russian textiles

The factory was established in the 1880s by Russian merchants on the banks of the Volga in a sparsely populated area not far from a thriving commercial town. According to local historical sources (Schelkov and Antonov, 1998, pp. 16–43), investors were attracted by the low labour costs, the availability of raw materials (timber and linen) and the strategic riverside location, which represented then

---

[1] At the beginning of 2007, the average wage for a worker at this enterprise amounted to 3,000 roubles, which compares poorly with the regional average of 3,500 reported in the industry a year before and the more so with the staggering 7,000 paid in one of the best factories in Ivanovo. The enterprise, only a decade earlier, was one of the best-paying employers, and the largest manufacturers, in the region.

the best route for freight. Most importantly, the needle trade was already well established in the locality with a flourishing cottage industry, which developed after the 1861 reforms had left most peasants without sufficient land to sustain their families. In less than a decade the factory grew exponentially, coming to employ thirteen hundred workers, almost as many as all the nine factories in the neighbouring town. Installed machinery grew threefold and capital invested five times by the end of the century, granting the factory a mention by Lenin himself as one of the most important industrial centres in European Russia – at least, according to the claims of the factory history book (ibid., p. 20).

Social unrest followed, with an increasing record of strikes and political mobilisation, making the factory once again the object of attention of the leaders of the working-class revolutionary movement. There were reasons for it: despite investment and profits the factory operated in the most dreadful conditions. It lacked the most basic sanitary facilities – principally ventilation – and paid extremely low wages. One third of the factory workforce was made up of children, and it was only by the end of the century that the authorities were persuaded to ban the employment of children under the age of 12. A local judge and social observer in the 1890s noted in his diary: 'a group of children from the factory, aged approximately twelve, dirtied with dust, run for a swim to the river. They had half a kilometre left. The majority stalled half way, long coughed and only after rest they quietly completed their journey. Most of them will not live even as far as the age of forty . . . this is the way the capitalist factory, like the legendary Moloch, swallows the children' (ibid., p. 21).[1]

War in 1914 and the 1917 Revolution saw the direct involvement of the workforce at the forefront of the revolutionary movement; but ironically, as nationalisation and workers' control were achieved, the civil war left the company town in a dreadful situation with no capital, raw materials or food provisions. It took several appeals to Lenin himself and endless struggles with the new Moscow authorities to restart production that recovered to pre-war levels only in 1925.

The late 1920s saw a further step forward with the construction of a hospital, a school and a massive social club; the properties of local aristocrats were turned into a health resort and a children's summer camp, the church into a confectionary. The village had become a town. Not much was added to the town's planning afterwards other than housing developments and production facilities, both of declining quality: first, the post-war red-brick houses built by

---

[1] The advent of socialism and lately of capitalism might have changed a lot, but the Moloch has continued to claim victims. It is a dark irony that I recollected a similar anecdote among workers at the factory concerning job-related illnesses. A woman remembered how her husband used to go for a swim, but amazingly his legs would stay dry as if they were watertight. She related the occurrence to his job in the bleaching shop where workers where left to work with all sorts of hazardous chemicals. Mortality was high among these workers, and no prevention and little help was offered by the poorly equipped local hospital. By the same token, night work and ten-hour shifts have been restored since privatisation.

German prisoners, then the notorious Khrushchev and Brezhnev prefabricated high-rises. Noticeably, none of the latter replaced entirely the former, so that moving from the factory on the riverbank, walking up the hills, one can observe the specimens of a century of workers' housing from wooden huts to the latest private developments of the local new rich.

A watershed in the social and economic history of this region is represented by the launch of the Stalinist industrialisation drive, which heavily penalised the light industry. Historians have just begun, on the basis of recently retrieved archival evidence, to reveal the extent of workers' resistance to wage cuts, tightening of discipline and food rationing, which in 1932 reached a climax with demonstrations and walkouts harshly repressed by the authorities (Rossman, 2005). The company town is directly mentioned in this work in relation to worsening living conditions, workers' reactions and political repression. There is no reason to doubt, then, as to why the company town followed very much the same fate as other industrial centres in the region transforming it from the centre of the conflict and contradictions of the fast economic development of the late czarist time into a somnolent and rather marginal provincial spot.

Anecdotal evidence surfacing from interviews at the factory corroborates this deduction. For Kolya, women workers' passivity, in particular their inability to put up collective action and their acceptance of the director's quasi-autocracy, should be understood as the long-term consequence of mass repression in those times. In his own words, 'Only those who kept their mouth shut survived it, and since then not a whisper has been heard; they are still afraid, I suppose' (Interview with shop manager, 2001). A veteran worker of the machine repair shop (see Introduction) referred to an episode in which a truck of OGPU agents came down to the factory to beat up and arrest people – including women, he emphasised with outrage.

Yet Stalinism did not seem to consolidate only on the basis of coercion. The gender divide in the working-class movement was crucial, as unveiled by Rossman (1997a, 1997b) and Glickman (1984), in allowing first the Bolsheviks then Stalinist authorities to defuse conflict and suppress workers' autonomy. The two key moments in this area were: the support for women's demands in the 1920s for better wages and higher status against male foremen, who had been at the forefront in the movement and monopolised its leadership,[1] while also being known and resented for their misogyny and continued abuse of young spinners and weavers. This concluded with some improvement in the status of female workers and, apparently, with the neat separation of male and female roles – the assistant foreman would become a male-only position responsible for technology while women foremen were left in charge of personnel; the development of differentiated patterns of bargaining: whereas open collective action, traditionally led by men, was suppressed leaving almost no trace, women instead resorted to less politically threatening actions based on 'the need to feed and clothe their children' and enacted and justified by the 'irrationality of

---

[1] Noticeably there is not a single woman among the leading figures named in the company-town history until the 1930s.

women'. These developments, as we shall see, have left profound marks in class and gender relations, shaping patterns of resistance and power relations in the factory.

If militancy became a risky business, and private initiative was banned, peasants and workers were offered plenty of opportunities for individual social mobility within the ranks of the Party-State and the enterprise hierarchy, as appears from the male genealogy of some respondents. Boris's family memoirs proudly mention his grandfather's role in the Civil War – a true Bolshevik with his huge Mauser machine-pistol who used to raid the countryside for grain requisitions to be shipped to the starving capital city but fell into disgrace because of the disappearance of one such freight – followed by his father – a decorated medical officer during the Great Patriotic War. As for himself, he had more modestly chosen to work in the factory as an engineer, like many in his generation, and enjoyed the sort of middle-class affluence achievable by Soviet standards in the 1970s and 1980s.

This is the focus of another manager's tale, disgruntled with the rampant corruption and the blatant display of wealth of corrupted officials and top managers. The table well stocked with beers while his wife was away, he reasoned: 'In my family they were well-to-do farmers. The communists forced us to give away all our cows, but they set clear rules: so if you were, let's say, a line manager you were entitled to a flat and a car, a higher position would yield a better car and a dacha, while top officials were allowed a two-floor dacha, a three-room flat and a Volga; now they try to grab as much as they can and there seem to be no limits' (Interview with line manager, 2000).

Another engineer in the quiet but marginal repair shop, reflecting on the intergenerational social dynamics in his family, pointed out more clearly the disillusion and sense of betrayal of these managers. I sit in his car as he tells me about his job; he is not happy with it and regrettably admits that he failed to continue studying since life seemed much easier back in the 1970s. His father had been the chief economist at the enterprise, a respected man and devoted communist; the car was a present from the director himself, who forced his father to accept it. The man never took advantage of his position, the son observed with regret, and it was difficult to reject his account as I observed the old man mending a makeshift greenhouse in his garden.

What these accounts talk of reflects very much the socio-economic changes in the country in the post-war period as they impacted on the perception of life chances and expectations. They provide an individual insight into the parable drawn by social mobility and then stagnation, furnished by apparent material prosperity, which translated in disillusion, passivity and modest accommodation to the system. A brief parenthesis in 1990–5 saw the attempt of the director to salvage his reign, sheltering the enterprise from the generalised crisis, but as the end of the decade drew nearer it was clear that the indissoluble link between the enterprise and the town, like the one between the State and the people, was strained to breaking point. Most of the managers who offered their account in this research have by now left the enterprise for shuttle jobs in more prosperous towns and regions or have left the town altogether. Demographic and economic decline has been recently manifested even in the administrative status of the locality being lowered from town proper to urban settlement.

The 2004 case-study passport: organisation, people and machines

The Upper Volga Textile Combine is an integrated cotton-processing enterprise. It is located in a company town in the crisis-ridden Ivanovo region that is dominated by the textile industry. The enterprise is the only employer in the locality.[1] The factory's main products include gauze and cotton fabrics for kitchen and bed linen production. The company has developed a profitable export business since the late 1980s, amounting to 5–10 per cent of its output. The bulk of production was used for barter with suppliers. The enterprise used to run all of the company town's social services; and, despite downsizing, they remain a heavy financial burden.

The organisational chart of the enterprise corresponds to a simple functional model (Lipsic', 2000).[2] The director, the chief engineer, and the main functional officers at the top constitute the administration (AKhO). Directly subordinate to the chief engineer, production is divided into four units: spinning, weaving, finishing, and a large maintenance section. Each production department maintains its accounting, wages, and labour offices. Departments are headed by a chief production manager, below whom are the shop managers. Equally important are cadre workers (foremen and brigade leaders), who have disciplinary and organisational powers.[3] Although formally the organisation is highly centralised, in practice it is decentralised and there is little standardisation of procedures. Power remains strongly personalised.

At the top, the executive director and the chief engineer hold decision-making powers on all strategic issues. They also have the last word on most petty questions – including individual cases of hiring, firing, holidays, and so on. The functional departments (in particular the personnel, and the labour and wage departments) are under-staffed and under-qualified. They serve as mere transmission belts along the hierarchy. The chiefs of production are in charge of overall production planning and budgeting for their units. However, it is in the shops, and between shop chiefs and cadre workers, that decisions relevant to workers are made. Hiring and firing decisions, disciplinary matters, and performance assessments are first made at this level, and are then moved upward for approval. Production managers are the backbone of the managerial structure. They form a parochial defence of their units' interests against the

---

[1] The Expert Institute selected the company town as representative of industrial decline in Russian company towns. The town is characterised by shrinking population, high unemployment, low economic diversification, and underdevelopment of the service sector. Together, these conditions have resulted in social pessimism and overall economic depression (Lipsic', 2000).

[2] Data and analyses pertaining to the organisation of the enterprise were found in the reports of consulting firms which advised the enterprise.

[3] Shop managers and cadre workers will here be collectively referred to as line managers, the direct representatives of managerial authority in the shops.

demands of the administration. Privatisation has not substantially modified this organisational hierarchy and decision-making process.

Currently, the workforce stands at 3,000, down from the 5,000 employees of a decade ago.[1] Two-thirds of the workforce is concentrated in the main shops and is predominantly female (e.g. Bowers, 1996; Rossman, 1997b, pp. 16–35). The main shops are staffed by female machine operators, male mechanics and auxiliary workers.[2] The position of machine operator in manufacturing is generally a well-paid male profession in Russia. In textiles, though, the operation of looms is left to women workers. This probably draws on traditional gender segregation, but also reflects the (allegedly) feminine skills matching the job requirements, such as manual dexterity. Jobs which require greater acquaintance with machinery and involve heavy or dangerous working conditions are assigned to men. Similarly, managers and specialists are invariably male, while women fill clerical and low status-positions (see Bowers, 1996; Rossman, 1997b).The Soviet wage system has hardly been touched. Workers are paid by piece-rate plus bonus, while ITR and auxiliaries are paid by time-rate plus bonus (Kirsch, 1972). Wages vary considerably between, and within, work categories and (covertly) by gender. Shop chiefs manage the pay system in a discretionary manner so as to augment their leverage on workers, though lamenting the overall abysmally low level of pay (Morrison and Schwartz, 2003).

The company was formally privatised in 1993, but remained in the hands of its Soviet director and his close aides. Declining revenues and growing costs were countered by stressing output volume. While maintaining enterprise paternalism, the management tried to tighten discipline and increase workloads. Mounting economic and social difficulties presented a window of opportunity in 1998–9 for a hostile takeover by an industrial–financial group pursuing an aggressive acquisition policy in the region. The outsider company, LTD – itself a subsidiary of a financial–industrial group – entered into business with the case-study enterprise as its supplier.

In 1998–9, LTD managed to acquire considerable influence over its operation through the so-called *daval'cheskaya schema*, a well-known Russian strategy for acquiring a company. Formally the parties enter into a processing-only trade agreement by which the manufacturer is supplied with raw materials in exchange for the finished product but is allowed to retain part of it. In reality, the manipulation of (high) input prices and (low) revenues by means of the

[1] The town population was 12,400 in 1997, and declining. Working-age population was 6,400, with registered unemployment standing at 508 (Lipsic', 2000).

[2] The Soviets had a liking for meticulous worker classifications. This was originally justified on the basis of adhering to the Taylor system of scientific organisation. Later it was used to fragment and divide workers. White-collar personnel were sub-classified as ITR, engineering, and technical personnel (including managers, but excluding clerks). Blue-collar personnel were classified between main production workers, who operate core business technology, and auxiliaries (such as loaders, cleaners, and maintenance workers).

monopolistic control of the enterprise's sales and supply channels allows the trader to plunge the target enterprise into indebtedness. LTD forced the case-study enterprise into bankruptcy and, though still under a temporary administrator, installed its people in the factory and dictated its policy.

Currently, the enterprise is waiting to be auctioned off, but LTD prefers to prolong bankruptcy procedures for fiscal advantages and as a means to intimidate the workforce. At the same time the new owners have worked hard to foster tighter production and financial discipline, but they have been cautious not to undermine the basis of shop managers' informal control.

5 Structures and strategies in transition

There is no such thing as Soviet management: management in Soviet times simply meant bosses picking up the phone to get things sorted out!
V. Khasbulatov, entrepreneur, owner of factories and co-operatives,
ex-convict

The discussion around the business plan has led me to think that the Russians fully understand at a conceptual level the technological and qualitative requirements of market competition but are prevented from putting them into practice. This is also the cause of deep frustration on their side: plunged into the day-by-day running of the factory, managers are forced to shelve their plans for modernisation.
Leo, chief management consultant, free thinker, Italian

In this chapter we introduce our analysis of the case-study with an overview of the firm's structure and strategies in the 1990s. The enterprise has been subjected to detailed reviews by business analysts who have highlighted the shortcomings of its organisational features and presented recommendations on how better to meet forthcoming challenges. The main point resulting from these reports was the anachronistic permanence of most Soviet features in its structures and its passive adaptation to changes in the external environment. In this chapter we try to make sense of these outcomes, providing a different theoretical approach founded on the assumption that the enterprise can be analysed as a complex economic, technical and social institution, which struggles to survive by matching internal resources with external challenges. This approach is put to work through the analysis of the real power structure and its interaction with the market and institutions in order to find a rationale behind managerial behaviour.

The overview of the corporate and organisational structure is aimed at presenting the relative weight of the various layers and functions of management, in particular the overwhelming role of the director and production managers in relation to functional organs and of social concerns over financial soundness. Following Fligstein's example (1990), this permits us to understand the constraints that this over-centralised organisation, with its production-oriented and populist managerial culture, poses to change in general and to market-oriented change in particular.

From privatisation in 1993 to bankruptcy in 1998, the enterprise tried different strategies to settle into the market, from Soviet-style expansion to downsizing and from barter to export deals. The exploration of these actions demonstrates that the slow pace of change and the ultimate failure to sustain an autonomous existence were not simply due to managerial conservatism or entrenchment. The interaction with an external economic and institutional environment appears actually to have nurtured the most cautious attitudes while acting as a powerful restraint on managers themselves in the pursuit of alternatives. Eventually, the position of the enterprise under temporary administration is analysed in order to ascertain the opportunities and limitations offered by outside ownership in fostering the effective reorganisation of management and the business.

With outside ownership, transition as a struggle for survival comes to an end, as the parent company insulates the combine from the immediacy of external threats. Problems are now internalised into the conflictual dynamics between the new owner and combine management. The outsiders' restructuring strategy reveals ambiguities and contradictions as they attempt to subordinate enterprise management without modifying its key features from bureaucratic centralism, and actual decentralisation, to paternalistic industrial relations. This leads to the detection of yet unexplored powerful internal constraints, introducing the analysis of production management and labour relations on the shop floor as the major determining factor in the settlement of restructuring issues, which is the object of the next two chapters.

Organisation, ownership and control: formal structures and real powers

The corporate and organisational structure of a firm can be analysed in order to provide an understanding of the relative efficiency of these arrangements. The analyses of the organisational structures and forms of ownership prevailing in Russia during transition, which have been made available by mainstream transition literature, have mainly focused on indicating their shortcomings by measuring their departure from established Western models. In the following sections, an attempt is made to understand the internal logic, stemming both from historical and contextual elements, of these arrangements and, hence, the reason for (limited) change and (overwhelming) continuity. The ownership issue and the governance structure are treated first, followed by a detailed account of the organisational structure. The conclusion will try to grasp the major characteristics and changes in the organisational features of the enterprise until bankruptcy.

Ownership and control: an employee-owned, managerially controlled enterprise

In 1993 the enterprise was transformed into a joint stock company. The privatisation was carried out according to the second option, which allowed employees to hold an absolute majority stake in the new company. Procedures and ownership structure, including behind-the-scenes dealings, were confided to us by a key informant:

> Privatisation started with the establishment of the 'people's' (*narodnogo*) enterprise. The labour collective is granted around 50 per cent of stocks. From such a stake no individual could hold more than 2.5 per cent of the stocks. Twenty-six per cent and 24 per cent of the remaining shares were divided up among physical and legal holders respectively. The former consist of pensioners and citizens of the company town while among the latter figure the largest stakeholders. The largest individual stake of 10 per cent was left, according to the law, in state hands. The second largest stakeholder, 8 per cent of shares, was (formally) another enterprise, a major supplier of the combine. In fact it was controlled by the general director by means of a behind-the-scenes interlocking agreement among the directors [of the two enterprises]. Considering that state property played no active role in decision-making, its part of the shares was controlled by the director too.
>
> (Interview with the head of the weaving department, December 2000)

Table 5.1 Share distribution

Typology of shareholders	Number of shareholders	%
Labour collective	2,955	49.87
Physical persons	2,023	26.05
Legal persons	5	24.08

Further episodic evidence suggests that top management increased its stake in the company by acquiring shares in the secondary market. In particular, the chief engineer claimed to have devoted a then substantial sum to the purchase of enterprise stocks.

The way privatisation was carried out meant that top management in general, and the director in particular, had, both formally and practically, absolute control over the new decision-making body of the enterprise. The coincidence between corporate and managerial structures meant that ownership became a function of managerial control, and its organs conducted a shadowy existence, mirroring the dynamics in the enterprise managerial power structure. The enterprise survived as an independent company for a relatively short period of time; with bankruptcy in 1998 a new administration and a new owner came forward. During this time managers maintain that the role of corporate institutions added little to the running of the enterprise. The director, as a result of the previously mentioned settlements, dominated the board. As for the representation of rank-and-file shareholders, the elections brought about mostly production cadres, supportive of the director, as representatives of the mass of workers and clerks. Therefore, meetings and reports to the board turned into empty rituals, something of a repetition of the sort of manipulation observed directly on similar occasions, such as the trade union congress or labour collective conferences.

Reactions to privatisation and the establishment of an independent company differed significantly between managers and workers. The head of weaving, who later sat on the board, recalled how 'privatisation produced at first a euphoric sentiment of freedom [*euforia svobody*] and a sense of proprietorship in the labour collective'. For workers, though, the whole affair – the constitution of the company, the distribution of stocks, the proceedings of the board and so on – was just 'a matter for managers', something from which they expected results but felt at the same time excluded. This reaction was sparked by a perceived sense of continuity with the past, the idea that nothing fundamental had changed for employees. There was also widespread uncertainty about the real long-term intentions of those in Moscow. For several years myths proliferated about the possibility of a complete reversal of the reforms. Later, in the mid-1990s, the steady deterioration of living standards, contrary to the expectations raised by democratic propaganda, fuelled doubts and suspicions about reforms among the rank-and-file, nurturing dismissive attitudes towards the rights and obligations of shareholders and private property in general.

For top management, independence meant the widening of the areas where decision-making at enterprise level was not constrained. From their point of view, privatisation appeared less a watershed change than a good point struck in a long-term struggle for independence. In fact, they felt that the increasing autonomy gained during *perestroika* was still challenged by political attempts at petty tutelage, questioning the formal acceptance of free entrepreneurship and private property. Moreover, powerful threats were posed by the growing power of suppliers and intermediaries, which made the market appear nothing other than a new battleground for the power struggle of this provincial company town with the 'Muscovites'. Therefore, to understand fully the emergence of such a form of corporate governance requires turning our attention to managerial structures and strategies, analysed in the following sections.

Organisational structure and managerial power in the 1990s: a business analysis

The organisational structure of the enterprise saw a relentless reshuffling of positions, departments and sub-units over the decade, without any significant change of its main features. When it was thoroughly scrutinised by management consultants in 1997 and 2000, both concluded that Soviet features had largely survived and advised substantial 'market-oriented' revisions. Findings from fieldwork allow us to supplement these business analyses with greater knowledge about the role and the functioning of individual departments and to achieve an understanding of the internal power structure. The formal analysis is presented first, highlighting the main features of a Soviet-type organisation as opposed to Western standards. Another section will follow, trying to present and explain its internal dynamics and unveiling some of the constraints to the changes advocated by consultants.

Looking at the organisational chart as it was in 1997, we can see that the enterprise presents a structure of a functional type with some significant variations. The organisation is highly centralised, with a large number of units and individual positions directly subordinated to the general director and the chief engineer. According to Soviet nomenclature, the structure can be divided into two different functional elements. The superior part of the structure, containing top management and central offices (*glavnye kontory*) was referred to as AKhO, the administrative–economic section (*administrativno-khozyajstvennyi otdel*). This was intended as a service structure of a bureaucratic type, performing control functions and handling the information flow between the planning organs and the director, on the one side, and production, on the other. Subordinated to the chief engineer, there are three separate production departments (*proizvodstva*) – spinning, weaving and finishing – plus a large maintenance and repair unit. Other operative departments like construction and transport, agriculture and social services are all assigned to director's deputies. Work among departments is divided alongside stages of the production process; shops are organised as sections of the production process, each of them containing a stage of the chain, irrespective of product lines or market destination. Production management is distributed on three layers: the head of production with budgeting and planning responsibilities, the shop chief and the foreman. Production and maintenance have their own administrative and technical offices subordinated to the head of department but operating in accordance with specifications of their respective functional main department.

The first consultant studying the enterprise's internal organisation found that this was set consistently with no alteration of the previous Soviet establishment. Their criticism and subsequent recommendations focused on two points. First, they argued, the functional model was inadequate given the scale of production and the large range of products dealt with by the enterprise.

As for the accounting department, the Western understanding of this function is, generally speaking, one of careful analysis of costs and margins in order to determine the contribution of each production line and service to overall costs and profits of the enterprise. It allows the assessment of resources and the potential of productive assets and determines which are the areas deserving development and which are those to restructure or close down. The staff employed in the accounting department was not meant to perform these tasks, hence was in no condition to do so. They were mere bookkeepers, registering data provided by other departments. As a result, the enterprise, which faced bleak financial conditions, was unable to implement a considered cost-cutting policy.

The lack of a proper sales and marketing department was identified as another major obstacle to operating successfully in a market economy. The existing commercial department was peripheral to the command chain and had no authority on price policy, design and development activities. Again, none of these functions was performed by, nor was in the capacity of, the present staff of the commercial department at the combine.

Consequently, the enterprise was advised to decentralise and divisionalise its core business organisation. In order to shift the focus from production to customer and, therefore, the managers' ultimate goal from physical to economic targets, it was recommended to establish and improve the operations of the above-mentioned departments and to co-ordinate manufacturing operations strictly with marketing.

The general response of the enterprise to Western recommendations will be treated as part of the overall restructuring strategy in the next section. Here it will suffice to consider the fate of the new marketing and design offices, the establishment of which was the only one of the consultants' proposals that enterprise management seemed to meet with enthusiasm.

The appointment of a designer, in itself a sign of willingness to change, was obviously not meant to produce a great change on its own. Unfortunately, like marketing, it was simply added to the existing structure and did not represent a first step towards thorough organisational reform. The problems that arose from its functioning are in any case a good indicator of the difficulty of moving away from production-oriented management. Design, as part of product development, appeared to be a function of the chief engineer, to whom the office was subordinated.

The enterprise had been assigned a design adviser as a member of the foreign consulting team; her arguments with the chief engineer provide a clear picture of the problem. All the time the issue of new products was discussed it seemed that they failed to reach an agreement because the main concern of the production manager was with technical feasibility rather than consumer appeal. In fact, the adviser used to lament that these engineers, as consumers, were quite ready to appreciate imported textiles but not equally prone to manufacture similar cloths as producers. In this latter case, their choice was driven by the desire to put technologies available to good use, irrespective of the end result.

As for the marketing department, it had a good start but was never allowed to make its own policy, let alone interfere with production plans. Several young graduates were recruited, headed by a young and ambitious economist. They initially dedicated themselves to market research, participation in fairs and experimenting with new technologies. Soon, though, it became clear that this new department was not to assume a strategic role, and its chief preferred to move to the more traditional but also more advantageous procurement office where, it was alleged, he managed to satisfy the needs of production much less than his own. A private report to the new owners by our key informant so described the situation with marketing in 2001:

A few words about marketing. Currently, at our enterprise, the marketing department performs essentially sales functions. Timid attempts to realise marketing activities are carried out without considering production requirements, volumes or competitiveness. Such an approach was typical of marketing [as it used to be in the West, CM] at the beginning of the 1980s. In reality, we began to do marketing from the basics and we are out of touch with the latest trends in the business: production analysis, costs and production volume, study of the difference between earnings and variable costs (profit margin), costs, prices, [competitive, CM] advantage. These analyses are not carried out at all. (Kolya, Internal Report to LTD, 2001)

In 2000 a Russian research institute conducted another comprehensive investigation at the combine (Lipsic', 2000, pp. 75–9). While praising management for its attempts to renovate production and find new markets, they found that the situation with organisation and personnel qualifications revealed widespread inefficiencies. In particular, they pointed out that internal organisation and decision-making processes were unreformed and the strategic marketing and finance departments were 'weak'. Management suffered from excessive centralisation and bureaucracy. There had been no transfer of powers to lower managerial layers, which forced senior management to deal with petty issues and waste their time on purely administrative tasks. Decisions required the approval of all units, which meant that decision-making was slow and production burdened with bureaucratic controls. They drew the following picture of the way financial issues were handled almost a decade after privatisation:

Financial accounts were predisposed essentially for fiscal and administrative control purposes; data processing was developing very slowly; management lacked a timely and useful flow of information; qualification of employees was very deficient . . . financial documentation was still hand-written . . . there was no satisfactory financial planning. The organisational structure of financial services was inefficient. All enterprises presented the following units: planning, finance and accounting. The activity of these units was uncoordinated and often they did very much the same things.

(Ibid., pp. 75–6)

The picture, here broadly outlined, delivered by business analyses, which inspire a great part of the literature on restructuring and transition, highlights the evident continuity with the past displayed by the enterprise and its consequent inability to face the allegedly emerging market. This outcome might lead us to consider this case as the end-result of managerial conservatism and Russian lingering backwardness.

Yet research experience in the field has proved that a conventional analysis can provide only a partial account of organisational issues. This literature, in fact, invariably retains the assumption of the full comparability of managerial positions and structures, relying on the assumption that superficial similarities might account for identity of functions and aims, and therefore regards Russian enterprise organisation as simply a backward duplicate of its Western equivalents.

To highlight the peculiar configuration of a post-Soviet organisation and to unveil the constraints which led restructuring on an unexpected path requires an account of managerial practices and informal relations within the factory and with the surrounding environment, which are the object of the next two sections.

Organisational structure and managerial power in the 1990s: a still-Soviet enterprise

In this section some general features of the enterprise organisation are presented, representing a substantive difference between Western and Soviet management. Despite the inevitable similarities with already well-documented Soviet practices, these have been elaborated by drawing on the experience of both Russian managers and foreign consultants involved in post-privatisation restructuring. They were generally understood and referred to as the main causes of misinterpretation of enterprise problems as well as barriers to the introduction of Western managerial techniques.

First, the system is deeply imbued with a strong hierarchical sense, which means that those further up the hierarchy, starting with the director and the chief engineer down to lesser production managers, count more than could be expected from just looking at the organisational chart. The uncertain scenario opened by privatisation reinforced the attitude of passive reliance on higher-standing figures.

Verticalisation is strictly interwoven with personalisation. Managerial jobs cannot be understood just in terms of abstract functional roles but should be referred to considering the role of individuals and their power in the hierarchy. This is why, as emerged during the drafting of the organisational chart, there are not departments to which individual positions are attached but, on the contrary, individual posts presiding over functions.

The focus on individuals also means that managers suffer from high exposure in case of failure and are therefore reluctant to take on new functions without guarantees of additional resources. Since access to resources in the enterprise is made dependent on bargaining powers and status, previously marginal departments are less prone to accept new responsibilities. This is even more the case in a situation in which growing scarcity is making inter-departmental co-operation less stable and harder to achieve.

High centralisation in decision-making is compensated by a *de facto* decentralisation of real management, due precisely to natural limits of the personalised forms of exertion of power and to weak informational support by functional departments. Consequently, a large gap exists between formal and informal practices and roles. Technological decay, uneven production pace and normative uncertainties widened this divide by forcing managers to look for easy fixes and compromises, which reinforced the lack of initiative referred to above – at least, in the conventional understanding of the term.

Furthermore, managers themselves have to rely greatly on workers' co-operation and support. The continued drive for higher output volume and the use of the piece-rate incentive system reflect and strengthen this situation, preventing any attempt to standardise and regularise the production process.

Ultimately, we should keep in mind that a Soviet enterprise was, first and foremost, a productive unit and its privatised successor has retained this feature. In fact, the downfall of the command economy, rather than boosting new market-related functions, has even increased difficulties in the shops, making technically skilled managers with responsibilities in production the backbone of the managerial power structure.

This early analysis provides some evidence in favour of the relevance of the Soviet legacy on enterprise behaviour, suggesting that such features make this organisation qualitatively very different from its Western equivalents. Further investigation of the functioning of the command chain and the characteristics of managerial work right after transition help substantiate this argument and unveil its consequences for restructuring.

Management in transition: managerial functions and hierarchical power

The organisational structure of the enterprise appears as a pyramid hinged on the person of the director. Looking at this figure is the best starting point for an in-depth analysis of its character and mode of operation. Literature on 'red directors' has long made clear that the nature and extent of their authority went beyond the formal attributes assigned to this institution. The director was not simply the all-powerful head of an organisation but also the leader of a community, the 'little father' to whom any of its members could turn, expecting a fair and benign intervention. Direct observation of the exercise of directorial powers confirms that the autocratic and paternalistic character of the organisation had remained intact at least until 1998–9. On this issue a foreign senior management consultant during an interview commented thus:

> The structure was certainly very hierarchical. Whatever the question at issue, it was the general director who had the last word. We can define it as a managerial firm with centralisation of decision-making – one of the kind that could be found in a Southern European family business as opposed to the impersonal management of the Anglo-Saxon model – and decentralised running of daily business. The 'Red Star', for instance, is more of an entrepreneurial firm with all the powers wielded by its director-businessman.
>
> (Interview with LF, management consultant, 1999)

In functional terms the general director was the only decision-maker in all strategic issues. There was no aspect of enterprise activity that he would not concern himself with and decide personally (Schelkov and Antonov, 1998). During numerous meetings held in 1997 in which I took part or had direct notice of, his presence was constantly required when a decision had to be taken, whether it was about the terms and conditions of a sales contract, discussing investment plans or bargaining with local authorities concerning the transfer of social assets. Conversely, functional managers, particularly from the commercial department, were more often than not absent.

A cross-analysis with interviews of top management executives proves that there were no staff personnel who could collectively or individually possess the knowledge and the skills to contribute significantly to the decision-making process at this level. The chief engineer instead played a significant support role, partly because he was in charge of the daily management of the production complex, partly because technical aspects were still the decisive parameters in every enterprise venture. It is indicative of their marginality that neither staff executives nor the CE have posed particular problems for the newcomers and none of them has been targeted for demotion or dismissal.

In the bureaucratic code of the enterprise the director was in almost all cases the only subject who could validate an internal order. Furthermore, he was the ultimate authority who could settle a dispute or meet a claim in the final instance. Normally, in cases of hiring and firing or disciplinary issues involving workers, as well as in cases of conflict among managers, it was the role of the second line in the hierarchical scale to intervene and to provide all the elements for a decision. Then, again, obtaining the signature of the director was always advisable, as my 'gatekeeper' taught me as soon as I started my fieldwork:[1]

> Once again running into the snow from the factory to the administration building, Kolya and I, papers in hand, to get a director's stamp. And I cannot restrain myself from asking him again what's so important about it. He replies – to have a signature from the director is a guarantee that no one will challenge us. Anybody else's is just paper, but with the director's it is different; they have to take it seriously. This is the way you do things here.

Significantly, when a complaint came to him he used to deal with it personally; there was no secretary or representative in between him and the other party, as one would normally expect of top executives in Western business enterprises. This function, though secondary as compared with real decision-making powers, was a fundamental source of prestige and authority. Operating through direct and personal contact without mediation was practically inefficient, as it overloaded management with dealing with petty issues, but symbolically was of enormous potential. The director's authority was also a source of legitimacy for lower managerial layers and, while it obviously limited their autonomy, it relieved them from taking full responsibility for their decisions.

A third and consequential aspect of the director's role was the strictly interrelated function of leader of the labour collective and benefactor of its larger working community. The analysis of this aspect will be carried out in the

---

[1] A detailed record of my first encounter with the director, representing a significant example of the form in which he exercised his power, is presented in the methodology section.

following section on strategies for its significant policy implications. Here it suffices to report how he liked to be presented to the public in official publications:

> Interviewer: 'You won't find anyone more popular than Ivan Ivanovich [the general director, CM] in town . . . everyone from workers to pensioners, from single mothers to the young have words of gratitude for Him . . . The town is sincerely grateful to Ivan Ivanovich for, in the most difficult years for his enterprise, he did not leave the town to stand on its own – says the head of the city administration.' (Schelkov and Antonov, 1998, pp. 57–69)

Management in transition: scale and scope of managerial work

In the previous sections it has been strongly underlined that one of the main shortcomings of the enterprise organisation was the excessive centralisation of decision-making. This refers implicitly to the scale of managerial powers (*polnomochie*) or the amount and relevance of issues decided by the highest enterprise authorities.

Managerial powers, though, presented another dimension, namely their scope (*krugozor*), no less rich in implications. The scope of managerial authority is to be understood as the horizontal extension of its powers, within the sphere of action of enterprise activities. So the general director's influence could legitimately extend within the region and beyond, stretching down to Moscow. The chief engineer was allowed to operate at enterprise level with the right to intervene on issues concerning clients/competitors. The heads of production departments were constrained within the section of the production process assigned to them, and so it was for lower managerial layers. This information, provided by a production manager, the key informant Kolya, confirms that non-production executives were not considered part of the command chain, suggesting that the problem with their work is less one of competence and qualifications than a more serious one of status and authority. Relevant implications were also raised by the informant about the general efficiency of this form of organisation, particularly in relation to the co-operation among departments.

In fact, as he explained, organisational reforms specific to the enterprise had already been attempted without success far before privatisation. In 1985 the enterprise experimented with the introduction of production control (*dispetcherizatsiya*), aimed at achieving greater co-operation among subsections of the production line. A new managerial position was appointed, the dispatcher, who was supposed to guarantee horizontal co-ordination of activities, and therefore achieve a regular flow of production between shops working under different production chiefs.

The reform failed to achieve the expected results, and the position was scrapped a year later. This happened, in the opinion of the informant, for a twofold set of reasons. First, the rigidly compartmentalised hierarchical structure was left unchanged. The dispatcher, placed in the shops, was in permanent conflict with higher-ranking managers who paralysed his action beyond shop and departmental boundaries. Second, these people did not receive 'managerial education' and had no 'managerial culture'; i.e. 'they did not take decisions'. Therefore the profound gulf between responsible and pro-active management and the reality of the limited scale and scope of the job which middle management had to confront represents another, more serious than expected, barrier to change.

Management in transition: assessing and rewarding managerial work

The permanence of a highly hierarchical and compartmentalised structure well after privatisation did not stimulate a rethinking of managerial work and therefore a reform of the job profiles and incentive system. At the same time, the new problems produced by privatisation led enterprise top management to intervene in the control system so as to regain efficiency. This resulted in a somewhat contradictory outcome in which lower managerial layers felt oppressed by a cumbersome organisation while top management complained of continuous attempts by subordinates to avoid responsibilities and conceal failure. The continuous remoulding of the control mechanisms (*organizatsiya upravleniya*) was so described by our major key informant:

> For the last decade, a great number of managerial organisational models have been experimented with: repressive with ritual subordination to the leader [*s podchineniem komanduyuschemu paradom*]; bureaucratic [*byurokraticheskaya*] with lots of stamps, papers and signatures; imitative [*uchenicheskaya*] with duplication of alien models; informal [*smazochnaya*] with the cancellation of reciprocal claims. Presently, all of these models can be found to a certain degree at the enterprise. The managerial structure in my view is cumbersome and unmanageable. There is no trust of subordinates towards superiors. (Kolya, internal report to LTD, 2001)

The analysis of findings from observation and interviews with production managers reveals the inadequacies of the mechanism of evaluation and stimulation of managerial work and the increased gap between formal requirements and actual practices it produced.

The enterprise has retained, for the entire period considered in this study, all the key features of the payment and incentive system existing in Soviet times.[1] Under such a system, managers, specialists and white-collar workers are entitled

---

[1] The payment system is treated comprehensively, for all employees, in a separate chapter. First, because, retaining the Soviet framework, managers were formally considered simply another category of employee. Second, the administration maintained a unitary approach to wage issues. Third, differentials in money wages were not altered and, despite preferential treatment, cadres with managerial functions did not gain the status of a superior, autonomous and well-defined category of employee.

to a monthly wage consisting of hourly pay plus a considerable bonus, which could amount to up to 100 per cent of the basic wage. The bonus is granted on the assumption that all tasks assigned to the manager have been successfully fulfilled. For as much as a wage system can be held responsible for results in managerial work, a system based on bonuses for individual task fulfilment, in an environment leaving little room for horizontal co-operation, would rather foster the insurgence of parochial interests and the pursuit of the bonus at every cost. This had been very much the case in Soviet times, especially with production managers, whose only real goal was output quotas in physical terms.

The enterprise kept output volumes as the only target for managers until the year 2000. The setting of targets by top management and the provision of resources available to managers in the shops had been changing, especially in the second half of the 1990s, making it difficult for the latter to achieve results and for the former to ascertain responsibilities. Managers first voiced to me their arguments about the dysfunctions of the managerial system during a routine meeting, held in December 2000, between the head of the weaving factory and one of his shop chiefs. My fieldwork notes report:

> The factory chief executive: In relation to the incentive system, it is still based on bonuses, which are in any case considered part of the regular wage. There's been no change in the managerial system; i.e. no Western-like model has been introduced. Managers (*nachalniki*) are judged on the basis of results – output by metreage and index of plan fulfilment – there is some consideration of production costs and quality, the latter only for export. Assessment of results is the sole responsibility of superiors. Soviet practices have not changed, problems are not solved openly, rather it is common practice to resort to trickery. In this respect there's been some change. In the past, production peaks were met by the use of extra machinery.
> A shop chief: We had lots of looms working in an efficient state and spare parts were available in large quantities. Now most of these machines lie idle because of lack of spare parts and shortage of personnel produced by lay-offs. Higher productivity is now achieved at the expense of quality and by extensive use of extra work because the labour cost is low. Consider that the relative weight of wage expenditures in production costs amounts to only 5 per cent of the total against 80 per cent of raw materials and 15 per cent of energy costs. The problem is that, while production plans vary according to demand, output volume is constrained into a narrow range by objective causes.
> The factory chief executive: The only way to avoid reprimands by top management is to study and carefully report all information about capacity, costs and production trends. It is more difficult to attract criticism when you can prove what kind of problems you are facing.

Top management has therefore continued to employ what was known in Soviet times as taut planning, the use of high, above capacity, targets in order to achieve the maximum level of utilisation of productive resources. Only now management could no longer rely on buffers between nominal capacity and assigned targets. Information on the state of the art in production continues to be the object of controversy as managers manipulate data in order to justify failures, while top management deliberately ignores the difficulties faced by subordinates. This makes it impossible to achieve trust and build the common knowledge necessary for careful planning and swift problem-solving.

The aleatory character of planning and assessment and the dramatic shortage of resources mean that top management has to intervene with individual managers in a personal and discretionary manner in order to keep pressure high for results. This produces, though, competition for resources and inter-sectional conflicts among managers of intermediate layers and hinders the smooth operation of production and the efficient allocation of resources among 'factories'. The head of the weaving department referred to this in a written questionnaire concerning relations with top management, i.e. mainly the chief engineer, and complementary departments:

> Particular attention has to be devoted to the securing of production supplies and to lobbying with the director on behalf of the department . . . [Our main problems, CM] are among others: the acceptance of yarn (complaints about quality, type, weight and humidity of yarn) [from the spinning department, CM]. Solutions are the following: filing claims; checking the adherence of claims to GOST [public legal standards, CM]; soliciting the chief engineer to punish spinning technicians for non-observance of quality standards. The same happens in dealing with the finishing department: just here our task consists in defending our department from complaints on the side of finishing (observance of quality standards and typology of fabrics).

Control and incentive systems were the object of continuous intervention by Soviet planners in the struggle to achieve greater managerial initiative, and specifically higher attention to quality and costs. They usually proceeded with the introduction of new targets tied to monetary incentives, relying on bureaucratic mechanisms for assessment. The conventional criticism of this approach held that the substantial inability to foster efficient management was due, among other things, to the absence of truly economic, i.e. financial, targets, which could provide subordinates with the only clear indicator for prioritising targets and controllers with an equally manageable tool for evaluation. Under the old director, there was no sign that staff management had acquired a greater role in providing an objective and impersonal control mechanism. On the other side, the urgencies of production, in any case, led personal relations between line managers along the hierarchy to prevail, transforming any new form of control into grounds for informal bargaining. The head of the weaving department provides a comprehensive picture of the degradation of control mechanisms that occurred over the transition period:

Since the end of Socialism there was no plan as such – rather it was merely contingent because lack of resources imposed flexibility. In three years I never lost my bonus for failing to meet planned targets. We used a fine-based system [*sistema strafovaniya*], i.e. bonus quotas were deducted from the wage for failing to carry out tasks. How is assessment carried out? Bargaining [*torgovliya*], i.e. there are neither objective elements of evaluation nor an impartial function in charge of assessment. It is up to the hierarchy to decide, with the last word in the hands of top management [*vysshoe rukovodstvo*]. It is therefore under these circumstances that, by means of relying on seniority and connections or using blackmail [*shantazh*], one acquires protection from top managers. Every month we work to fabricate justifications for the non-observance of some kind of instruction. Those rewarded are not the ones who produced more and better but those who manage to throw on someone else the responsibility for one's own failures.

Management in transition: wage system, wage differentials and managerial status

Retaining the Soviet wage and incentive system implies also the preservation of Soviet categories, which do not differentiate among white-collar employees in the same way that their Western counterparts do. The Soviets recognised the role of officers with managerial functions, the cadres, which also included, though, blue-collar workers such as foremen, supervisors and brigade leaders. Yet, on the one side, there were executive posts, primarily among staff managers, which did not enjoy the powers and functions generally understood for senior management. On the other side, payroll categorisation was based on qualification rather than on function, so that managers (*rukovoditeli*) were included in a much larger group, ITR, comprising all qualified office personnel. The fact that no intervention has been attempted in this area has serious implications. A key informant so commented on this point in an internal report:

> It is impossible to decide personnel issues without a well-thought-out payment system. A year ago [2000, CM.] different systems were considered, reforms started; and from the beginning, in my view, we allowed a big mistake. For all activities, employees' categories, a single system for work assessment has been adopted. (Kolya, internal report to LTD, 2001)

If all white-collar employees operate formally under the same system, differences in status and actual power and responsibilities are reflected in significant wage differentials. So, as exemplified by a list of wages for top executives, managers continue to be paid very differently. In particular, the low wages for many specialists and staff managers have fed the low consideration for these functions, diminishing their own self-esteem while preventing new recruits from entering these professions. Top management seems particularly preoccupied with keeping wage differentials unaltered. This policy, as we shall see further on in greater detail, is inspired by the need to maintain the higher status of production managers and, more generally, the delicate social balance within the labour collective as a whole. The most significant fact that in any case inhibited an active wage policy since privatisation was the downward trend of the real value of take-home pay, which demoralised the entire managerial personnel and was responsible for a dramatic outflow of qualified personnel, particularly from 1998 onwards.

Managers, staff and line: what do we need ITR for?

In the previous sections we have learned that the enterprise was governed almost single-handedly by the director and his aides, that a thin line of production managers administered operations on his behalf, while staff management was quite marginal to decision-making. Enterprise-level studies mentioned above tell us at length about how bureaucratic the administrative machinery is at the enterprise and how badly equipped its personnel are in carrying out new, strategic, market-related activities. It remains to understand what these people are actually doing and why they have been left untouched for so long by the axe of restructuring. Some basic figures about their staffing levels, location within departments and relative wage costs might help identify the consistency, role, status and problems posed by enterprise white-collar employees.

Table 5.2 Distribution of employees

	Managers	ITR	Auxiliaries	Total
AKhO	59	145	15	219
Production departments	51	111	14	176
Total	110	256	29	395

Number of non-productive employees at the combine, 1997[1]

At the enterprise the number of 'non-productive' forces amounted to around four hundred people, including managers (*rukovoditeli*), specialists (*spetsialisty*) and office workers (*sluzhaschiya*). Their absolute number might seem

---

[1] These figures are my own calculations from official enterprise data made available to me on behalf of the consulting firm operating an EU-sponsored restructuring programme. The information was collected more or less formally at shop and office level with the help of Kolya, who had been entrusted with providing support to the foreign consultants.

impressive, but if we consider their proportion[1] relative to the overall workforce it is a mere 10 per cent of the 3,882 people officially employed by the enterprise in January 1997.

Another noticeable fact is the high number of office and department chiefs, ranked *managers* in the table, while office workers as such were almost non-existent. This is because there were plenty of technical and planning offices monitoring every aspect of enterprise activity or piece of equipment. This also explains why, despite centralisation, there were almost as many bureaucrats in production as featured in central offices.

The almost consensual anxiety among managerial and workers' ranks alike that ITR was an unbearable bureaucratic burden can be better understood if we look at the wage costs that come with it. While accounting for only 10 per cent of the workforce, the white-collar employees' wage fund[2] amounted to one third of that of the manual workers; this would strike the average Soviet man and woman as exceptional figure, and certainly is a huge financial burden for the enterprise.

In order to understand the role and the fate of these people it should be noticed that their functions and earnings[3] are quite diverse indeed. Managers proper, i.e. decision-makers, amount to a handful of deputy directors in the AKhO and around one-third of the white-collar employees in production. The large mass of non-productive forces are therefore staff managers, divided more or less equally between engineers and other science specialists, working in monitoring or maintenance and repair, and economics graduates employed as

[1] Granick (1960, pp. 167–71), in a pioneering work on Soviet management, noted that 'not only Russian plants have a lower proportion of administrative and clerical personnel than do Americans . . . but the trend since 1940 has been downward'. The data shown in his work, between 15 and 20 per cent, indicate that, if this proportion remained unchanged, our enterprise fared quite well in saving on white-collar staff. On the other side, Russian plants were normally operating on a much larger, often below-efficiency, scale, which means that the lower proportion of white-collar employees stands against an inflated workforce. This is more evident in the case of the textile sector where in capitalist economies, since the 1970s, large establishments have been washed away by a tide of downsizing and outsourcing to smaller productive and service units.

[2] Wage costs in roubles per month for non-productive forces were 616,311,150 roubles according to official enterprise data provided by the Labour and Wage Office in May 1997. The wage fund of manual workers amounted to 1,880,819,799 roubles per month. The commercial exchange rate in the course of the year fluctuated between 5,000 and 6,000 roubles per $US.

[3] A quick look at wage costs among departments yields the impression that production-related services, and therefore technical specialists, fared much better than trade and financial units. In the AKhO, for example, the 32-strong staff of the chief engineer earned collectively about 50 million roubles while the same number in sales and marketing totalled only around 32 million. The engineering department, featuring mostly maintenance and repair works, achieved an even more substantial 78 million with 48 employees. Not surprisingly, these are the shops and offices which experienced redundancies later in the 1990s.

planners, accountants, trade specialists et cetera, but fundamentally controlling the conduct of production managers.

As for technical specialists, there seems to be a consensus at least among production managers that they are essential to the good functioning of the enterprise as a complex technological system. As Boris Anatolievich, then the chief mechanic of the weaving department, put it:

> You should understand that we need a large engineering department because unlike Western enterprises we have to do most of the repair and reconstruction ourselves. I perfectly understand how people work in the West; if, let us say, a piece of equipment breaks down you pack it up and send it to the producer. But, then, again, everything works smoothly up there, repair is not an everyday business, and in any case you have to make arrangements for this service and they do not come cheap. The printing machine we got from England was bought without guarantees and hardly any instruction. We had to adjust it to our systems and now it is only us who can deal with it.

The autarky imposed by the planned economy remains a necessity as scarcity continues to plague production, this time because of economic constraints. The point was clearly made by the toolmaker of the carding shop regarding the need to repair damaged spare parts:

> In order to save money, they purchase sub-standard materials that we then have to rectify and so we lose in terms of quality. I will give you some examples: there is a spindle made of plastic, it breaks when it falls. We had to manufacture one of wood ourselves. This valve, the original is a metal cast; they say it is too expensive so we have to make it ourselves in plastic. Still, while it was hard to find, the price was one and a half roubles, while our own one costs fifty roubles.

This judgement might not be intended for all specialists and would not prevent extensive criticism by line managers of opportunism and amateurism in the work of auxiliary services. Shop-level managers and technicians often pointed out that, because of 'not working for the plan' and 'being autonomous units', auxiliary services were less than diligent and reliable in carrying out their job. Yet, admittedly, unsatisfactory pay and lack of personnel did contribute to undermining the quality of their work.

Here the problem is 'double subordination' (*dvojnoe podchinenie*), one of the basic arrangements of Soviet economic organisation. It had been designed in Soviet times to prevent line managers from spoiling resources to achieve the short-term goals of the plan and concealing information to avoid the blame of superiors. While presenting itself as a nuisance to production managers, and an anachronistic one after transition, this was and still is indeed a key function of staff management.[1] This system continues to operate in so far as the work of production managers has been left very much unchanged.[2] Its contradictions, though – at least, within production – became particularly pressing only after bankruptcy, when the combined effect of tighter plans and outflow of cadres sparked a bitter conflict over resources and responsibilities between production and auxiliary services.

The staff–line divide, institutionalised by professional, organisational and wage discrimination, with the ensuing perennial conflict between categories, contributes to organisational stability also at another level. The victimisation of auxiliaries, reaffirming shared values about the nature of productive work, the corresponding status of different groups of employees and the legitimacy of the hierarchy as a whole, in fact provides enterprise administration with an important ideological tool for social control. There are, therefore, solid arguments militating in favour of retaining a large apparatus of staff management. Then, again, considering the costs it entails, the functional role played by staff management has to be understood within the context of the economy of scarcity to which the financial hardships produced by 'hard budget' external constraints now make a significant contribution. This will become more evident when treating the case of administrative and clerical personnel.

Managers, staff and line: the apparatchik in transition

Clerical and administrative personnel were the quintessential apparatchiki; it was they whom enterprise employees generally had in mind when voicing criticism of ITR. The low consideration for these workers certainly owes a lot to the traditional Soviet disregard for non-manual and non-technical professions. It was a clerical employee, a senior accountant, who provided me with the most straightforward formulation of this ideological conception. In a quite emotional speech she argued that:

> One hundred people in the AKhO earn as much as the whole enterprise. They do nothing, especially the personnel and the marketing department. It is a scandal that white-collar employees earn more than workers; in the end these are the ones who produce. We simply live out of their work.

---

[1] The distinctive feature of Soviet staff management as a control system and some of the problems related to the behaviour of its members are clearly delineated in Gregory (1989, p. 511).

[2] This might seem a typical vicious circle, in which the unaccountability of the staff manager is paramount to his/her reliability as information broker and norm-setter, but permits the former to be inefficient (see Gregory, 1989, pp. 514, 523). The reform should have put an end to this dilemma by precisely subordinating both staff and line managers to the discipline of profit. The description of the control and incentive system shows how Soviet inter-managerial dynamics have sharpened rather than been subdued, but it is the analysis of the manager–worker relationship in the following chapters that will attempt to provide a rationale for such a case.

To be sure, you would not find many managers supporting this 'communist' view in such terms, and most people in the AKhO might be quite cynical about enjoying a privileged position. Yet our experience of discourses at the enterprise indicates that prejudices against ITR were widespread and universal. In the tense atmosphere dominated by bitter competition and a perennial search for scapegoats, which established itself in the crisis-ridden transitional period, they were the common and easy targets of character assassination. So, when I approached the new director to secure formal permission for them to be interviewed, he stigmatised with derisive remarks their early unwillingness to concede interviews: 'Ha! They do not want to talk. I do not understand what they might be afraid of. They know nothing!' In the opinion of most production managers, too, planners and accountants were 'mere clerks who know nothing'; a fact confirmed by their heavy reliance on precisely those production managers they were meant to control. Not surprisingly, our main informant denounced how these uneven relationships in the shops brought about the systematic forging of data.

Workers, and in particular cadre workers, were more rather than less critical towards ITR, whom they described as being a parasitic group serving the interests of senior management. The main points in these arguments were the fact that white-collar employees regularly 'escape blame for failures' and therefore 'do not risk losing their bonus', that 'they enjoy protection from senior management' as 'they always support the administration', often by staffing the trade union committees. Accusations of involvement in corruption and theft in relation to procurement deals or in cases of disappearance of large amounts of output were also quite common.[1] What made administrative staff so vulnerable was the fact that most of these professions were staffed by women while the administration and command hierarchy was dominated by male engineers and male cadre workers. The resentment of the mostly female workforce towards this category was also grounded in the belief that these women enjoyed a privileged lifestyle, shorter working day, clean environment, better access to services, which were better-suited to a woman's needs.

The aleatory character of their jobs, the low level of qualification and the poor credit enjoyed in the collective make administrative workers a vulnerable category amenable to manipulation by senior management (see Clarke, 1993). The eminently 'political' role played by ITR in the enterprise represents a clear sign of continuity with the Soviet organisational and social framework and is

---

[1] Workers did not point necessarily at ITR only; general reference to senior management or simply management made a rare appearance. Since most interviewees were cadre workers, close to shop managers, and in any case interviews were often held in their offices, one may suspect a strong incentive to show compliance, however genuine it might be, to the argument of sustaining the common interests of the shop. The most sceptical among managers, though, were quite adamant in directing their blame at higher levels, as workers did when reckoning the whole of management (nachal'stvo) in their condemnation. One may conclude that, whatever the level of consciousness of these actors, they might find it more convenient to address their claims safely at ITR rather than risking direct confrontation with the director and his aides.

fully understandable within that context. Yet it tells us more about what they do than about why they continue to operate in such conditions. To understand it requires looking into their specific functions, seeking for their contribution to enterprise activities and the constraints to significant change in their jobs. One point we should like to stress is that the transition from plan to market did not make *ipso facto* the skills of these employees obsolete or their jobs anachronistic. Whether this was the case depended very much on the effective changes to the normative, organisational and relational contexts relative to their sphere of activity.

At the level of central offices there were, for example, two departments, the Labour and Wages and the Accounting (i.e. Finance) offices, which displayed a remarkable ability to survive changes and lay-offs. Their chiefs not only managed to avoid relocation or replacement but also got promoted, despite the fact that these were the strategic economic departments where Westerners would expect a high turnover. In the case of the former, the fact that no changes either at legislative or at enterprise level intervened on labour issues meant that norm-setting and wage calculations required only partial and gradual interventions within the limits of pre-reform rules. Furthermore, the sensitivity of such an issue as wages called for extreme caution and a good deal of dissimulation at the top, which these bureaucrats are quite good at, leaving all the rest to the skilful manoeuvring of production managers themselves. Even when changes were relevant, like in fiscal or trade areas, they were neither consistent nor univocal and more importantly what remained very much the same was the attitude of the counterparts, such as state officials, banks and trade partners.

To fend off the stubborn determination of the taxmen, the intrusiveness of creditors and local politicians required the manager primarily to circumvent rules and conceal data – a job similar to the tactics employed in Soviet times against ministerial petty tutelage. On the other side, the lack of investment funds and complex partnership or sales deals made the call for up-to-date financial and planning services purely academic. Another key issue was to guarantee secrecy. When I questioned my main informant as to why a proper financial department had not been established before and the fifty or so handwriting accountants replaced by computers, he confided in me that:

> After the advice of foreign consultants we began to think about establishing a finance office but we did nothing about it because the terrible state of our finances put us in a very delicate position. The director thought that a move in this direction might bring sensitive information into the open, endangering the enterprise's position *vis-à-vis* intrusive creditors and suppliers.

Significantly little information leaked as to how the enterprise managed its funds and arranged its export deals, even when foreign consultants attempted a thorough scrutiny of the enterprise's situation.[1] This leads us to remember that trust is among the scarcest currencies in Russia, and the heads of administrative offices, traditional stalwarts of senior management, continue within certain limits to be rewarded for their loyalty and support.

What has been said above does not mean that the situation with main departments was simply frozen, as changes in Sales indicate. Apart from the short-lived attempt to launch a marketing activity, the former commercial department had to adjust to the new position of the enterprise in the market. With the exception of an economically significant but quantitatively limited export activity, the enterprise was forced into processing-only agreements to access vital cotton supplies; what was left from it was for the most part sold on a barter basis for general supply purposes. Procurement rather than sales or marketing became the key office in the area, while the strategic hard-currency deals and cotton-based agreements remained in the hands of the director. This last development suggests two lines of argument.

One could at first regret the fact that functional departments were not allowed to take charge and develop skills and experience and certainly speculate on how the imbalance of power worked as a hindrance to this end. Then, again, it is difficult to overlook the powerful constraints that external relations imposed on the enterprise.

Managerial strategies: the enterprise versus the market and the State

Enterprise management had reportedly acquired substantial autonomy in investments and export in the *perestroika* period; from 1993, once the enterprise was transformed into a joint-stock company, they were set free to decide about organisation, output and staffing levels, while conversely being forced to find customers and suppliers autonomously. Therefore, management was expected to elaborate its own strategy and operate in a supposedly free market, constrained only by the resources internally available and by external regulatory and economic constraints. The vision and the operative conduct of the combine's management, on the one side, and the limits and obstacles they encountered in practice in the external environment, on the other, are the object of analysis in the following sections.

---

[1] The round of interviews with the heads of administrative offices, which I conducted in 2000–1, encountered an equally high level of resistance to releasing information. All of the deputy directors, unlike production managers, required written permission to concede interviews. Even so, 'heavy' units such as accounting and procurement gave an outright refusal to co-operate while others, such as sales, marketing and personnel, proved to be very little informed about their own affairs. All displayed uneasiness at touching on sensitive issues, such as redundancies, conflicts with production management, and bankruptcy.

The history of the enterprise during the 1990s presents most of the elements of what has been defined in the literature as a 'survival strategy'.[1] Senior management was admittedly committed to retain 'what has been built in the past', referring to both productive and social assets. Despite this ideological commitment, there was, since privatisation began, the understanding that radical changes were necessary, in particular technological innovation and productivity growth to catch up with Western efficiency standards. Tangible measures were in fact carried out in this direction, such as investment, cost-saving innovations, changes in labour organisation, and redundancy of unproductive personnel and units.

The determination of enterprise leadership to pursue change grew towards the end of the 1990s, when high indebtedness, fading state support, and dependency on suppliers convinced management that the current configuration of the enterprise was unsustainable. As suggested by manager-respondents themselves, it is possible to distinguish a period of gradual adjustment, from privatisation to 1997, and a second up to 1999/2000, shorter in time but abundant in fast-developing changes, when dismissals and lay-offs were precipitated. In both cases, managerial strategies fell short of restructuring, and the bankruptcy procedures initiated in those years apparently make the case for such a conclusion.

It would be unwise, though, to consider strategy only in terms of managerial agency and its direct consequences, bringing on to management alone the full responsibility for the event. If strategy is intended instead as the retrospective reconstruction of the enterprise path of development, then external relations come to the fore as major determinants of the managerial course of action. The 'market' and the 'State' will appear to have had a much more ambiguous role than expected, undermining in fact the bases for any serious attempt to restructure.

Managerial strategy in the 1990s: from expansion plans to the struggle for survival

In the late Soviet period, the combine was in every respect a successful enterprise – at least, by Soviet standards. As many managers reported, often with nostalgia but not without a sense of disillusion, 'output was counted by

---

[1] Survival, i.e. the struggle to stay afloat against adverse and uncertain conditions, was for most enterprises, especially in the immediate aftermath of transition, the only option available (Clarke and Kabalina, 1994; Hendley, 1998). Here survival stands for the ideological approach of management that understands 'the survival of the enterprise . . . in terms of its survival as a productive unit, and above all as a labour collective' (Clarke and Kabalina, 1994, p. 12). Clarke also maintains that the three main strategic options available to management – the others being the market-oriented approach and rent-seeking (Clarke and Kabalina, 1994; Grancelli, 1995) – should not be understood as mutually exclusive. It should be pointed out that, in this particular case-study, evidence seems to suggest that profit-seeking rather than rent-seeking was another key ingredient of enterprise strategy.

millions of metres' and 'profits were high'. The factory was proud of the state of its technology, too. In the 1980s, I was told, the director had managed to obtain a large consignment of machinery originally planned for another destination, a fact that also spoke for his political influence and business consciousness. What really made the pride of the enterprise and its director, and boosted managerial self-confidence, was the 'visionary' decision to install the STB 330 weaving looms[1] for export production.

The enterprise managed to export to Italy, triangulating with a Yugoslav partner in order to circumvent the EU quota system. In 1991, thanks to this partnership, it was able to purchase ten second-hand Italian looms, the newest machinery still available to them, expanding their export capabilities. The same year the enterprise carried out another major investment, the purchase of an English yarn-dyeing system. This, reported our informant, was the last major investment carried out at the enterprise, for since then liberalisation, privatisation and economic crisis had jeopardised initial managerial plans. These events in fact resulted in a series of shocks for the enterprise. First, there were the financial difficulties produced by price liberalisation and hyperinflation. My notes on the main facts that occurred at the enterprise in the decade, as reported by my key informant, record that:

> In 1992 the enterprise obtained a loan from a State bank at a yearly rate of 80 per cent, to be returned by 1995. The loan was granted only to a few among the most solid enterprises. The enterprise was forced to take it since working capital was lost following the monetary reform by Prime Minister Pavlov and the enterprise experienced difficulties in cotton purchase. To make it worse, at the end of the year interest rates jumped up to 440 per cent and payments and fees rose accordingly. It came as a result of Gaidar's statement that there was no need for Russian textiles. The loan allowed for keeping on with production but threw the enterprise into financial quandaries. The director expected growing debts eventually to be written off by the state/regional budget, according to previous Soviet practices, to compensate for maintenance by the combine of employment levels and the social sphere (an expectation which was to prove groundless).

Problems, though, were not limited to the availability of funds. The collapse of state procurement led to the break-up of inter-enterprise supply chains and produced physical shortages. Cotton supplies, which were key to the survival of this industry, came to a halt just after the collapse of the Soviet Union and continued to be a troublesome issue thereafter. As the director himself declared,

---

[1] In 1997 there were at the factory more than 1,000 looms of which 80 only achieved the minimum width in fabric output that makes it qualified for export. The fabric obtained therefrom could be used for bed linen manufacturing. In case shorter width might be necessary, the use of a cutting edge could turn those looms into a double head, saving considerably as opposed to shorter single looms. This emerged from trade talks with foreign clients, in which I participated, having accompanied the enterprise delegation on its trip abroad.

'what creates problems is the embargo imposed by the Uzbek government . . . even in these circumstances we have found our own way to acquire cotton from our old friends . . . It is precisely these connections that help our production stay afloat' (Schelkov and Antonov, 1998). Shortages of raw materials had immediate repercussions on technical and human conditions of production. The director on this point noted that:

> Serious complications have arisen with raw materials, which means degradation of technology, nervousness, fall in output and financial complications. Only because of acute shortage of cotton, the enterprise in 1992 has worked quite worse than in the previous years 1990–1. But if we compare this fall with [the situation in, CM] other factories, then it will appear one of the most moderate. Every enterprise has stayed idle on average for two months while we did for two weeks all in all. During the year, the wage has been raised by 13.8 times and reached no less than 18000 roubles, second place in the Trust. Then in order to economise we did not resort to closures of educational institutions like similar enterprises in the region. We did not stop housing construction [but went on with building programmes, CM]. There is much talk about privatisation of individual flats, [but, CM] we keep running the waiting list. Substantial resources are devoted to subsidiary departments, in particular agriculture. Some time ago we bought up part of the *sovkhoz* and now activity is directed to reconstruction and re-equipment. (Schelkov and Antonov, 1998)

Lack of funds for restructuring and the problems in production mentioned earlier prevented managers from reaping the advantages offered by privatisation. Kolya points out that in 1993, out of the free-hands 'euphoria' produced by privatisation, 'top management expected to proceed rapidly with massive lay-offs so as to catch up with Western standards with little consideration of the state-of-art in production. The labour market turned out unfavourably, buying out the best workers and leaving the enterprise in constant need of skilled personnel.'

The enterprise therefore was able to weather the initial post-privatisation shock by relying basically on its long-established connections with the local Party and suppliers. This did not come without a price. Politics required employment, and therefore capacity, to be maintained at high levels. The unsophisticated and unstable market-oriented production was marked by quantity rather than by quality. Expansion plans were downscaled, and the Soviet principles of management prevailed in inspiring decision-making. The director stated in such a way 'the goals for the current time': 'survive in the approaching market; avoid loss of cadres so as to hold on to the present position and also to preserve our [output, CM] volumes capacity'.

The period from 1993–4 up to 1996–7 was characterised, according to our manager-informers, by the attempt 'to make the enterprise profitable by increasing output volumes'. The approach was for most managers a taken-for-granted of their 'socialist' education. As our key informant confessed:

> Investments continued to be considered only in view of increasing production volumes and modernising equipment. Decisions were made on the basis of availability of financial resources rather than on expectation of orders or profitability. We had been taught at the *Institut* that the more solid enterprises were the largest and the well-being of the enterprise was ensured by the continuous growth of equipment and production.

In any case there was more than an ideological pledge or cultural backwardness to account for this choice. This strategy responded, first, to the objectives already stated for capacity and employment and to the more general political understanding that in so far as the enterprise remained large its social visibility would attract special consideration by the authorities. On the other hand, growth of output became the only means of surviving in a market dominated by barter. Once again the confidences of my key informant help clarify what elements led the situation in this direction. Reading from my notes:

> After the collapse of the centralised supply system the enterprise adapted to trade autonomously, mainly by barter. Since 1994 the 'Mafia' has entered the textile market. In fact, notwithstanding its low profitability, the short cycle made it attractive for those seeking short-term returns against small-scale investments. Gauze entered the top ten for most barter-trade goods – fuelled by exaggerated expectations of state support and a renewed wave of orders due to the conflict. Problems with cotton supply at national level led to the establishment of RosKontrakt [state agency in charge of the reactivation of the supply line from central Asia, offering financial support to agents, CM], yet funds ended up stolen or diverted. The combine decided to solve its cotton hunger by working on a processing-only basis. The agreement consisted in receiving cotton supplies on terms of processing-for-a-share-of-output. The raw material left available went to feed other production lines, which could be sold on the market for a return. The combine decided to boost processing-only goods production with the gradual introduction of the *Ital'janskyi grafik* so as to increase cotton supply for the whole enterprise. The Soviet textile sector had long worked under a three-shift rotation system referred to as *Ivanovoskyi Grafik*, i.e. Ivanovo's timetable, because of the historical concentration of the industry in this region. The system was one of the hardest in USSR industry. It consisted in alternating 6 days of morning shifts, including a single night shift, and 5 days of afternoon shifts. There were two rest days at the end of each period but no end-of-week full-scale interruptions (white-collar employees, though, have always had a regular working week and so do most managers and auxiliaries). Rotation of workers' gangs allowed for continuous production, with limited stoppages for maintenance and re-equipment. The new system features six working days – two for each shift (day, afternoon, night) – increasing the monthly

load of hours worked on the four shifts from 538 to 713, with the increase resting mostly on the night shift which grows from 14 to 49/56 hours per month. Output and revenues grew accordingly and so did the pace of production. Yet, because workers had less time to rest and worked longer time with limited supervision, output quality and labour productivity decreased.

As a result the enterprise, unlike other neighbouring combines, kept production going and survived, but accumulated a debt burden unsustainable in the long term and saw a deterioration of its working conditions. Public records confirm that 'still in 1995 the enterprise was putting out the highest volume of production in the region, totalling 134 billion roubles. The whole sum though was ending up in expenses' (Schelkov and Antonov, 1998). In fact, barter negatively affected enterprise business in many ways. As it did not permit the ascertaining of the real value of the goods exchanged, it tended to depress the virtual return from sales. While the enterprise was eager to get rid of its goods for badly needed spare parts, raw materials, such as fuel, gas and cotton, were bought at above-average prices. The end result was a constant weakening of the enterprise trade balance.

As far as barter was employed to obtain supplies and deal with intermediaries rather than final customers it made it impossible for the enterprise to develop commercial skills, favouring the transfer of commercial activities from the director to a dedicated department. It also prevented market signals from reaching the enterprise and making marketing and product development the leading functions. Leo, the senior consultant leading the restructuring project in the field, during an interview observed that:

> The key problem is the absence of retailing; there are no shops, an enterprising trade sector that could operate as a medium with customers and allow producers to establish the market value of their goods. The manufacturers offer their goods to clients as it is, without considering that for each kind of good there is a wide range of offers from specialised firms. These are the outcomes of barter, which makes it impossible to ascertain the relative value of commodities. Barter in itself would not be a problem as far as it is performed by operators directly in the market.

Instead, as a manager put it, procurement-oriented trade consisted in 'exchanging our rubbish for theirs'.

Furthermore, since barter trade could hardly guarantee regularity of consignment and certainty about the characteristics and quality of goods purchased, scarcity continued to plague production. Therefore, increases in output and barter trade created more problems than they were meant to solve. Other than financial difficulties and marketing problems, they allowed, or forced, the continuation of Soviet practices in the shops.

The 1996–9 period: from foreign-led restructuring to insolvency

In the second half of the 1990s, the director and his aides made a last attempt to save themselves and the labour collective by employing a more drastic strategy of cuts. In the mean time they tried to take seriously the offers and suggestions that foreign consultants, sent to the region under a joint EC–Russian restructuring programme,[1] were putting forward.

Consultants produced an analysis of the state of the enterprise and presented a business plan with recommendations for restructuring. I was able to examine these materials and participate in their presentation to Russian senior management in 1997. The analysis presents elements that confirm managerial concerns for the situation in the market and set the most problematic tasks related to restructuring. The business overview consists basically of a traditional market analysis, placing the Russian textile industry and enterprise individual business in the context of the world and domestic market in order to sort out their most valuable business opportunities and feasible perspectives of development. The analysis refers to structure, strategies and operational mode: since the first topic has already been treated at length, here the argument is limited to the remaining two areas of concern.

According to the consultants, the enterprise current activity was characterised by chronic scarcity in cash flow, huge rates of idle productive capacity, low profitability of current output and lack of direct and/or long-standing relationships with partners/suppliers.

The combine continued to operate large shops where relatively new machinery lay alongside 'archaeological' equipment, which wastes raw materials and requires steady maintenance work. Since a great deal of output was given in barter in exchange for supplies it seemed that these productions were justified solely by the ability to obtain supplies, which was still far from self-financing, let alone allowing profit margins.

It was admitted that the current enterprise organisation and its management were consistent with the situation in the industry and the 'market' in Russia.

At an all-industry level, the lack of co-operation among individual enterprises was remarked on. Enterprises did not show any interest in developing – or any ability to develop – a division of labour and persisted in manufacturing the same kind of goods, resulting in destructive competition. They had not been able to set a common stand towards suppliers and final customers in order to strengthen their position in terms of price and quality. As a result their contractual power was low and many of them had virtually become a mere productive unit under large financial–industrial groups or ambiguous intermediaries.

---

[1] The project fell into the framework of a broader co-operation agreement between the Russian Federation and the EC (Tacis) to provide support for the transition towards a market economy. This specific project was aimed at rescuing this sole-industry area, badly affected by the ongoing slump in production, which was a cause of major political concern for the high level of unemployment and pauperisation. The Management Consulting Firm, in collaboration with other leading firms with expertise in the field of machinery and cotton, successfully bid for the project tender.

In fact, the collapse of the command economy had not delivered anything close to competitive open markets. On the supply side, the 'retreat' of the State had meant partly a mere change of the legal status under which former state agencies operated, partly the entry of new subjects like banks, investment funds and trade intermediaries. The lack of funding, limiting the choice of suppliers, strengthens the position of these subjects. These companies pursue a rent-seeking strategy aimed at ensuring their monopolistic position instead of fostering investments and business-oriented restructuring. On the demand side, the positioning of the enterprises was equally weak. With shrinking state orders, the textile industry was supposed, like any other consumer-oriented industry, to be led by mass consumption. Again like other consumer-goods manufacturers, they found themselves overtaken by foreign competitors. Many enterprises were forced to look at exports of cheap commodities as the vital source of revenues, while their market share at home was at stake. As a result, it was argued, these enterprises were operating in survival mode with no chances to survive in the long term.

In order to haul themselves out of the present dire conditions and retrieve their position as viable business makers, the selected companies were assigned a business plan. The plan consisted of three parts: the restructuring of the organisational structure; the implementation of immediate actions to regain efficiency; the development of a comprehensive strategy.

The measures to regain efficiency in the short term were all urged by the aim of cutting running costs and increasing productivity. They usually included energy conservation, waste reduction, lay-off of unnecessary workers and dismissal of auxiliary activities – first of all, the welfare system.

The strategic proposal included the following medium-term actions: upgrading of the productive capacity of the factory to raise the standards of its output to the requirements of the world market; reshaping the product range to focus on the most marketable articles; improving the enterprise outward profile to deal directly with customers and suppliers; dismantling the welfare system. Given the serious shortage of internal financial resources and the already high level of indebtedness, argued the consultants, the only way to plan investments rested on partnership with foreign manufacturers. On the contrary, the domestic market was regarded as too insidious and lacking expertise for partnership or financing. Expectations were placed instead on the local authorities to cope with the unemployment resulting from factory lay-offs and the dismantling of the welfare system. It was their duty to elaborate a retraining scheme and plans to foster the development of business activities other than textiles, to absorb redundancies and to accept having the enterprise welfare system switched on to their budget.

Among the many measures contemplated by restructuring, cutting jobs and closing unproductive outlets was certainly the most needed but was also a quite difficult and painful one to carry out. Other than the fear of discrediting management and the director, there were the complications already pointed out in relation to white-collar employees. Without changing the overall labour and production organisation, any redundancy would create holes in the staff, making the work of those remaining harder. For these reasons production managers resisted and utterly refused the lay-off of cadres and workers. For this very reason it was difficult in the first place to determine which were unnecessary workers, as staffing was decided at lower managerial levels where informality and approximation reigned.[1] Senior management adopted a three-pronged strategy:[2] they favoured the natural loss of cadres due to the low level of wages; transferred administrative staff into production jobs; resorted to outright lay-off for peripheral outlets and socially marginal categories.

Already, in the first half of the 1990s, the enterprise got rid of the worst among its employees – first of all, alcoholics. Furthermore, in the 1992–4 period there were no new recruits. The closure of schools, nurseries and shops brought the enterprise working population down to around 4,000 from the initial 5,000. Another thousand were to be lost in the period under consideration. Beginning with the redundancy of 400 pensioners, more redundancies were achieved with 'the merging of the construction and transport department into the economic-transport unit (*KhTO*)'. Factory canteens were also either shut down or made into private businesses, as was the health resort. Housing was eventually transferred to the local authorities, though maintenance of flats continued to rest on factory resources.

As for labour productivity, the whole operation was a failure as the natural loss of cadres more than compensated for targeted cuts, forcing the enterprise to recruit the very same people, unskilled and under-qualified, they had been trying to get rid of. My key informant pointed out that 'When I entered the factory as assistant foreman I was replacing the last cadre without formal qualification. Now the process has reversed'. In any case the problem was that the structure of costs did not change. First, because unprofitable shops were not shut down, they were awaiting investment and technological reconstruction; second, the bulk of the social and town-maintenance services continued to burden the enterprise budget.

The failure to carry out investment was the outcome of a combination of factors, but managers pointed to the disappointing relationship with potential foreign partners and, second, to state intervention in identifying those to blame for the bad fate of the operation. Together with the foreign consultants, a plan for investment was drafted to be used for gaining a credit line from banks; having their own money, senior management decided in any case to send a delegation to Western Europe to shop for equipment and look for contracts.[3] Their objectives were ambitious: a new set of second-hand weaving machines

---

[1] I had a taste of it in 1997 when collecting data for the foreign consultants in the shops about the manning of production lines. There was a tangible tension with managers over decisions to classify workers' jobs, whether direct producers or auxiliaries, as they felt clearly that in the latter case they could qualify for dismissal.

[2] Information provided by the chief of the OtiZ (department of labour and wages) in a written interview.

[3] I took part in this business trip, sponsored by the EC project, as a translator and a guide to the Russians.

had to be purchased, a new automatic spinning line was to be acquired with a barter deal; contracts for export of fabrics were also discussed, and the possibility of sourcing cotton in European markets emerged. Despite disagreements which emerged during talks, from financing to technical details, revealing serious differences in trade behaviour and techniques, it was a stunning surprise to hear that talks had collapsed without results at the end of 1997. With the help of my informants I attempted to produce an explanation; my notes tell it as such:

> With the Italians in 1997 we attended a course of business strategy which allowed us to focus on cost accounting and profitability assessment when deciding over production matters. The business plan we elaborated at that time did not incorporate these elements and in fact was rejected by banks. Italians were also meant to help with export and investment. The director eventually decided to reject their offer for sales of fabrics when he discovered that their real value on the Italian market was three/four times higher than our selling price, while they were asking for a few cents' discount. As for investments, we planned the purchase of weaving machines and were considering an offer on a barter deal for spinning. The former failed when our funds were frozen in 1997 as a result of restrictive monetary policy, and the latter talks failed as we insisted on purchase rather than barter. We did not like the fact that Italians were trying to buy cheap from us and impose unfavourable deals, trying to compensate with promises of handouts to those managers participating in talks.

The role of public authorities was no less detrimental, as it was referenced in both periods in several complaints by enterprise managers. The director in 1998, when the situation had become desperate, expressed all his disillusion in this outburst:

> The first sign of the forthcoming disaster appeared in the years 1996–7. The collective 'lost itself' when they borrowed at an 80% annual rate to buy raw materials . . . Then our problems with sales also began – remembers [the director, CM] with sorrow – which we never had before . . . interest mounted up and . . . our bank account was frozen for two years. Immediately afterwards several social setbacks also appeared: non-payment of wages, stoppages, lay offs and so on. The situation became untenable: non-payment of wages ran up to nine months. [Interviewer, CM:] Will it continue for long? [Director, CM:] It will while the government pursues its truly genocidal policy towards the textile sector . . . Paradoxically in our times it has simply become unprofitable to run a good business! Where is our own state leading us, to full disruption, to misery, to social break up? (Schelkov and Antonov, 1998)

One could disagree with the wording, but the substance of this argument was unquestionable. As suggested by Leo, the senior consultant leading the restructuring project in the field, the absolute lack of industrial policy was striking. In his own words:

> The enterprise has to face harsh competition in the market as a result of wild liberalisation of foreign trade. Personally I find this latter decision quite counterproductive. Under such conditions you do not favour competition, you simply wipe out the whole industry. Russian industry is now in a situation comparable only to that of some countries in the immediate aftermath of WWII. But post-war liberalisation in those cases was conducted much more cautiously in order to allow for adaptation and gradual restructuring.

The role of the State, at the level of central authorities in Moscow, was indeed mostly remarkable for its absence. There was no selective liberalisation of import-export, which could stimulate competition while fostering foreign investments; nor was there financial or fiscal support to national exports or credits for the purchase of machinery and raw materials. It took years to stabilise trade relationships with cotton-producing CIS countries, and when this happened it was to the advantage of a new lobby of intermediaries. They channelled low-quality cotton to Russian producers while selling the best of their harvest abroad, and this with public money supposedly destined to guarantee supplies to local producers. 'Foreign' cotton remained instead out of reach because of high import duties and lack of hard currency.

Another very unusual issue relates to the situation of the nearby military installations. Formally the base did not exist, so fuel and gas bills as well as infrastructure, including a railway terminal, were a further financial burden for the enterprise. According to managers, it was a matter of political expediency not to raise the issue with the authorities; this explains their anger and disbelief when political support failed to materialise in a situation of desperate need.

The role of the local administration was more ambiguous. They in fact channelled funds to the enterprise as long as they could, as confirmed by the director of the local association of textile manufacturers. Then, again, this fostered confusion as to the division of roles and responsibilities between the economic and the political sphere. Leo, who witnessed talks between the enterprise senior managers and the governor, inferred that:

> The regional administration has greater powers than its Western counterparts. Enterprises are held under tutelage. The administration has agreed to channel credits to the enterprise to cover its debts but has refused to take on the costs of the company town welfare system; it maintains that this is a step that can be made only after reassurances from Moscow. The administration has also refused to liberalise trade, lifting a heavy fiscal and administrative burden and a high levy of 10 per cent to 15 per cent on profits. The administration justifies its fiscal policy with the need to subsidise loss-making enterprises.

Left without allies, short of funds, including working capital, 'the enterprise fell on speculators, basically cotton traders, taking advantage of these troubles' (Schelkov and Antonov, 1998). What ensued was, at factual level, a short-lived struggle for control between outsiders and the director that ended with a declaration of insolvency and consequently his ousting. The dramatic ending of this crisis meant also, and more significantly, the failure of this last attempt at restructuring as part of the long struggle of the enterprise to operate independently in the post-reform economic environment. It now appears clear that the enterprise, its structures, strategies and mode of operation maintained most of the pre-reform features, or at least continued to respond to Soviet managerial principles. Nevertheless it is equally evident that: management was neither unaware nor ideologically opposed to adaptation;[1] restructuring was in fact pursued within the limits set by knowledge and availability of resources; the enterprise, owing to demonetisation and scarcity, was in fact very much constrained in its strategic choices. Therefore, it was rather the case that managerial behaviour was a rational response to external inputs and that such a continuity with the Soviet past should not be interpreted as managerial resistance to market competitive forces but as an adaptation to the *modus operandi* of those very forces.

---

[1] Despite the widespread belief that Russian managers did not understand the market economy and wanted to live 'under socialism', the chief of the consultants' delegation in Ivanovo came to the opposite conclusion, observing that environmental barriers were overwhelmingly against any modernising strategy at enterprise level.

6   The consequences of outsider control

Restructuring, *noun (management)*
1 major rearrangement of staff, systems or finance within a company or a
*group of companies: '**restructuring resulted in the loss of 500 jobs'**.*
Oxford Dictionary of Business English, 1994

New shops have sprung up in the streets, quality housing is being built, and
even factories have seen up-to-date equipment being installed but, the old
Soviet command system has remained substantially unchanged.
(Interview with Kolya, 2007)

Bankruptcy, takeover and the gradual absorption of the case-study factory by a trading house is by no means an isolated case. In the last decade the creation and expansion of financial–industrial groups, usually taking the legal form of holding companies, has changed the economic panorama in the region. And textiles have come last in this process of concentration. Therefore, further analysis of enterprise management requires putting its structures and strategies into this new wider organisational context.

There are important theoretical and policy implications, too, in favour of considering the new role of holding companies and their new owners in pursuing restructuring. First, outside ownership has long been praised by mainstream transition economics for providing the context for effective enterprise restructuring. Practically the emergence of holdings in the Russian economy has raised the expectation, and sometimes it has been accompanied by the promise, that these agents might transfer their financial and marketing capabilities – as well as the wealth amassed during early transition – into the real economy.

Yet financial–industrial groups taking over enterprises encounter difficulties in carrying out restructuring (Johnson, 1997). Managerial resistance is openly blamed by new owners, but their commitment to real change has come under scrutiny. Case-study research indicates that, whatever their level of involvement in modernising and relaunching manufacturing activities, new owners rely heavily on traditional Soviet practices (Clarke, 2004; Kabalina, 2005).

This chapter will review and analyse restructuring carried out at the combine as part of the overall process of reorganisation of the trading house into a holding company. A second holding company is taken into consideration for comparison, to which some of the respondents from the company town moved after failure to carry out restructuring in the combine convinced them of the need to look for a more promising work environment. The two cases considered present very different strategies, one – the trading house – characterised by a lukewarm approach to restructuring and orientation to short-term profits while the other – the holding recently turned into a corporation – allegedly committed to long-term modernisation, but at present the two display similar outcomes. Analysing their formative stages – from takeover to restructuring – from the viewpoint of the management–ownership relationship pinpoints the limits and contradictions of the holding as a new form of economic organisation torn between the competing goals of: (1) pursuing short-term financial targets and organisational and technological development; (2) asserting traditional, i.e. Soviet, authority and achieving efficiency, which implies promoting managerial autonomy.

The key finding is that the route to successful restructuring lies in overcoming Soviet-type personnel and production management. This is unlikely to happen without thorough technological change at enterprise level and organisational change in the holdings' command structure. These early experiences of restructuring also reveal how building trust between managers and owners represents an essential precondition for pursuing these goals.

Industry structure and holdings' strategies: consolidation and monopolisation

By summer 2005 there were five holding companies[1] dominating the textile industry in Ivanovo and the upper Volga region. Each of these groups is clearly identified with a business leader who combines ownership and leadership of the group and its constituent parts (sometimes in association with partners with a much lower profile). For their influence over local and sectoral affairs, and their political ties, they have become known as oligarchs. These companies have taken control of two-thirds of the largest and best-known enterprises in cotton textiles (as well as businesses in linen and clothing) and conducted a wave of

---

[1] The official title under which these firms are registered is either 'Trading Company' (*Targovaja Kompaniya/Targovoj Dom*) or 'Holding' (*Kholding*). These companies control three or more enterprises through stock ownership (in the majority of cases with a 100 per cent stake, only in three cases out of 22 do their shares amount to 50 per cent or less). They have full control over the appointment of managers, and the activity of enterprises is planned and directed by the holding headquarters. Enterprise activities are also integrated in the holding supply chain.

closures.[1] Together, they own a majority stake in the regional textile industry. All but one have been established within the region, and some own stakes in other activities, but for all of them manufacturing in the sector and the region represents the core business. The independent sector by contrast has been shrinking, with five out of ten enterprises going out of business since 2000 alone. Research findings suggest that these trends are the direct result of the oligarchs' strategy of consolidation and monopolisation. Here we shall review the policies that have accompanied them and their effects on the industry.

The leaders of holdings and trading companies have often claimed to have saved the industry and to be committed to its reconstruction (Smirnov, 2000; Ivanov, I., 2005), yet new owners have attracted a string of criticism from a plurality of sources, which provide a comprehensive account of their policies and their shortfalls and contradictions.

Light Industry trade union top officials lament that the oligarchs keep 'buying and selling enterprises, shutting down factories and moving workers and equipment to other establishments'. A top manager who worked for the two largest groups provides the following explanation:

> The buying and selling of enterprises by different groups resembles a 'domino game' in which each group seeks the ideal combination to satisfy their production and sales plan; but only a few go as far as carrying out reconstruction and re-equipment. Oligarchs have also tried to get hold of prestigious establishments in order to raise the leverage of their groups, making it easier to obtain loans from the banking system and support from politicians. (Interview with holding's production chief executive, 2005)

The other point made by union officials is the marked continuity in production 'based on few products giving immediate returns such as gauze for medical use and grey fabrics for export' – the sort of goods on which most of the producers in the region survived in the 1990s. The state of decay of machinery and equipment with obsolescence at above 70 per cent (Preobranzhenskaya, 2005) clearly indicates that modernisation has not been a priority.

It is evident that, at least until recently, oligarchs have preferred extensive growth to innovation, making the most of existing production capacity. They have tapped into existing markets with a policy focused on a narrow range of low-quality staples. In this context volumes and prices are determinant factors. Consequently, they have tried to put competitors out of the market by: seizing production facilities and supplies, including labour; and driving down prices, relying primarily on cuts to labour costs and tax dues. The manipulation of bankruptcy has been a key tool in such pursuits. One stratagem has been artificially to maintain enterprises under bankruptcy. Bankruptcy, in fact,

---

[1] Official statistics are quite unreliable as control and ownership often do not coincide; many large establishments have been split into smaller legal units which figure in statistics as Small Enterprises. A list compiled by our gatekeepers calculated that out of 37 large textile mills 27 had fallen into oligarchs' hands, seven of which have now been shut down.

'allows paying less taxes and forfeiting payments to the pension fund' (Interview with holding senior manager, 2005) and, as workers and trade unionists pointed out, it puts strong restraint on pay rises. Here it is also important to note that under such an arrangement ownership rights and corporate governance are left in a grey area, preventing the consolidation of these businesses. Since such a scheme cannot be protracted indefinitely, companies have found a more sophisticated and legitimate tool to retain the related fiscal and labour-cost advantages. Our sources explain that:

> With the end of the year 2005, companies have their last chance to restructure, turning large enterprises into a collection of small firms (i.e. with less than one hundred employees), register the newly established enterprises as 'small business' and file tax payments (till the end of 2007) according to a simplified scheme, which means paying roughly 50 per cent of a 'big' business tax burden. (Interview with holding's production chief executive, 2005)

Monopolisation of supplies and cutting of costs also seem to inform the handling of labour in the form of containment of labour costs and labour-hoarding. Factory closures appear to respond to this strategy. Some of the largest factories in Ivanovo city have been turned into department stores and rented out as office space leading to the 'gradual disappearance of the textile industry in the urban area'. A journalist investigating holdings' strategies reports that:

> The industry is migrating into the province where labour-market conditions are more favourable. In rural centres there are no alternative job opportunities and women workers are more than ready to tolerate low wages and bad working conditions or absence of a proper employment contract for higher pay. (Interview with journalist, 2005)

The shift towards marginal areas and marginal workers in an industry that has suffered a dramatic loss of cadres and has difficulties recruiting qualified personnel is likely to produce negative effects on discipline, productivity and management. According to workers and managers at one large mill affected by the transfer of machinery and workers from redundant factories by the parent company, such an operation had been chaotic and devoid of any apparent purpose other than putting competitive pressure on 'autochthonous' staff and depriving competitors of valuable cadres and equipment. Labour-hoarding appears to be a widespread practice and to have other purposes, too:

> Each holding controls a relatively large number of enterprises but only a few are real businesses; the others only exist for fictitious redistribution of revenues in order to hide profits and retain the loss-making status.
> (Interview with journalist, 2005)

These practices also indicate that current employment levels are unsustainable and a substantial number of jobs might be at risk. As for wages, trade unions have denounced the existence of an under-the-table agreement among large groups in order to keep wages down. Paradoxically, though, tax avoidance has allowed large groups to pay higher wages and retain some social services, sustaining the hoarding of labour at the expense of independent producers.[1]

Thanks to all these measures, oligarchs have been able to pursue a policy of high volumes and low prices, cornering local competitors. The use of price-based competition has also meant that concentration and consolidation at company level have brought greater stability to individual enterprises operating under the corporate roof, but have not stabilised the market, as their representatives claim (Interview with the director of the Ivanovo Region Textile Industrialists Association, 2002). From an interview with a local journalist and political consultant it emerged that:

> Two manufacturers' associations exist which are constantly conflicting, which has so far made it impossible to stabilise the market. The issue at stake is the attainment of an industry-wide collectively agreed policy on prices, raw material supplies and the like which should stabilise prices and prevent dumping . . . In reality, the oligarchs have so far delayed a normalisation because they have profited from such a situation. Independent manufacturers have long survived thanks to higher quality standards and the retention of the social sphere. Dumping is the preferred strategy to undermine their businesses and take them over. (Interview with political consultant, 2005)

The expansion and consolidation of holding companies has granted them a virtual monopoly in the industry, while retaining large areas of inefficiencies, under-employment and obsolete production capacity. They have stifled genuine competition and prevented the growth of entrepreneurial enterprises. These achievements have been possible by exploiting semi-legal practices with the active involvement and support of corrupted local authorities.[2] The economic sustainability of this strategy has been made possible by cuts to real wages and reliance on the flexibility of a marginal female workforce.

---

[1] In 2003 the director of a successful independent firm denounced unfair competition by large groups. Last year the firm was forced to close along with other neighbouring similar enterprises following the alleged involvement of a local oligarch. A senior manager, working for the latter but with a previous career as a businessman, confessed that his employers are poised to prevent entrepreneurship which they perceive as a threat.

[2] Both private businessmen and red directors have profited from the lack of transparency over property rights and the failure to establish a wider institutional framework regulating economic activities, including rights and mutual obligations between public and private actors, employers and workers. The success of the former over the latter has not *per se* stimulated greater appreciation for the rule of law: the emergence of holdings has produced not new owners relying on corporate governance but oligarchs.

These considerations require some specifications. First, it should be observed that the preference for quantitative growth and market manipulation over genuine competition and cost-saving innovation is consistent with the social character of this first generation of traders and speculators and the fundamentally parasitic nature of their early business activities; yet to appreciate the constraints that they experience requires an investigation of the way companies are internally organised and managed, which is the focus of the next section.

Second, these practices have been common to all companies to a greater or lesser extent; yet, as they differ in size, origin and type of leadership, their role and commitment in reproducing or changing them is likely to be different. Some holdings rely on only a handful of enterprises and have tried to focus on safe niche markets such as work clothing or army procurement. The largest groups have gained a dominant position via horizontal expansion while appearing now the most vulnerable. The following sections will focus respectively on the two largest groups, investigating their organisational and management structure.

Management and restructuring in holding companies: two case-studies

Outsider takeover and outsider control: consequences and questions

In 1998 the 'Upper Volga Textile Company' was filed for bankruptcy i.e. declared insolvent, put under tutelage by the authorities and became totally dependent on creditors. A year later all its economic indicators had appreciably worsened; the director was forced to leave office; and its leading creditor, the 'tolling' contractor LTD, obtained full decision-making powers over the management of the company. The employee-owned company was disbanded, replaced by a temporary administration regime with the official task of restructuring the enterprise to full recovery so as to avoid proper bankruptcy. By the beginning of 2000 the old director had lost hope of recovering his position, his supporters at the enterprise were removed or forced to quit; meanwhile local politicians achieved a deal with the newcomers as for their responsibility in running the company town. Who are the outsiders? How did they manage to takeover the enterprise? And what is their strategy? These issues are outlined in this section. This will recast the problem of restructuring and introduce our analysis of outsider policies carried in the following chapters.

In order to understand the takeover, two points should be kept in mind. First, this event fits into a general trend, not limited to the industry and the region, which saw industry-led groups, based on Soviet personal ties and supply chains, being supplanted by financial–industrial groups, operating as intermediaries and therefore in control of access to markets and credit (Johnson, 1997). Second, the takeover was a multistage and multifaceted process:

(a) It required not only economic superiority but also political clout;

(b) It was not limited to the assertion of legal rights of outsiders but entailed direct actions, including the 'physical' assertion of authority, aimed at asserting the full subordination of the old enterprise employees to the new owners. The change was therefore ambiguous in terms of its efficiency outcomes and uncertain as to the conflictual nature of its evolution, not only at the top but also at the bottom of the enterprise hierarchy.

The Trading House: structures and strategy

The structure and scope of operations of LTD and its parent company, the 'Trading House' (TH), were outlined by the president and leader of the latter, Anatolii Zaryanovich, in an interview given to the factory paper.

> The Trading House has operated in the textile market for more than seven years. There are more than fifty enterprises in our sphere of influence, from different industrial sectors and in different provinces and republics of the Federation. The main task of the LTD company, as part of the Trading House, is the production of textile goods, competitive in the local as well as in foreign and near-abroad markets, the processing of cotton, the production of yarn, grey cotton and mixed fabrics, the production of apparel and also the development of new products. We process up to 1500 tons of cotton a month. The supply of cotton, on the basis of direct contractual relationships with cotton-producing republics, is performed by the company ITR, which is part of the Trading House too. Sales, marketing and participation in fairs at home and abroad are all managed by another associated firm, ITOT. The Trading House also includes enterprises working with linen and manufacturing linen fabrics but even ones operating in other industrial sectors. (Smirnov, 2000)

The origins of such a successful business are much less clear, and according to confidences from insiders, they have to be sought in the 'dark economy' that sprang up in the late Gorbachev period.[1] Our key informant, after a stage at the TH headquarters in 2002–3, reported at length about its history and later developments, which I summarised as such in my notes:

---

[1] One of the few interviewees that I managed to question on this issue was an engineer, once an independent entrepreneur, who was working as an LTD controller at the combine. He confirmed that the TH had a three-pronged structure (cotton procurement, handling of processing contracts, sales of finished goods). He specified that its mode of operation in relation to manufacturing enterprises was one of provision of services and continued intervention whenever technical problems or conflicts arose. In the latter case the Trading House sought the unofficial support of Moscow- and *oblast'*-level authorities to foster its case. He eventually added that it might have been difficult to extract information from them; in fact he advised me not to, as they 'run a dirty business'.

The founding party of the business was a group of friends, who started as illegal retailers of consumer goods in the late 1980s. They managed to become dominant in the cotton trade in the region through connections in the criminal underworld. The Trading House is now well organised and staffed with young, qualified professionals but they have not changed their way of doing business. They deal with partners on the basis of half-legal/half-criminal (*blatnoi*) relations. They aim at achieving virtual monopoly over every aspect of the business regardless of costs. A remarkable example of their aggressive policies is given by the very circumstances of Kolya's recruitment. After having being forced out of his place at the combine he was called back by LTD to work on a restructuring project at another enterprise formally owned by a 'vassal' firm. When the latter invited him to stay, LTD imposed its veto and pressed for him to move to a different site. Presently he has been allowed to regroup his old managerial team at the combine. When I asked: 'What's all this for', he replied: 'This is the wrong question. The issue is not "what for" but "against whom".' They want experienced cadres and do not care about overstaffing; they pursue this strategy for no purpose other than stripping qualified personnel out of the market, against potential competitors, their nominal allies included.

The hegemonic plans of the TH extended beyond the bilateral relationship with individual plants to encompass the reorganisation of the regional industry under the auspices of its own textile manufacturers' association. In fact, after privatisation, the Soviet associations grouping the forty-two textile enterprises in the region reunited into a single joint-stock company, Ivanotextil, but then centripetal tendencies prevailed reducing it to an empty shell. The new association,[1] 25 members strong, has now taken a leading role in co-ordinating the activities of its constituent members in order to stabilise the market and foster recovery through co-operation. Organisational features, achievements and goals of the association and its founding members, the merchant houses, are well expressed by its director:

> The industry has suffered heavily from a decade of crisis but is recovering. An important role is played by the regional framework and this is a guarantee for the future. The lead has now been taken by the merchant houses, which are gradually taking over the factories/enterprises. The current strategy of

---

[1] The association I refer to in this case is one of three currently existing and the strongest in number of associates. There is enough evidence to suspect that the association is a creature of the TH. Until the year 2000, A. Zaryanovich served as its president. The director of the association, who volunteered this information in 2000, showed himself during the interview to be on good terms and in fact to be quite familiar with LTD operations and the specific case of the combine. He spoke passionately in favour of LTD's restructuring 'mission'. He had a quite different opinion of previous industry leaders, the 'red governor' and the competing Ivanotextil, which the combine's previous director had been very fond of.

merchant houses is to constitute micro holdings so as to bring enterprises once again under a single roof. Holdings will manage finance and trade, leaving production and personnel management at enterprise/factory level. The association is actively supporting this strategy; for example, we managed to obtain an *oblast'* law which formally recognises these new corporate structures. The association is also working hard to foster co-operation so as to overcome the structural problems existing in this market. In the first place, we managed to put an end to price fluctuations (up to 20 per cent) due to the seasonal character of the industry which forced enterprises to work at a loss (or stay idle) during summer. The management system under the Soviets was not entirely wrong. In my opinion a great mistake was made when enterprises were allowed to manage their businesses independently. They never dealt with buying and selling and failed badly. These functions, i.e. trade and finance, have to be returned to specialists, the holdings.

Furthermore, when I questioned him hard about the responsibilities and intentions of traders towards enterprises he admitted that 'Traders have accumulated high profits [at the expense of enterprises, CM]', though he added 'but now they are ready to take responsibility'.

Therefore, the TH had so far operated as a mere intermediary but was gaining greater involvement in production even when this did not formally appear in terms of direct ownership. Enterprise management was quite sceptical about the prospective contribution of outsiders, claiming it was a mere speculative, and dubious, business which was simply tightening its grip on enterprises the better to squeeze them. Then, again, the hostility between the two groups (the Soviet managerial elite and the new Russians) could be better-interpreted as a conflict over resources, neither of them having a greater legitimacy in managing the industry on the basis of past performance. In any case, the hostility of enterprise management explains the difficulties faced by the newcomers entering the industry and their efforts to legitimise their role, partly depicting themselves as modernisers, partly by making reference to best Soviet practices. On the other side, the purely commercial, and speculative, nature of their activities so far raises the question as to whether they possess the ability and determination to carry out restructuring. Their involvement with the combine presents an opportunity to investigate this issue.

'Conquest', or the hostile takeover

LTD was one of the combine's suppliers and rapidly became a major creditor; in this capacity it sided with the bankruptcy public authorities in overseeing enterprise activities after insolvency. The circumstances surrounding these events became inevitably the object of claims and counterclaims from both sides (Schelkov and Antonov, 1998; Smirnov, 2000).[1]

---

[1] Without reaching the climax of other Russian cases of hostile takeovers publicised in the press (see Dakli, 2000), this conflict did not lack the vocal bitterness and the dramatic consequences proper to them. The director and the representative of outsiders

In the first place, enterprise management questioned the very legitimacy of the declaration of insolvency. As reported earlier, in fact, a substantial amount of enterprise debt burden could well be attributed to costs arising from the non-productive sphere, social and even military installations. It was therefore a political decision to proceed with bankruptcy.

Another disputed issue was the rightfulness of LTD's intervention. Its leaders claimed that it was the enterprise management's fault, not having observed the clauses of their agreement, preferring to pay out other creditors, therefore allowing for LTD credits to run high. Our key informant, though, had an entirely different story to tell on this point. Until then, he explains, the combine director had taken care to distribute liabilities evenly among partners/suppliers in order to avoid precisely this kind of situation. However, when a state administrator was dispatched to the enterprise to put things right, he began to accept offers by LTD to contribute to expenses or financial obligations[1] which in principle should really have been postponed, given the state of enterprise finances. In this way, enterprise managers maintain, LTD bought out the company. This controversy calls for several considerations:

(a) First, the fact that the fate of the enterprise was decided with the help of political clout comes rather as a confirmation than as a surprise, as it is commonly found in literature (Clarke, 1994; Johnson, 1997). This stands in favour of managerial arguments.

(b) On the other hand, it is equally evident that, once the enterprise plunged into crisis, the authorities, whatever personal interest they might have had in interfering with it, were still called on to solve the situation. Being themselves short of funds, they had to rely on those investors, namely the Trading House, which was very able and willing to intervene.

Yet the main argument raised by management was that the very financial situation in which the enterprise lay, and its inability to restructure and recover, was due to its unequal relationship with suppliers. The contractual regime under which the enterprise and outsiders co-operated is known as *daval'cheskaya schema*.[2] The director claimed that this system deprived the enterprise of decision-making powers and, with the outsiders dictating enterprise policies to their own advantage, it was impossible for the enterprise to recover. To the

accused each other in the press of responsibility for the bankruptcy. The positions of the opposing factions were then voiced in interviews and conversations held at the factory during my fieldwork.

[1] Namely, purchase of materials and machinery, and payments to the wage, social and pension funds, which had been so far postponed (the former) or frozen (the latter).

[2] Literally commission-based production, a kind of agreement similar to a processing-only contract which had become very popular among textile producers in the region after the 1998 monetary crisis. As we said before, it consisted in the enterprise processing raw materials provided by the outside contractor, agreeing to deliver a certain volume of output in exchange for a quota of cotton.

contrary, outside contractors claimed that they had little say in enterprise affairs as it swallowed resources, which they provided in order to recoup the original debt. It would not be immoderate to maintain that both sides were perfectly right in their own respect. The problems with this kind of agreement, in principle not unique to Russia, are the ones proper to barter for supplies. It cuts off the enterprise from the market and leaves it working as a mere production unit.

The system is particularly pernicious in view of the need to restructure. This can be explained by comparing the present relationship with the one the enterprise entertained with higher bodies under the planning system. Under the current agreement the enterprise receives a minimum plan, which is the output agreed for delivery, but it is responsible for saving on resources provided by outsiders in order to cover its expenses and make a profit. As a senior production manager noted, the enterprise was never in a condition to produce much more than the quota due to the outsiders as traditional inefficiencies prevented them from 'making the plan'. From this perspective it can be said that market reforms did achieve their goal, i.e. to subordinate the enterprise to hard budget constraints. The enterprise was made responsible, i.e. financially liable, for its failures, which is where insolvency came from. But it did not go any further than this, rather making more acute than relieving Soviet problems.

Therefore, whether outsiders intentionally used the scheme to strengthen their grip over the enterprise or simply viewed it as an easy way to raise profits, it was clear that once brought into direct management of the enterprise they had to modify their approach and carry out reforms. This is what – at least, formally – they were set to do according to the above-mentioned declaration of intentions.

'Occupation', or the second stage of the takeover

From 1999 to summer 2003, LTD, directly or indirectly, intervened systematically in enterprise affairs, bringing changes to almost every aspect of its organisation and procedures. The organisational chart was constantly revised; managers received new instructions on quality standards, rewards, wages and penalties. Changes were not limited to procedures but affected people, too: the enterprise saw a new director almost every year, and key production managers were replaced. Here I provide an outline of the changes that affected the managerial layout of the enterprise, leaving more substantial issues of labour and work organisation, the overall change in the social constitution of the organisation, to the following chapters.

The 'new' philosophy inspiring the actual restructuring of the enterprise derived from the above-mentioned idea that the enterprise should once again focus on production. An immediate consequence, quite visible in the new organisational charts, was the slimming down and regrouping of the main departments. In particular, the commercial department disappeared altogether and marketing was filed for disbandment.

The president of the TH further specified the measures and tasks to regain efficiency. First, the number of ITR had to be reduced; he judged it intolerable that one-third of enterprise employees were still out of main production jobs.

Second, both managers and workers should plan and carry out their work more carefully, putting an end to squandering of materials, waste of resources and delivering of defective products.

To these ends, over a period of two years several actions have been brought forward, featuring forms of indirect and direct control as well as incentive mechanisms. Beginning with lay-off, already in 2000 the chief of the OTiZ had to declare that 'lay-off and transfer of staff into production' were ongoing and 'further reductions in staffing levels' were expected. This was achieved with the reduction of Planning and Sales into pocket offices and the withdrawal from the social sphere. More general cuts to auxiliary and maintenance jobs, visibly in the chief engineer's department and in Production, were also lamented by production managers. Natural wastage and transfer into other units helped to make the process socially less painful[1] and blurred the impact and the visibility to the observer in terms of employment decline.

A different issue was the cut in manual jobs in the shops. Notwithstanding traditional Western views on this point, the director of the Association reassured me that no such thing as a 'massive lay-off' was going to happen. First, because 'we do not look at the Western option, the automated factory, [second, because] . . . our problem is to keep high output volumes'.

If the new owners did not mean to get rid of their new employees in great numbers, certainly not in the initial period at least, as to gain their consent and please politicians, they were much at odds with the way people worked. If production has to be the focus of enterprise management, then 'the rouble' should become 'the main criterion for good or bad' (Smirnov, 2000), warned the president of TH from the columns of the factory paper. The appointment of the chief accountant as managing director, a mature woman with no prestige, breaking a long-standing tradition that the chief engineer should take the vacancy, was the clearest materialisation of this precept. So managers very soon saw their wage made dependent on additional elements rather than just on volumes, such as quality, costs, and level of waste. All managers interviewed in this period indicated that their responsibilities had grown, direction was more authoritarian and there was less room for compromise.

It is not that changes were simply entrusted to individual initiative; controls were also introduced. The two last organisational charts show how the security department grew into a diversified body fighting embezzlement, waste and theft of funds and materials through physical and bureaucratic routine checks. The Quality Control unit was also revitalised, with the appointment of a prestigious

---

[1] The social impact of displacement for office workers varied greatly. Certainly accepting the offer of a job in production (which was due by law, if available) was generally traumatic, if accepted for lack of alternatives. Many regretted the loss of benefits such as shorter and more regular shifts (especially for women who staffed the lower ranks in offices), better working places and the status of 'intellectual workers'. It seems that opting for the private sector or relocation in the factory was mainly conditional on availability of connections in one or the other area while age and education or 'entrepreneurial spirits' might favour success at a subsequent stage.

and skilled chief, previously head of spinning, and the assignment of more personnel, deployed both in factories and in the laboratory. Last but not least, LTD began to send its own people into the factory; controllers appeared in the shop chiefs' offices checking on the state of production and the correct implementation of orders. Weekly and monthly briefings were also scheduled at the offices of factory managers to review the implementation of the plan.

These initiatives, no less than the previously mentioned controls, produced traumatic effects on managers who felt unjustly harassed or simply pointlessly disturbed. As a result, for at least a year, production management fell into a state of complete confusion as fear spread among managers and their subordinates of punishment by demotion. It seemed quite clear that the newcomers played on personal jealousies and factional rivalries in order to secure control over the labour collective and defeat those still on the side of the old director.[1]

LTD therefore, not without costs and contradictions, installed itself into the enterprise organisation and began to integrate (subordinate) it in its system. The question arises how these events were survived and perceived by managers and what real changes they brought to their daily work routine. An interview with the newly appointed chief of quality control yields the first impressions about lights and shadows in the new administration's plans. On her appointment and its general meaning in the new course, she maintains:

> I have been transferred to this position because of my determination; the previous chief has been demoted for lack of character . . . In the past, until *perestroika*, we had a strong department for technological control, which oversaw the qualitative aspects of production. This was put aside and abandoned after *perestroika*. Now LTD pay a lot of attention to quality, there is competition and they are ready to spend money on it. Now we keep count of every *kopeck*; they have taught us to value money. The budget is fixed centrally, and if you need more you have to provide justifications for extra expenses, though usually they let you go with it.
>
> (Interview with the head of the quality control department, 2001)

None the less, neither her work nor the general state of production management seemed to be perfect and faultless, both in practice and in conception. In fact, as she put it:

---

[1] The main target of these 'punitive expeditions' turned out to be precisely my key informant Kolya, then working as head of the weaving factory, and his closest associates. When he eventually left the enterprise in February 2001, the domino effect drove out of the factory many valuable specialists while breeding disillusion and anger among those workers who felt personally loyal to him. It is quite an irony that, in early 2003, LTD rethought its decision, giving him the job of chief engineer. As a result he managed to get rid of all those 'incompetent careerists' who had previously taken advantage of his ousting. The moral here seems to be that the newcomers could not easily dispense with the ideas and experience of the old cadres.

The main problem lies in the laboratories; they are subordinated to production, and their judgement can be influenced. When possible I try to have a word with them; I am on good terms with the senior managers there . . . Well, there is bargaining – between production and the administration. I am afraid there is no planning, centralised management. Our working conditions do not allow us to have an unquestionable plan. Production departments cannot foresee what is going to happen. We are still in transition. In the end, they are the owners; they want to decide how to spend their money and want to see results.

(Interview with the head of the quality control department, 2001)

Trading House's takeover, and management resistance

The crucial limit of holding–enterprise relations consists in the forms of planning and monitoring used. The replacement of physical with financial indicators and the greater attention to costs and quality have materialised within a very traditional format of planning and administrative control furnished with little autonomy and rewards for enterprise managers. The takeover of the Volga Textile Combine by the Trading House represents an exemplary case in holdings' initial policies. The takeover took the form of increasing interference by the holding's supply units in the enterprise's affairs aimed at controlling flows of resources, and only secondarily their rational use in production; the latter being viewed very much as a direct effect of the former.

The leader of the holding denounced 'the habit of managers "to live under socialism" and their inability to adjust to market conditions and pay attention to costs' (Smirnov, 2000), and promised to bring efficiency and reward hard work, while tackling indiscipline, theft and idleness. The measures adopted were, among others: direct control over production management with regular visits by the holding's directors and the permanent presence of their deputies at shop level; changes to the wage and reward system featuring mostly fines for failures to meet targets; administrative control of any activity involving the use of enterprise property subjected to approval and monitoring by the new security department. At the same time, production targets were raised with the expectation of achieving full utilisation capacity. These initiatives had a paralysing effect on production, limited line managers' ability to manoeuvre and brought havoc in the shops.

The pressure to achieve more with less without any reward or expectation of modernisation led to a breakdown of morale and open conflict with the owners. Our key informant, who was then leading the insiders' team after the red director was forced to leave, was removed from the key post of head of weaving production and quit in protest, followed by a number of engineers. They were replaced by the second lines, often female staff personnel with no experience or expertise other than their loyalty to the newcomers. The actual outcome after two years of 'occupation' was intensification of work and bureaucratisation of management without organisational or technological change. The enterprise achieved greater output at lower costs but at the price of loss of cadres, breakdown of co-ordination and workers' demoralisation expressed by low productivity, poor quality and discipline violations.

Despite their original claims, the holding's top managers had run a very Soviet productivist campaign centred on individual responsibility, high production targets and stifling regulation. Not surprisingly, this called forth a traditional form of resistance, ranging from the walkout of qualified personnel to absenteeism and theft by workers and continuous bargaining over planning targets by production managers. If managers' and workers' resistance was partly inspired by enterprise patriotism and attachment to their autonomy, it had a solid justification in the understanding that the new policy would simply lead to intensification of work without compensation. Enterprise managers in particular expected commitment to re-equipment and improvement in quality of supplies as evidence of breaking with the Soviet past, which in fact did not materialise. Having secured control over the enterprise but realising the long-term untenability of the situation at the factory, the new owners reinstated the old leaders.

The Trading House, restructuring and its limits

New owners so far have not emerged as great innovators, preferring cautious, piecemeal re-equipment to full-scale reconstruction and adaptation rather than revolution in management. Yet the conflict with production managers has not been simply a struggle for power disguised as an ideological battle. Attempts at restructuring reveal a striving for control and an urge for efficiency becoming an issue of growing concern with the new owners. An interesting case is represented by the 'reconstruction' activities carried out in the 2002–4 period at the combine and another production site, bankrupted former state enterprises, recently purchased by the above-mentioned holding.[1]

Before Kolya could return to his company town, the TH leaders wanted him to get acquainted with working in their corporate structure and possibly put his loyalty and abilities to test. After a period of training at their headquarters he was dispatched to another town and put in a position of responsibility within a team in charge of restructuring a newly purchased company.

The first site had long been idle before the takeover took place; it therefore represented in the managers' own opinion an ideal setting for restructuring, in that they did not expect resistance from a pre-existing labour collective or managerial structure. Other facilitating factors were: a high managerial turnover, whereas the reconstruction team would exercise full discretion in recruitment, targeting young qualified specialists and experienced cadres; the same 'green field' effect would operate for workers; here the availability of a large pool of

---

[1] Here we report and discuss accounts provided by production managers, including our gatekeeper Kolya, who have made their career in senior company positions over the last decade, working at different sites and taking active part in technical and organisational change. Interviews and observation took place during two visits in 2003 and 2005, supplemented with updates via electronic correspondence.

unemployed and pauperised workers, former employees of the bankrupted enterprises, allowed more room for manoeuvre on issues such as discipline and productivity.

The key components of the restructuring initiative consisted in a comprehensive set of changes in production management encompassing: (1) a new organisational layout with a shorter hierarchy, achieved by cutting the position of production department chief and introducing dispatchers; (2) a reorganisation of production featuring new layout and installation of more advanced second-hand imported machinery; (3) market-driven planning, which should have originally tied output volumes and assortment selection to clients' orders rather than to existing production capacity (admittedly 'planned and attempted but not fully achieved'). Despite this, managers in charge reported that the experiment had generated satisfactory business outcomes and boosted mutual confidence with the holding's leadership, prompting the latter to return Kolya to his native enterprise to implement similar actions. During 2003–4, he was appointed chief engineer, assembled a managerial team made up mostly of loyal autochthonous managers and set out confidently to reproduce the successful restructuring case in his initial workplace – this time, though, with patchy and eventually disappointing results. One of the newly appointed dispatchers, Vitya, provides a vivid insight into the entanglements which crippled the reform process. First, dispatchers are allowed to operate only during the line managers' time off (night and weekend shifts), so their actual impact was limited. Second, managerial style is unchanged: 'They arrive at eight in the morning when problems have already piled up and sit down waiting for reports to come from foremen . . . Personally I do not understand what we need these managers for' (Interview with dispatcher, 2005). Finally, re-equipment, in his experience, has been badly run and displays a disappointing lack of commitment and planning: he explains how shops were flooded with faulty machinery from other factories with no clear guidelines about its operation, and once shop personnel fixed it no reward was provided.

Workers are equally vociferous about the state of dismay in the shops. A controller in the finishing department interviewed in 2005 commented that the enterprise is not cutting staff but actually employing more workers, including those with poor discipline records. In her view this is one of the causes of poor performance, resulting in a blame game with the hierarchy. Another relates to the use of employees from redundant factories leading to conflicts between outsiders and autochthonous workers, who perceive the newcomers as rate busters.

The holding's managers, at the same time, have not abandoned the Soviet habit of visiting production managers with demands about output and costs, bypassing enterprise leaders – something reminiscent of ministerial petty tutelage. The chief engineer lost the confidence of his closest subordinates, who expected protection against the holding's heavy tutelage, while failing to deliver to his employer. In his view, the halt to the reform drive was due to the combination of 'structural constraints and an unfavourable market conjuncture'; among them:

> (a) ownership failure to back orders and promises with resources and powers necessary to turn them into reality, (b) a strategy based on high output volume failing in the face of export stagnation, (c) the resort to survival strategies based on cost reductions rather than innovation.
>
> (Interview with former chief engineer, 2005)

Clearly, change without investment proves unsustainable, and individuals revert to familiar Soviet practices as they guarantee at the same time the fulfilment of production targets and the tutelage of parochial interests. Yet it remains to see whether this is just a case-specific outcome due to the technological and cultural backwardness of managers and owners. For this reason a second case is considered in the following section.

The Holding Company: a modern patriotic business

Evidence of similar problems in ongoing restructuring at a rival textile holding[1] indicates how the aforementioned obstacles are not solely the product of conservative corporate policies and technological backwardness. This second company presents itself as a modern business aimed at developing rather than just profiting from textile manufacturing. The holding's own newspaper responded recently to criticism, addressing textile oligarchs with these words:

> the founders of the holding are true patriots aimed at making their business a modern national company in the country's light industry . . . the textile Holding Company does not shut down factories, neither turn them into 'fancy' trade centres or carry out massive layoffs. It sees constant wage increases and improvements in working conditions. Stability and development cannot be achieved overnight but our advancements to these ends are there for everyone to see. (Ivanov, I., 2005)

More significantly, its market strategy seems more advanced. In a recent interview, the director of one of its factories pointed out how purchases of state-of-the-art machinery since 2002 have turned its facility into a leader in finishing of textile goods. He singles out cheap imports and counterfeits as a major threat to be fought through continuous change in design and quality (Okhotnikova, V., 2006). Respondents working at the holding confirm that the company is at the cutting edge in the region for product and process innovation. The holding's policies mark a difference also in management and personnel areas. A key informant maintains that ownership promotes management development, fights

---

[1] The holding was established as a textile company in 1992. Local informants indicate that the starting capital originated in financial speculation related to pension funds and had no involvement in speculation with the textile markets like the Trading House. The enterprise currently employs nine thousand people in six enterprises.

enterprise parochialism and seems responsive to suggestions from below and to customer needs.

At the time the interview was taken, in summer 2005, the owners had entrusted a thoughtful top manager with reviewing internal practices and carrying out a gradual rationalisation of internal procedures. Practically, this involved the conduct of seminars with plant managers for both educational and mobilisation purposes. Promising developments in corporate culture and integration of plant managers encountered definite limits in the mode of operation of the company. As pointed out by the chief of quality control in the aforementioned factory, technological obsolescence and the 'Soviet' mentality of line managers still represent formidable obstacles. The consequences are that these new policies find little response in production; attempts at improving quality in practice always run the risk of jeopardising planned output.

The outcome of these experiments clearly indicates how both ownership and managers have fallen back into Soviet relations. Distrust prevents establishing stable working arrangements between ownership and plant management and, consequently, bringing changes into production: like Soviet experiments, 'reconstruction' proves unlikely to retain its momentum as it fails substantially to modify relations between the actors. At the same time, despite initial failure, this experience has turned out to produce visible advances in the attitude of top managers and owners towards restructuring. Structural problems remain in two crucial areas of management, both at above-plant level and in production. Though clearly related, they pertain to two different sets of social relations, respectively those characterising worker–manager relations in production and ownership–management relations within the command chain. Findings from the two case-studies allow further investigation of the latter by analysing the structure and management of the holding.

The structure and management of the holding: Soviet management and capitalist contradictions

The parent company[1] is owned and run by several partners. The holding is a diversified company, operating in textiles and in food processing as well as in financial speculative activities. Two partners are in charge respectively of the finance and development and the international relations departments. They are in charge of developing a variety of schemes and activities whose common aspect is 'to make money by any means available'. In pursuing this goal, they have specialised in two areas, respectively seeking legal loopholes to conceal profits and avoid taxation and setting up off-shore companies and investment schemes abroad. The organisational structure constituting the textile business resembles a relatively traditional set of functional and production departments.

---

[1] The organisational charts presented and analysed hereafter were provided confidentially in 2005 by key informants working in senior managerial positions at the holdings' plants. Detailed accounts refer to the Trading House, but the same general features and problems can be extended to the Textile Holding.

The way in which their activity is planned, monitored and assessed is described as follows.

Each department, or 'project' as they are referred to in corporate jargon, actually consists of one or more legally independent firms. Each firm operates as an independent business and is assessed by financial indicators. Quality Control is in charge of reducing the number of customer complaints; Procurement is in charge of redistributing revenues among participating enterprises through pricing of inter-firm trade and so forth. The positioning of each project within the hierarchy is dependent on its economic contribution to overall profits; therefore its prerogatives, authority and budget are not set once and for all but keep varying. This leads our key informant to conclude that 'the objectives of these projects are at odds with their functional role as service structures providing for the development of the core business [i.e. production, CM]' and 'the holding is at the same time a multidivisional company engaged in manufacturing and trade of goods and a financial pyramid aimed at the highest returns in the short term'.

The management of the holding is still personalised and highly centralised. As our key respondent put it:

> The holding is structured as a pyramid with a little 'czar' or 'Brezhnev' at the top, whose decisions are unchallengeable and embodied in the plan . . . The structure of the 'Trading House' is a perfect embodiment of this polity. There are seven 'infernal circles' in between him [the owner/leader, CM] and the manufacturing enterprise and three separate lines of command, respectively functional [such as supply or engineering services, CM], administrative, presiding over each enterprise, [like Soviet ministerial *glavki*, CM] and hierarchical, down from partner-owner to the head of textile business and the head of manufacturing below him. These structures are often in conflict between each other. This is basically nothing less than a re-enactment of the Soviet model. (Interview with chief of quality control, 2005)

Continuity is even more evident when looking at the operational aspects: the dominant form of management remains the plan, a rigidly defined set of objectives, with little room for adjustments and feedback from below. The benign and co-operative attitude taken by the second case-study towards plant management finds, in their opinion, a definite obstacle on this ground. The uncooperative attitude of production managers and to an extent of all levels below the parent company top circles is directly related to the continued reliance on the centralised planning system and the constant state of uncertainty and powerlessness it conveys along the managerial hierarchy. As our respondents put it:

> 'We live in constant danger of being victimised by superiors for acting outside the rules.' This in turn remains inevitable since 'in the past unevenness of production was caused by shortages of state supplies, now the

possibility of disruptions relies heavily on the owner, i.e. whether he will pay gas bills, wages to workers and so forth, otherwise everything shuts down'.

(Interview with chief of quality control, 2005)

This evidence indicates that the acquisition of stakes in manufacturing by the holding, and its concentration in the hands of oligarchs, has left the trading company structure unchanged. Its growth in scale and scope has produced a proliferation of intermediate bodies creating problems of co-ordination. Soviet management has proved essential for restoring production but also an obstacle to innovation. Oligarchs, like red directors before them, have so far profited from production but have yet to learn how to make production profitable.

Summary and conclusions

For the past two or three years holdings have struggled to impose an even production pace and responsible behaviour on managers and workers, and are far from finding a definite answer to managerial distrust and workers' resistance and their continued reliance on Soviet practices. Kolya suggests that, despite much criticism, the new owners know and tolerate these practices very much for the same reasons the previous authorities did. He calls it *obman*, deceit, the bargaining game in the managerial structure between an 'absent' centre and the 'irresponsible' managers. It consists in the administration providing fewer resources than required for achieving the targets they have themselves planned. The efficient combination of factors remains the sole responsibility of production and lower managers, who are constantly kept under pressure.[1] The disproportion between the planned results and the resources available, which results from taut planning, is an insuperable instrument to achieve good results at low costs but also a formidable barrier to planning and modernisation and the introduction of Western managerial techniques. So far it has been taken for granted that the only way to make the enterprise into an efficient firm is no less than thorough restructuring and that conversely to prevent it means the continuation of Soviet practices.

To understand why marketisation, hard budget constraints and even outside ownership could not achieve this goal, and what it means for the enterprise to reproduce these practices in an entirely new economic and institutional context, requires us to walk down into the shops and open the box of social relations in production. As for the outsiders, it will help to explain how they dealt with the unresolved contradictions from which they had so far profited. Their strategy and the conditions for restructuring can only be analysed in relation to the constraints imposed by these relations.

---

[1] This practice corresponds to what the literature on Soviet management called 'taut planning'.

7 Controlling workers: the policy of productivity in transition

A five-year plan in four years;
On three shifts;
With two hands;
For one (little) wage.

Folk saying – Russian textile workers

Vy delaete vid, chto platite zarplatu – my delaem vid, chto rabotaem
[You pretend to pay us wages and we pretend to work].

Folk saying – Russian textile workers

In this chapter an analysis of the functioning and change in the reward and incentive system will be carried out. This is made on the understanding that this was, and still represents, a key managerial function and therefore is crucial to understanding what sort of adjustment, if any, is taking place in post-Soviet management. Payment systems are usually defined as being aimed at providing employees with reward and motivation, which we shall rather translate in the sense that they simplify the function of controlling labour. This is obviously by far not the only means by which employers can regulate, and increase, the productivity of their subordinates.

In between the two world wars, then on a larger scale in the post-war years, manufacturing industries in the West have seen the emergence of ever more sophisticated managerial and technological devices, which if not eliminating certainly pushed into second place the combination of the piece-rate and the 'watchdog'.

In Soviet enterprises, as explained in the historical section, the form assumed by the labour process meant that incentive pay remained the predominant form for controlling labour and increasing productivity. What we have in mind for change is therefore not simply the introduction of a more 'rational' incentive system but a relative change of its weight in carrying out managerial functions.

Observation of managerial behaviour, carried out now for several years in the case-study environment, convinced us that, not surprisingly, this is still a crucial area in managerial work. Enterprise administrations have found that the old payment system was, under the new circumstances, less effective and almost unmanageable. Nevertheless they have been extremely reluctant to change it precisely because their reliance on the workforce has increased rather than decreased relative to the Soviet period. On deeper scrutiny, it has been noted that it is the more aggressive managers from production who are liable to propose and sustain change as they are the ones who have to buffer the inadequacies of administration policy in the face of growing worker discontent. At the same time, their proposals, even when put in place, demonstrate the limits of a conception of labour organisation still relying on the idea of incentives as a key command lever.

Between 1999 and 2001, a wave of takeovers in the local industry radically modified the property framework, prefiguring also a change in strategy. Nevertheless the idea that outsiders might undertake what old managers were, as the mainstream literature claimed, unwilling to do or incapable of doing does not meet with comforting evidence. It is certainly true that the new, widely adopted wage systems, with their stress on performance and other 'quality' indicators, their attentive differentiation for professional figures, describe formally a move from pay-by-results to performance-related pay. Still, the enormous social and cultural change that stands in between the two is not visible or not consistent.

Managerial circles continue to be very fond of incentives and rely heavily on workers' motivation, sustained and nurtured by enterprise paternalism. This choice, it is candidly admitted, is not devoid of problems and contradictions. Yet the efforts are concentrated at striking a balance which would retain, rather than reverse, the old order. In this vision the payment system is viewed as a crucial device for social control, including its discretionary informal use by managers, and the factory/enterprise as a mere production unit, founded, socially and organisationally, on the exertion of this control.

This chapter consists of four sections. In the first I shall outline the characteristics of the formal and informal mechanisms of the Soviet wage system. In the second and third I shall present and analyse the evolution and change the system underwent under the effect of transition and the action of the old and new management of the combine. Finally, I shall report on the implementation and response by line managers and workers so as to understand the limitations of reforms, the rationale of retaining the old system and some important modifications it has undergone under transition.

The 'socialist' wage system and its post-reform legacy: formal and informal practices

This section is devoted to the description and analysis of the formal and informal institutions of the payment system established under socialism and maintained by the enterprise well after privatisation. The wage system and the highly articulated system of benefits and incentives functioning under the Soviet system were highly centralised. Wage structure, pay scales, grading and incentives were drafted and defined in Moscow, at ministry level, and were substantially uniform across industries, reflecting Party policies in the field. Liberalisation and factual decentralisation in the early 1990s, then the severing of formal ties following privatisation, set the enterprise free to make its policy decisions. In practice it left enterprise managers in charge of administering the system without the resources and the guidance once provided from the centre. Until 1998, the wage system did not undergo any formal review at the enterprise. The institutions and practices referred to here are therefore the ones which managers inherited as official policy from the 1980s and continued to operate until the late 1990s.

The formal settings

The payment system at the enterprise featured two basic forms: piecework, which comprises most manual professions, and hourly pay, applied to white-collar workers or ITR. Both categories received a bonus that, for direct manual workers and production managers, was tied to the fulfilment of the production plan. The analysis will focus on the piece-rate wage, given the strategic importance of its earners and the centrality of its administration in managerial work.

In the factory the two major production departments are spinning and weaving, with a quite similar professional structure and pay scale. Piece-rate workers in their shops comprise machine operators, weavers and spinners, mostly female, and foremen assistants, in charge of light repair and maintenance work, a male-only category. Highly paid but scarce in number are the fitters, dealing with more complex technological services.

The regular wage of these categories consisted of a basic wage and a bonus. The former was made up of two components: the flat-rate pay, amounting to around 30 per cent of the basic wage, and the piece-rate, which occupied the remaining 70 per cent. The bonus for plan fulfilment was calculated at 75 per cent of the basic wage.

The incentive mechanism hinged on the piece-rate. This was calculated on the basis of production norms, a statistical average of output per machine per hour, and the price, or tariff. Norms could differ; as a manager put it: 'It is well known that [piece-rate] computation is made according to a formula and depends on the tariff, the normative capacity and the production norm. But if the tariff is the same for all spinning workers, yet capacity is dependent on the sort of yarn produced, therefore production norms cannot be the same' (Ivanova, 2001, p. 1).

The standard tariff varied among categories and could be corrected upward or downward by coefficients. A higher tariff was paid for overtime, first-quality output and nights or Sunday shifts, while lower tariffs applied to *prostoi* and cases of idleness, or second-quality output.

Prostoi is an indicator of idle time due to stoppages. Idle time was accounted for separately and, in cases where workers were not held responsible for halting production, it was paid for compensation at a lower rate. In practice this system allowed workers to get away with the corresponding loss of output. *Prostoi* was reported by foremen and was an important component of shop-floor bargaining.

How did it work? Informal practices

It is well known that the Soviet wage system was much less motivating than it might appear at a formal analysis; managerial attempts to buy workers' co-operation led to manipulation of incentives and proliferation of extra wage payments, which in turn undermined the financial rationality of the system. The study of the actual functioning of the system in the case-study offers supportive evidence, providing greater insight and some industry-specific peculiarities.

In order to explain wage formation we should first identify the responsibilities of different managerial bodies in assessing and rewarding workers. In this, as in other areas of decision-making, powers were concentrated in the hands of the director and a few other senior managers. Middle managers formally had no powers nor did wage offices, present at central and departmental level. On this point our key respondents were quite clear:

> The wage or time and methods officials are only in charge of statistics; they are mere 'clerks'. The administration is the only one in charge to solve these questions, but managers can influence their decisions because they assess workers' performance and they provide all the necessary information.
>
> (Interview with the head of the weaving department, 2001)

Observation of daily managerial work reveals that: wage officials were fully dependent on managers to make their calculations; managers were constantly dealing with workers' grievances; they were actually able to mediate with the administration and tended to find individual solutions within the limits of the system and its resources. The way line managers describe how wages were paid displays the centrality of their role as well as revealing some frustrating limits posed to the exertion of their discretion.

Our key respondent has been working now for a decade at the enterprise, occupying the positions of shop chief in spinning and chief of production in weaving. He had been in charge of calculating the wage fund and was active in proposing and implementing its reform; he is therefore particularly qualified in explaining the real functioning of the system. He explains that the 'piece-rate and premium wage', as managers called it, was generally paid in full to all workers. In his argument this was due not to a well-tuned system but to lack of incentive and to bad design.

He justifies his argument on the grounds that the piece-rate had in reality a much lower weight in the wage than would appear at first sight. In fact, 'if we consider the three components of the wage, the hourly pay, the piecework and the bonus, and we calculate their per cent contribution to the total wage, we obtain respectively the following: 17 per cent for flat rate, 26.9 per cent for piece-rate, 56.1 per cent for the bonus' (ibid.). Since 'the hourly pay *and* the bonus can be both considered fixed components, then piecework in practice makes up less than 30 per cent of the actual wage' (ibid.).

Technological constraints also have their part. He observes that 'nobody could fail to meet the norm [i.e. they were set very low, CM] and, even so, only the hooligans were penalised with the loss of bonus'. In his opinion the specific character of textile production does not allow output to vary significantly. He explains that in weaving and spinning 'all you have to do is do up the threads when they finish or break to avoid machine idleness, if any other factor is excluded. It is a routine task and given a certain number of machines it cannot yield substantial variations in output.' In fact, he argues that piece-rate does not add anything to the performance of textile machine operators. He even wondered why the Bolsheviks in the first place opted for this system in his industry. In his experience, the practice of storming, stimulated by this incentive, demonstrated its harmfulness as workers try to overcome bottlenecks by violating technological discipline and safety rules. Though, elsewhere, he gave plenty of evidence that managers must tolerate it in so far as they are pressed for output targets.

Technology alone, though, does not tell the whole story. The rigidity of the system, as it emerges clearly from the statements reported above, was at least equally dependent on established conventions between workers and managers. He himself openly stated that 'the bonus must be paid'; and line managers, interviewed on this matter, were all convinced that the bonus was an integral part of the wage. This also implies that plan-fulfilment was guaranteed. In fact production norms had not been revised for years.

This is not to say that the large majority of workers were not concerned with meeting managerial expectations for plan-fulfilment or that it was indeed an easy task. Workers considered making the norm a paramount task and they had to put a lot of effort into making sure that they accomplished it.

Yet the piece-rate and the related bonus were not considered in themselves as an incentive – that is, a flexible means in the hands of managers to discipline workers. As a manager noted: 'in the last years of *perestroika* we had probably the highest wage in the manufacturing sector but this had no effect on productivity and morale' (Interview with the shop chief of the weaving shop n°. 1, 2000).

The limits of the formal incentive system based on scientific assessment of results were overcome by personal bargaining between workers and managers. Managers were admittedly urged to use a stick-and-carrot tactic to discipline workers and elicit their co-operation.

'At the Institute', our key respondent reminds us, 'we were taught that the job of managers consisted in exercising authority by using both the carrot and the stick.[1] To make sure that subordinates do fulfil their tasks, the manager has to educate them by paying by results' (Interview with the head of the weaving department, 2000). The wage system, tied to individual performance and offering a wide range of means to differentiate earnings, is used by the experienced manager as a tool to graduate rewards and punishments among subordinates. The character of this relationship is strictly personal: it can manifest itself in a simple one-to-one relationship or be extended to a collective whose leader, a good mechanic, brigade leader, foreman, shop chief, demonstrated managerial abilities.

Managers had several means to achieve workers' co-operation in a direct and effective way. These ranged from the discretionary decision over recruitment, relocation and promotion of workers to distribution of bonuses and individual rewards. The existence of six levels of grading, numerous professions and piece-rate differentials provided a wide range of earning differentials. Line managers were directly in charge of recruiting, training and promoting workers, and they consciously used their discretion on these matters to discipline workers.

We have observed that, irrespective of their aspirations, background and formal education, people working at the enterprise entered their working place at a lower step on the ladder. They progressed over time under the guidance of their direct superior combining experience, further education and evidence of law-abiding behaviour. Access to better jobs generally implied further education, which the enterprise offered on its premises, including special training courses and the more formal schooling at the branch of the technical Institute. Managers usually selected candidates, offered tuition, advised and even instructed their candidates before exams.

Workers who had no aspirations or skills to become cadres and enter positions of authority could still improve their condition and earning opportunities by moving to a different production shop or working station. It was in the manager's hands that a worker be trained to work on a certain machine or be judged sufficiently skilled to be allowed in his shop. In principle the system allowed also for reverse measures, though social and political conditions made it more difficult for a manager to punish, demote or relocate workers to lower positions. Our key respondent found that 'these measures are unpopular'.

The most simple and immediate way to implement the pay-by-results policy was, and still is to a certain extent, literally to agree with individual workers or brigades to pay a lump sum, usually under the guise of a bonus, for the accomplishment of a specific task. As a manager put it: 'you have to pay [i.e. bribe, CM] a man if you want the job to be done' (Interview with the chief mechanic of the weaving department). This is a quite vast area, which clearly borders on informality while being tied for payments to the use of official incentive funds.

---

[1] Or 'knut i pryanik', as it is known in Russian.

In so far as current practices in the shops may give a hint of how bargaining took place also in the past, our observation leads us to conclude that the use of individual incentives at the factory strongly resembles practices usually described in the literature as informal bargaining. The case suggests two specifications. First, managers stressed the centrality of continuous bargaining at individual level literally to buy workers' co-operation. This practice was intended as the communist, i.e. official, way to deal with workers' grievances and motivational problems.

Second, a clear pattern was observed which differentiates between professions as to the frequency and consistency of bargaining. Skilled workers, the technicians in charge of repair and maintenance services, were more likely to deal directly with the shop chief to schedule their work plan and settle their payments. The quote reported above regarding the need for extra payment, referred in fact to male workers only: 'women would do their job anyway', he added. Women did actually raise grievances, usually concerning tariffs, norms and bonus coefficients. Differentials also arose thanks to differing productivity between individuals or shops. Nevertheless, machine operators had less room to exercise control over their work, and for them the bargaining was confined to minor adjustments within the system. This phenomenon can be fully understood only if keeping in mind the fact that male workers and managers felt a strong sense of comradeship among themselves *and* a higher standing over their female colleagues, therefore feeling under lower pressure when dealing with them. This is consistent with the fact that the sector scored high productivity rates, as the tighter plan targets would suggest, and yielded high 'profits'.

So far we have discussed the functioning of the payment system with reference to monetary pay and incentives. Yet it is well known how in the Soviet system money played a much lesser role than it does in capitalist societies. In particular, key goods and services were made available directly by enterprises and were made dependent on workers' status as cadres. This system was tied to the peculiar political and social features of the socialist states and has therefore no equal to any incentive scheme in the capitalist world. In the managers' opinion it was an essential pillar of the social structure of the enterprise, playing a greater role than any other monetary incentive. We shall therefore report it in the following section before making an appraisal of the payment system as a whole.

Non-monetary incentives: the moral and material rewards of cadre status

Bonuses and other handouts administered more or less informally by shop managers all represent forms of monetary reward. However much their consistency, denomination and mechanism of distribution may have changed, they are still very much the same today. Therefore, if analysis were limited to those aspects of the payment system, the idea of continuity would certainly be exaggerated. As our key respondent put it: 'throwing a five-rouble coin in someone's hands was not the way to make, or reward, cadres in Soviet times. Every alcoholic could get a bonus for a good piece of work.' Under socialism, alongside monetary rewards there were moral (political) ones, which were of incomparably greater importance. Generally they consisted in the awarding of an *orden* (badge of honour) and were administered on consideration of both political activism and work professionalism.

Their superiority over material incentives has to be judged on a twofold argument: an *orden* raised the social status of the holder for life; if he behaved carefully he could be safe that his/her opinion would not be challenged both at work and in political bodies. Privileges of a more mundane character were also part of the package and, again, they could not be reduced or suspended. Kolya remembers that: 'When the latest consumer goods were assigned to the factory for distribution, he would be offered purchase without queuing; if cars were available, he had only to go and get it; the same would happen with an apartment.'

Therefore, this form of incentive added to the sense of security of workers, both socially and economically, in a way monetary incentives, as they were designed and have largely been maintained, could hardly compare. The end of the socialist institutional framework and the centrality assumed by market-like transactions has made these incentives obsolete but has left a void that material rewards – inconsistent and episodic – can only struggle to take up. The problem here is not simply to elicit workers' effort but to rebuild their confidence and consent on a stable and solid base. This necessarily includes restoring the moral and material status of cadres, also as an incentive to attract new recruits among the young. Our key respondents seemed confident that high, stable wages giving access to a Western-like level of private consumption could be a solution. Unfortunately, current trends suggest that, as one of them put it, 'so far no Ford has appeared in Russia, who understood that his wealth can be erected on people's welfare'.

The major characteristics of the payment system can therefore be categorised as follows. Piece-rate administered under Soviet conditions of production means highly differentiated salaries and continuous bargaining. Its more visible negative features were: excessive pressure on workers to achieve norms, marginalisation of managerial work, distress for managers involved in bargaining, and budgets strained by unplanned growth of the wage fund. Managers, though, were still very fond of it and more oriented to reform than to replacement. We discussed with our respondents whether it was not the piece-rate system in itself that was the problem rather than its design or targets. They argued firmly in favour of the virtue of the piece-rate system as opposed to flat hourly pay as a means to elicit workers' efforts, asserting that 'workers won't work otherwise'.

Bonuses are a relevant component of the wage system. In the first place there was the bonus for plan fulfilment, consisting of 75 per cent of base salary, but this was a regular part of everyone's earnings at the factory. In Soviet times other bonuses were administered in relation to specific campaigns, the latest known were related to the introduction of the brigade system, the anti-alcohol campaign, quality improvement et cetera. Several respondents stressed the importance of socialist competition. All of them were actually used by line managers to provide extra pay to motivate workers.

Prostoi[1] was extremely important in the calculation of individual wages and had relevant effects on labour costs. Each worker – the ones considered here are weavers – was assigned a number of machines whose output was used to calculate her wage. It was not unusual for some of them to lie idle during the shift, or stay out of work even longer, because of breakdowns and repairs, lack of parts or yarn et cetera. In this case the worker would obviously lose the equivalent output; furthermore, she would risk failing to fulfil the plan if output losses were considerable.

Generally workers would raise a claim to have the loss compensated and not considered for bonuses depending on plan-fulfilment. It should be underlined that, even before the crisis began, this practice fell under scrutiny as a result of increasingly frequent stoppages and the need to tighten up financial and organisational discipline. Since the practice was still in use, though restricted, after wage reform, as we shall see, we can also observe that managers tended to attribute stoppages rather to objective causes than to conscious negligence of workers and so were inclined to accept workers' claims.

Bonuses and piece-rate differentials, their availability for discretionary and discriminatory use by managers, constitute not the only but certainly the most important means in the traditional, Soviet way of management.

In order to comprehend how wages actually worked as a means to elicit workers' efforts and maintain managerial authority we have to consider the circumstances under which production was carried out and how relations between workers and managers were maintained. In Soviet times, on everyone's admission, conditions of production were optimal, the enterprise output was counted in millions of metres, and accounts registered high profits. Still, results and benefits were not equally distributed among shops and employees. Production managers had to fight their daily battle against the well-known vagaries of Soviet production. The most significant recorded here were lack of co-ordination along the production line, permanent conflict with the central offices which pressed for plan-fulfilment and failed to deliver on key procurement, and the poor quality of technology which imposed constant concern for maintenance and replacement.

All this diverted the manager's attention from his main business and constantly threatened the achievement of his or her goals, production targets. We have to add that subordinates varied greatly as to their skills and motivation since traditional disciplinary measures, principally firing, were unavailable. One of the main tasks of production managers, other than overseeing technology, consisted in carefully selecting the skilled and reliable people to whom they could safely delegate tasks and on whom they could rely in case of difficulties. The system was ingrained and often distorted so as to guarantee that these workers would be recruited, rewarded and retained.

---

[1] The output loss, its compensation, and the 'virtual' output entering wage calculations are all referred to in factory jargon as *prostoi*.

The system was an essential device in the mechanism that structured and reproduced the social relations in the enterprise, the stability of which was in turn perceived as a precondition to the normal organisation of production. Therefore, the old management felt no need to modify it significantly till its distortions on the current activity of the enterprise were no longer acceptable. In the 1992–8 period the administration was dormant on this issue, and the story is more one of retain than reform. The nature and effect of the latest reform spurred by outside owners is less obvious, appearing both conflictual in its implementation and controversial in its conception. We shall look at both in the following sections.

Crisis and reform: the wage system in transition

During the 1990s the wage and incentive system remained substantially unchanged. Still, the radical modification of the technical and economic conditions in which the enterprise operated made its flaws even more evident, fostering partial modifications. A vicious circle was established between declining purchasing power of take-home pay and low workers' motivation, on the one side, and technological deterioration and lower productivity, on the other. Senior management lost control over the growth of the wage fund, and line managers saw a growing gap between the ability to elicit greater efforts and the corresponding results. They responded by using target-related bonuses, increases in the incentive component of the wage and finally the introduction of collective bonuses. The growing bargaining power of managers did not stop productivity decline, and put it into question the very effectiveness of the piece-rate system.

1990–6: business as usual – the system retained

At least until 1997, combine senior managers did not address openly and decisively the issue of productivity policy and, more generally, worker–manager relations. Radical changes to the wage and incentive system did not enter the restructuring agenda. This despite the fact that discipline was poor and productivity declining. They actually tried to cope with it in other forms, relying on the assumptions that it was poor technology, low incentives and the weight of the less able and motivated that hindered productivity and poisoned an otherwise harmonious atmosphere among members of the labour collective.

The director took a position of least resistance, expressing his determination to sustain and even extend the productive and social assets of the 'labour collective', relying on the efforts and loyalty of its manager and worker cadres (see interview with the general director in Shelkov and Antonov, 1998, pp. 57-69). Reviewing productivity issues, he focused on introducing new machinery or improving manufacturing techniques, clearly avoiding any reference to grand schemes in the field of work organisation.[1]

It should be noted that traditionally an increase in production 'norms' was usually tied to technological renewal, as confirmed by a prescriptive article included in the last collective agreement. Yet it does not seem that norms played any role in raising productivity, showing in this sense continuity in informal bargaining practices. As shop managers confirmed in interviews, norms did not really mean anything, they had not been raised for decades and their recent adjustment had no bearing on efforts to get more work done.

Nevertheless, since 1990 the plan had been discontinued, and both supply and sales had to be managed differently with far-reaching effects also on the way work was carried out and paid for. On this point our key respondent explains:

> With the supply of cotton uneven and uncertain, it became impossible to meet planned targets at prescribed deadlines, we worked as much as we could once we received the material. [Therefore], managers paid the settled wage plus bonus pay irrespective of piece-rate calculations . . . payment was made under considerations of the way they worked. [The way they proceeded was] to talk with foremen and see how their shifts were performing.
>
> (Interview with the head of the weaving department, 2001)

From the point of view of a scientific approach aimed at matching rewards with results, this occurrence was a further drift away from a rational system of wage calculation. In practice, this meant an increase of managerial discretion but also greater room for complaints and ensuing bargaining. Managers and foremen might now have an upper hand over individual workers or shifts but for the most part they were, or felt themselves to be, compelled to pay full wages despite the deepening negative trends in productivity and discipline. Enterprise administration, in turn, lost any possibility of command over the wage funds and planning a more efficient use of resources.

Transition also required that the enterprise had to pay for supplies and cope with rising costs; and this meant, according to the strategy then adopted, producing more and faster. This prompted the piecemeal introduction of the fourth shift. This decision boosted both absolute productivity and wages but also posed problems of manageability. The introduction of the extra shift was subject to approval from the production management, who had to guarantee the necessary increase in the staffing level. This was one reason why line managers resisted or procrastinated. Whatever the case, staffing did not seem sufficient at any time, leaving shop managers to cope with it by agreeing with existing workers on longer working days and extra work (*sverkhurochna*). It seems as if shock-work was reappearing under a new guise, compensating for the high levels of absenteeism and low individual productivity. At one time, some shops

[1] In reality, managers were well aware of restructuring options based on 'Western models' and harboured plans of deep restructuring and massive lay-off. However, they were forced to shelve them as the crisis deepened their reliance on workers, making such plans unpopular and economically unsound.

tried to cope with 'under-staffing' by introducing twelve-hour shifts. This was, though, a temporary solution. The practice continued, but as a rule longer shifts were bargained at individual level.

The other option was to ask employees to work on rest days. In all the latter cases extra work was not made compulsory, but workers felt a strong pressure to comply. Self-interest – that is, the need to supplement a meagre wage – had its part, but so did the pressure of managers and fellow workers to fill vacancies and not to let them down. In terms of labour costs this solution was effective in the short term. In current managerial discourse it meant the achievement of greater flexibility in the use of the workforce, saving on the cost of recruiting extra workers, who tended also to be even less productive. Yet one can only imagine the consequences for both production and a worker's life of a twelve-hour shift. The extensive recourse to extra work indicates at one and the same time the reproduction of traditional bargaining practices centred on line management and the growth of managerial powers. This confirms how much their early idea of transition did not contemplate any structural change to worker–management relations. They simply imagined using the free hand gained by privatisation in order to strengthen their discretionary power over workers.

Yet our judgement of the behaviour of the enterprise management would be partial and unfair if we did not mention the gradual emergence of alternative strategies and the difficulties encountered in implementing these new options. Managers in fact explained that their expectation of productivity gains lay in staff reduction, an idea again quite familiar to scholars of the late Soviet reforms. What they had in mind was a selective cut, addressing the unproductive and 'antisocial' elements in the labour collective. Looking at experiences from other enterprises, in 1995 the legal adviser went as far as advising a guided bankruptcy. Some managers embraced the idea, but then the director put it aside. Later, the 'unproductive' became all those workers who did not directly or indirectly contribute to production, so they proceeded to some internal reshuffling or cutting of service units.

As was sadly recognised by the department of labour and wages, all this did not produce any significant change in the wage-fund balance. Our key respondent pointed out that the failure of this strategy was due to the unexpected activation of the labour market, which significantly reduced the traditional hold on key sections of the workforce. 'The enterprise did not recruit in between 1992 and 1994,' he said, and 'to the contrary of what we expected we lost the good ones and had to keep and recruit more of the bad ones' (Interview with the head of the weaving department, 2000).

Reward to retain: wage and personnel policy

If the wage system was to operate effectively, a new variable had now to be considered, namely its ability to retain and recruit workers. This was an absolute novelty to the management, used to a uniform wage scale spread across the industry.

The initial strategy of the director to retain all the elements of the past welfare as well as the 'insularity' of the company town might have stemmed the flood. In the second half of the 1990s, though, the outflow of specialists made evident the shortcomings of the conservative approach. It became clear that the current level of wages could not satisfy the most needed skilled workers and specialists. This might at first surprise considering that, as explained before, the socialist system was in practice very flexible and already favouring these categories. Still, if one bears in mind the relevance of the non-monetary component and the role of incentive funds, now curtailed or disappeared altogether, it is immediately understood that differentials in the current monetary wage were insufficient to remunerate the exceptional work of cadres.

The more so because inflation was eroding the purchasing power of salaries and money was acquiring the highest consideration among the employees. Therefore a decision was made to raise the wages of fitters and mechanics, mostly foremen assistants, altering the traditional wage differentials. Managers recount that this decision led to a spontaneous uprising of both the other workers and the ITR, forcing the administration to retreat. The problem was left in the hands of line management, who had to juggle with funds and norms in order to save their specialists.

The 1997–9 crisis and attempts at reform: the triumph of the bonus.

Managers resolved to experiment with changes to the wage and reward system in the 1997–9 period, believing that it no longer provided a viable form of stimulation; indeed, labour productivity had fallen sharply, and workers seemed no longer to be motivated. Such a decision only came after a profound crisis had strained the cohesiveness of the labour collective, heavily compromised managerial authority and those regulatory mechanisms like the wage and reward system, eventually forcing managers themselves to search for new approaches to control workers and manage production. Crisis was manifested in several forms; we shall now look at those which had an immediate impact in production, and the responses which they attracted from managers and workers.

First of all, growing external pressure in the form of higher input costs and narrow margins on sales had imposed increasingly harder financial constraints on expenditures. Furthermore, a sky-high debt charge led the authorities to freeze enterprise resources. The response by top management was to begin a cost-cutting policy, including staff reduction, cuts to current expenditures and obviously a postponement of any plan of capital renewal. Coupled with a policy aimed at output increases, this series of circumstances produced a deterioration of technical and organisational conditions of production in the shops, frustrating managerial attempts to keep production flow under control and depressing workers' earnings and working conditions. Yet the consequence with greater and immediate effect on people's lives and morale was the non-payment of wages, which led to the accumulation of a full year of wage arrears in the 1997–9 period. Let us see now how workers and managers experienced and interpreted these phenomena, and how the wage and reward system came to be identified as a distorting mechanism and therefore a key tool for corrective action.

The situation in production in 1997 is vividly and thoroughly referred to in an interview given by the then head of the weaving department to the labour collective's weekly newspaper:

> We work in difficult conditions, first of all production overheats continuously because of physical–mechanical conditions of the yarn. I am sorry, we have not been forced to deal with cotton of such low quality before. Breaks have grown sharply and we had to compensate workers for two months because they worked with low quality cotton. Secondly, we failed to keep pace with the production schedule because of irregular provision of yarn from the spinning and preparation shops. As a result, *prostoi* have grown and final output has fallen. In order to increase material incentives for workers and managers, daily and monthly output targets have been set and rewards are administered for plan-fulfilment. The work schedule also has been reinforced, with the first shop now working round-the-clock on four shifts. Still we cannot meet the expected output targets, basically for two reasons. First, as mentioned, because of lack of yarn, secondly, which is much more complicated, because of the human factor. A sudden generation turnover and a sometimes ill-conceived cadre policy have led to such a situation that the professionalism of weavers and assistant foremen has notably declined. It has to do not with training but rather with dedication. They lack the will to learn and work slackly. We cannot deny that we are living in hard times, many circumstances affect people's life, among them non-payment of wages and the hardships of everyday life. Those problems, which should require immediate actions, are first the deficiency of spare-parts. The machinery is on average 10–15 years old and obviously machines break quite often. Because of the lack of spare parts we may have up to 30 machines idle for a shift. Obviously now their purchase is not a problem, it's just that we cannot afford them. The epidemic of thefts continues to be equally worrying among our miseries. This is one reason why our production lies in much worse condition. All measures taken by the administration have turned out to be ineffective. We have installed alarm systems in all warehouses. It obviously gives results but until people understand that they are robbing themselves, until they stand up to preserve enterprise assets, there will be no change. (Svetlakov, 1997, p. 2)

The concern of the production manager focuses on the fall in productivity and the lowering of output quality, which directly affects the fulfilment of his targets. As a top manager in charge of the whole weaving department he also has concerns for the major determinants of this situation. He individuates the interplay of objective, i.e. beyond reach of production managers, and subjective factors, the 'human' component. The non-co-operative attitude of workers appears to him as a justifiable, still worrying, phenomenon and an unprecedented one – at least, in its scale. Solutions, though, amount to nothing other than the re-introduction of 'elements of the planned economy' as the interviewer defined them, i.e. target-related individual rewards. Not surprisingly, they were short-lived.

An interview with his successor, made at the end of 2000 but covering the whole period, allows a more detailed look at the dynamics of the wage and its interactions with relations in production. The new head of production, our key respondent Kolya, had to face a situation that, while depicted in his own words as very similar to his predecessor's, was aggravated on both sides of the hierarchy. On the one side, there was the greater determination of the administration to introduce order into production to gain efficiency and, on the other, workers' disillusion was probably at its highest level. Between 1998 and 1999, we should keep in mind, the enterprise reached the bottom of its crisis: production halted for the first time, leaving workers with food rationing. Then bankruptcy meant a shift in decision-making power in favour of creditor's hands and in rapid succession the replacement of the director himself. Now traditional concerns for output growth were not replaced but combined with requirements for higher quality and lower costs, and workers were made the object of a discipline campaign by the administration.

'In 1998–9', our key respondent observed, 'we experienced a worsening of technological discipline' (Interview with the head of the weaving department, 2000). On the state of manager–worker relations, required to comment, he burst out: 'We have to force employees to work!' (ibid.). In his opinion, this had much to do with the ill functioning of the wage and reward system. My field notes on the point say:

> A look at trends in the structure of the wage reveals its distortive effects. The *prostoi* coefficient has been growing steadily, as a result plan is over-fulfilled but real output declines. Actually, the piece-rate amounted to only 30 per cent of the salary, the rest consisting of bonus (*premiya*) and *prostoi*. Productivity had fallen to 17 metres/hour.

As he himself reasoned, the natural deterioration of working conditions, accelerated by the introduction of the new shift, augmented stoppages and breakdowns, depressing productivity. But the practice of compensating workers in order to preserve their earnings meant that lower output did not result in lower wages. As a result, top managers lamented, reward lost any real relation with work. An earlier response, under the new head's mandate, did not differ substantially from previous interventions:

> At the beginning of 1999, a first move was attempted in order to reverse this trend with an increase to 100 per cent of the plan-fulfilment bonus. Admittedly the advantage was that the relative weight of piece-rate theoretically grew and so with it the interest of the worker to increase output. The disadvantage was that clearly workers were more than ever determined

to achieve their planned target . . . at the cost of actual output. As a result productivity on gauze fell from 23 m/h to 10–12 m/h.

(Interview with the head of the weaving department, 2000)

Before turning to the wage reform it remains to examine what were the causes of workers' discontent, and why traditional interventions did not relieve it, and then see how it worked to lower productivity. The shrinking of resources available to managers for bargaining with workers against the required upward adjustment in productivity meant that the wage and reward system inherited from socialism lost any sense. As our familiar respondent put it: 'managers had been left with the whip to govern' their subordinates. The chief of the wage and labour department (OTiZ) explains: 'The old piece-rate and bonus system basically disintegrated as a result of the abysmally low level of wages' (Interview with the chief of the OTiZ, 2000).

Such a situation, though, did not produce generalised and overt conflict but individual responses, which further depressed productivity and revenues. The new unfavourable circumstances in which the enterprise found itself, coupled with technical and organisational flaws of Soviet times, combined to produce this effect.

Workers already strained by higher workloads and longer working hours could not possibly react but with tricks and discipline violations against attempts to elicit further efforts. The individualised payment system halted co-operation among shifts and between machine operators and maintenance workers, while cementing collusion between operators. As many put it: 'why give way to repairs if machines can still produce and let someone further on sort it out' (Interview with an assistant foreman, 2000). The shop chief agreed that any measure to speed up production, though unorthodox, was understandable in view of the need for greater output (Interview with the shop chief of weaving shop n°. 1, 2000).

The gender divide further complicated the situation, with female machine operators on the one side and technical personnel, generally male, on the other. The first under greater pressure to produce and bring the plan home, the second more scarce in number, owing to voluntary outflow, and difficult to manage for lack of appropriate incentives.

In March 1999 the decision was taken for a full-scale reform with the introduction of a collective system of payment, the brigade system. Brigades were established at 'zone' level comprising machine operators and assistant foremen servicing the 'zone' over the four shifts. Each brigade was put on self-financing (*khozraschet*) and asked to sign separate contracts. As far as the wage structure was concerned, we had the following:

The individual piece-rate coefficient was integrated with an indicator of the 'zone' overall output to force workers into greater co-operation.

Plan-fulfilment bonus (*premiya*) rose up to 200 per cent of the basic salary.

Furthermore the key question of *prostoi* was eventually made the object of a cut-throat decision. First, a ceiling was established to the amount of *prostoi* eligible for compensation. Second, decision-making over this matter was passed over from foreman to shop chief.

Immediate results were visible: shop statistics recorded a stabilisation of productivity at the higher pre-crisis level while average salary grew, too. Now workers were paid according to results, managers maintained; the piece-rate coefficient weight rose to 35 per cent of the overall take-home pay, and wages grew on average by 2.5 per cent. Also differentials – at least, among brigade members and within shops – were reduced making life easier for shop managers forced to deal with recurrent complaints and permanent bargaining.

Admittedly the new system was only a partial and short-term solution to work-organisation problems. The major defect was its applicability, since each brigade had to sign a separate contract and some could differ significantly from the collective one.

Its introduction, rather than being planned from above, was proposed and designed by top production managers and then extended gradually with the collaboration of middle managers in order to achieve consent and smooth down technical or organisational inconveniences. Like the introduction of the new work schedule, the new payment system encountered resistance and suspicion by middle managers. The field notes on the situation in the shop report:

In November 2000, our key respondent occupies the post of head of the weaving department. He has managed to introduce a new payment system, the brigade system. The new system has not been extended automatically to all shops. As he maintains, change should be introduced with 'democratic' methods, not imposed from above. He is therefore trying to convince his friend and subordinate, the shop chief, to adopt it in his shop. The shop chief is not convinced about the effectiveness of the new system. In fact, to him it does not appear new at all. He asks whether his superior has in mind the constitution of 'communist' brigades of shock workers. The situation in the shop seems to lean in favour of the pro-brigade argument. The shop chief asks for his superior to adjust the coefficients for wage calculations of several workers: the problems lie in the fact that the piece-rate depends, among other things, on the number of machines operated and obviously there is not an even number for all workers. The situation is further complicated by the fact that some machines are better than others, so workers fight for the best 'zone' and then complain to him. The head of the department assents to his request but insists that the new system, by equalising wages with the collective coefficient, would smooth down differentials and so the complaints. The shop chief did not provide a clear explanation for his opposition; a response, though, can be looked for in the workers' attitude to differentials, which emerged vividly also in this shop.

The reform also led to a substantial increase in wages; still it did not help with the continuous complaints by workers over wage differentials and discrimination in the allocation of resources. Traditional intra- and infra-category differentials were left in place. Yet the deterioration in capital stock and continuous changes in production programmes meant that differentials between brigades and shops continued to manifest themselves and earnings remained volatile. Stress on quality, cost reduction and rationing of raw materials and spare parts was constantly used to justify wage cuts and loss of bonuses. On this ground both workers and shop managers felt endangered, as the latter were considered ultimately responsible for workers' failures. Managers could use their discretionary powers to match the best workers with the best-equipped working stations, but this inevitably raised jealousies and complaints.

I could observe how the situation in the shops had reached an explosive climax when a shop chief summoned the chief wage accountant of the weaving department to face grievances by workers. From my notes:

> Workers' representatives argue that the wage has remained substantially unchanged despite the introduction of the fourth shift, they complain that other shops receive better pay without specific justifications and lament bonus losses on excessive strictness of quality control. The shop manager confirms the claims, maintaining that his shop has been discriminated against in setting the piece-rate price. The wage office employee rejects accusations, though remarking that poor quality and the high level of *prostoi* were possible causes of differences observed. She is basically unable to face the argument and ends up simply defending the authority of the central wage department to act according to the data available.

The argument was probably no novelty to all participants. What appears to be new is the determination from above to impose decisions at the expense of managerial authority on the shop floor. Managerial support for workers' claims reveals the extent to which the new policy was endangering traditional bargaining practices on the shop floor.

We discussed these issues with the head of the department at the time these problems emerged, and he agreed that the core problem was precisely the retaining of the piece-rate and bonus system and its underpinning philosophy of voluntaristic mobilisation. If technological discipline was to be achieved, workers should be guaranteed a reasonable wage for an acceptable work plan. In his opinion, the piece-rate component had to grow up to 60 per cent, a homogenisation of production targets provided, and piece-rate workers themselves had to be reduced to only 30 per cent of the staff total, essentially machine operators and assistant foremen. Quality had to become the cornerstone of rewards. He was equally adamant that without investment and radical revision of the managerial structure the traditional Soviet informal practices were the only control mechanism available. A wider-shake up in the area was therefore expected but it came to coincide with the greater involvement of outsiders in the enterprise management. Its analysis has to include the different interventions in the payment issues that they carried out in order to consolidate their hold on employees.

The 2000–2 outsider control: a new wage policy?

When outsiders effectively took over the situation at the company, wage policy was certainly one of the major areas in which they had to intervene. First, they had to decide what to do with wage payments. Since 1997 wage delays and wage arrears had built up creating an enormous financial and motivational problem. Second, they had to review wage policy – that is, to intervene on differentials – if they wanted to counter the outflow of skilled personnel. Third, they had to inaugurate a new policy in line with the idea of 'Western' efficiency and modernisation they constantly spoke of as their aim. This included new incentive pay, which will be discussed extensively later, and a change to prioritised professional categories, in order to favour managers and economists.

Wage payment and wage arrears

LTD, the outsiders' company, agreed to repay gradually wage arrears and to restore regular payment of wages. The first action was made conditional on the financial performance of the enterprise and was clearly linked to workers' increased efforts in restoring high productivity levels. We should recall that the enterprise had fallen into financial difficulties since 1997, culminating in 1998 in the paralysis of production and complete default on wages. As a result, workers had accumulated huge arrears, which were 'frozen' and were meant to be paid separately, like other consolidated debts. They are therefore referred to here as 'historical' arrears, for their computation and payment was distinguished from delays in payment of current take-home pay. In mid-2001, looking back at the previous year, official reports[1] said that 'historical' arrears had been substantially reduced from 4,630,000 roubles to 'only' 606,000. The high level of 'current' arrears remained instead substantial, running at a high 6,420,000. This last arrangement should not be overlooked because delay in current payments meant that workers were now receiving deferred wages, for example April wage in July, May wage in August and so on – that is, devalued ones.

Workers, several times, took collective action on these matters. In April 2001 they were refused the right to celebrate Easter holidays, still not on the official holiday calendar, with the justification that the enterprise could not afford to discontinue the production process even for one day. Workers therefore raised the issue of wage arrears and threatened stoppages. The directorate then countered with the threat to remove bonuses. Eventually an agreement was reached, which contemplated payments to production workers only, excluding ITR and auxiliaries.

The worker who reported this story commented angrily about the event, observing spontaneously that the administration had been able to head off workers' protest by making concessions to a privileged category. This is especially remarkable for a worker, a female low-paid quality controller, who demonstrated herself in other circumstances to be much less confrontational and

---

[1] Data presented by the chief engineer at the trade union conference in May (Smirnov, 2001b).

was often well disposed towards the newcomers. She previously commented, in fact, that the outsiders were at least able to pay salaries while the previous director had failed to meet his promises. [1]

Again, later in August, an enterprise trade union meeting offered the occasion to present LTD leaders with a request to anticipate arrears repayment on the grounds that workers were unable to meet education expenses for the approaching school year. Workers maintained that their wages were too low to withstand these costs. The scornful reply by the LTD president was later reported in an interview the factory paper. It can be safely synthesised as follows:

> 'I want you to understand this clearly', he said, '. . . notwithstanding the enormous financial efforts in modernisation sustained by our firm, we still do not see the expected results.' Then he continued complaining about 'falling productivity, absenteeism, discipline violations' and so forth. He pointed out that 'in the spinning shops, after the introduction of the new wage system, workers can easily earn up to 3,000 roubles a month', therefore concluded that 'we have the impression that in their majority workers simply do not want to earn a good wage'. (*Privolzhskyi Rabochij*, 2001d)

Another measure contained in the financial adjustment package, of little significance in itself, but with pernicious consequences, was the reintroduction of cash payment for meals consumed in the factory canteens. Prices in the past had been heavily subsidised, and the collective farm guaranteed a steady supply of fresh foodstuff. During the crisis the administration decided to deduct the costs of meals from wage dues, reverting in practice to in-kind payment. Workers were obviously unhappy with it, as they preferred to see cash instead of increasingly worse food. In any case, the decision to restore payment, at much higher prices than in the past – up to 20 roubles for a full menu – resulted in workers deserting the canteens and resorting to consuming their home-made meals in the shops. Doctors declared this practice a serious health hazard and related it to an increase in registered cases of infections. The fact that now many managers and ITR were heading home for their lunch break was also detrimental to work-time discipline. Furthermore, the *de facto* loss of this service meant that women had now to take on this burden at home. The economic rationality of the decision was doubtful, bearing in mind that deserted canteens had now to be run at a loss, but perhaps this move anticipated their definitive closure. Anyway, workers met this measure with resignation. As one

---

[1] The woman in question is currently working as a quality controller in the finishing shops. She has been one of my key informants, particularly for issues regarding women workers. She used to be the chief of one of the factory canteens before cuts to ITR positions and social services forced her to take a blue-collar job. As with others suffering the same fate, her demotion was the result of ostracism targeting her as a single mother with serious family and personal problems.

woman commented: 'Women in any case must cook for their family, therefore there is no need for canteens' (Interview with female worker, 2001).[1]

The ability of management to defuse collective action and the timidity of workers' moves were quite apparent. This can only be understood considering that workers were neither used to nor intended to bring forward their claim at enterprise level, through collective bargaining. In reality, as demonstrated by these cases, workers raised their grievances in a collective fashion only occasionally, prompted by external circumstances. The problem tended rather to be solved on a personal basis in the shops. It was in this context that workers felt justified raising their grievances either individually or in small groups, at shift or shop level.

If workers regularly resorted to managers for any problem related to pay, payments of arrears were no exception. In one case a worker turned to the shop chief to discuss the problem of delays in wage payments. As we have seen, workers were paid deferred wages; the worker quite rightfully explained the point and wondered why people should not be paid the 'real' current wage. He underlined that it was unfair for them to be paid less than they actually earned. I cannot fail to notice that this was in fact the first time I myself heard about this problem in these terms. The observation was correct but for the case that the worker was posing the problem in terms of a personal arrangement with the manager. The manager in that case did not dismiss the request but outlined that it was rather the job of the trade union to sort out these questions.

More commonly, workers appealed to the manager to request advances on the arrears due. Once having a walk with the shop chief's family we came by a worker who warmly greeted and thanked the manager. The former explained later to me and to his wife that he had successfully applied, at the worker's request, to the administration for the receipt of his wage arrears. The worker, he told us as a justification, was in urgent need of cash to buy a new flat. He was meant to pay for the flat by selling a room in the communal house where he used to live. Yet he was not allowed to sell without a signed contract for the new house and, at the same time, he could not sign the contract without a prior cash deposit. Obviously he had no money of his own to sort out this bureaucratic jam.

Several conclusions can already be drawn. The new administration proved to be extremely attentive in making the most out of the economic and financial difficulties of the enterprise. At the same time, they proved equally cautious in building up their legitimacy as new owners, avoiding direct confrontation with the labour force as a whole. Restoration of regular payments was in fact important to restore a minimum of confidence and facilitate the outsiders in breaking through managerial resistance.

Malignantly, the outsiders' adversaries commented that the move was a propagandistic carrot thrown at the workers, nothing less than a poisoned

---

[1] Looking at the early Soviet banners propagandising the new communal facilities as a way to liberate women from the traditional family burdens, one could not suppress the feeling that their disappearance was also marking the obfuscation of the rights connected with it.

chalice for the enterprise, now elevating its indebtedness to, and its dependence on, the outsiders.

In order to defuse conflict they continued to rely on traditional practices. As far as they were forced to take general measures, they managed to transform them into sectional problems, reinforcing conflicts and divisions among the workforce. This will be shown more clearly in the next section about differentials. By doing this they were transforming what could appear as a right, to which everyone was entitled, into a privilege that could be granted only to those who deserved it. In this way they confirmed and reinforced the paternalistic and hierarchical nature of social relations in the factory. This was only possible by allowing, in fact forcing indirectly, middle management to deal personally with wage-related claims, as emerges vividly from the analysis of the implementation of the wage-system.

Pay scale and wage differentials

The new administration also came under pressure to review its wage policy in order to retain and recruit specialists and skilled workers. This called for a review, altering wage differentials between occupations so as to favour specific categories; and, second, for the definition of a wage level sufficient to shelter the enterprise from trends in the labour market. The conflict that arose around differentials shows, nevertheless, that the search for consent among the workforce had to remain the main drive in this area of wage policy.

Being located on the border with the much richer Moscow economic area, the local labour market suffered a constant drain of cadres. The situation was made acute by the practice of individual enterprises retaining workers from scarce professions with an aggressive wage policy. Despite all the official calls for unitary action among industrialists and the condemnation of unfair competition, this practice did not seem to come to an end. This problem was strictly intertwined with difficulties in attracting and training young professionals, making old cadres a more crucial resource. The result, as a manager underlined, was that 'in the past there did not exist any difference in pay for the same profession in the same industry when now differentials are proliferating' (Interview with the head of the weaving department, 2001).

Already under the previous administration the wage drift in the labour market had made unsustainable the policy of retaining historical differentials among categories. Yet a generalised increase in salaries in favour of fitters and mechanics led to an uprising of both operators and ITR, heading off the attempt.

The same fate was to meet the outsiders' plans to shake up the entire pay scale, privileging managers over workers and economists among them. As our key respondent commented: 'ITR and workers reacted with obstructionism, making the newcomers think better of it' (ibid.). The respondent further commented that:

A European policy aimed at planning wage scales consistently with skills and professions needed at the factory was bound to fail as it requires too many resources and a strong bargaining power of the employers. The lack of appeal of industrial jobs in the province seriously undermines the threat of dismissal and to the contrary reinforces the bargaining power of selected categories. Therefore, the newcomers, in an opportunistic move to consolidate their grip over the enterprise, are forced to adopt traditional Soviet tactics. (ibid.)

As already seen above, they accepted making partial concessions to this or that group of workers in order to silence them and avoid a direct generalised clash with labour or managers. Some data on the wage level of selected professions and groups of workers provide evidence about the structure of differentials and its evolution.

Table 7.1 Average wages

	Average wage[1]	Average wage[2] (weavers)
1998	–	850
1999	585	1,050[4] 1,780[5]
2000	958 1,227[3]	1,800*
2001	1,359	2,200*

[1] Data provided by the chief engineer at the trade union conference, 25/05/2001; [2] Data provided by the department chief; [3] End of the Year; [4] After first bonus increase; [5] After brigade reform; * Estimates by production managers.

The few available data might be patchy, though some conclusions can still be drawn when supported by further evidence from interviews. The first, not surprising element is the high differentiation between production workers, including machine operators, and the even better-paid foreman assistants, and the rest of the workforce.

Table 7.2 Wages of selected managerial positions in December 2000*

Gender	Position	Stipend
M	Managing Director	5,000 roubles
M	Chief Engineer	4,300 roubles
F	Chief Economist (vice-director)	4,000 roubles
M	Vice-director for General Affairs	3,000 roubles
M	Quality Control Chief	2,000 roubles
M	Security Chief	3,000 roubles
M	Chief of 2nd Dep	1,000 roubles
F	Chief of Personnel Dept (cadres)	1,500 roubles

M	Legal Consultant	2,000 roubles
F	Chief of Secretarial Office	1,000 roubles
F	Senior Economist of the Planning Dept	1,280 roubles
M	Chief of Wage & Labour Dept	2,000 roubles
F	Chief Accountant	4,000 roubles
F	Chief Accountant Assistant (accounting)	2,000 roubles
F	Chief Accountant Assistant (finances)	1,900 roubles
F	Chief of Computing Office	1,000 roubles
M	Chief of Procurement Dept	2,000 roubles
F	Chief of Sales Dept	1,600 roubles
M	Chief of IT Dept	1,600 roubles
M	Chief of Health & Safety Dept	1,500 roubles
F	Chief of Training Centre	1,300 roubles
M	Senior Engineer for Construction	1,500 roubles
M	Director of Transport-economy Dept	1,800 roubles
F	Vice-director of Transport-economy Dept	1,600 roubles
M	Director of Central Tech. Laboratory	1,500 roubles
M	Vice-director of Central Tech. Laboratory	1,400 roubles
F	Director of Spinning Production	2,400 roubles
M	Vice-director of Spinning Production	2,000 roubles
F	Director of Weaving Production	2,400 roubles
M	Director of Finishing Production	2,400 roubles
M	Chief Mechanic	2,500 roubles
M	Chief Mechanic Assistant	2,000 roubles
F	Chief of Trade & Catering	1,450 roubles
F	Chief of Housing Dept	700 roubles
M	Chief of Health & Sport Complex	1,200 roubles
M	Editor of Factory Paper	1,000 roubles
F	Director of Technical School	580 roubles

*Data contained in a general director's memorandum as published by the factory paper (*Privolzhskii Rabochij*, 2000). Salaries do not include benefits.

This is particularly evident for the crisis year 1999. At that time, evidently the administration struggled to maintain its core workers by substantial increases in wages, leaving the others the choice of accepting wage cuts or leaving. Since staffing levels fell from around 4,000 to less than 3,000 between 1997 and 2001, especially as a result of spin-off of the social sphere and auxiliary jobs, this might be seen as an accompanying measure, which facilitated dismissals. Shrinking staff can also account for the narrowing of the gap in later years. At the same time, the growing concern of managers for the loss of cadres, amid crisis and non-payment of wages, should remind us of the extremely limited room for consistent strategies and the enormous side-effects of the crisis on the quality of staff.

Comparing workers' wages with data on individual positions of managers and ITR reveals that the divide between workers and managers, including senior managers, was not so clear-cut. Neither responsibility nor education was in principle a guarantee of higher wages. Production workers could claim and in fact earned higher wages than the bulk of ITR, as deduced from the fact that workers' wages were already higher than those of many office chiefs. Both senior managers and workers reasoned that office workers were of little use and therefore did not deserve such high pay.

Obviously there were privileges attached to the position that could outweigh the disadvantage of the low pay. A former Komsomol officer now working in production remarked how 'for a woman it is much better to work in an office. The working timetable fits family duties, and the working place, quiet and clean, is more adequate to women' (Interview with woman worker, spinning shop, 2001). Workers also lamented that managers had obvious social clout, which could shelter them from fines and reprimands. Last but not least, key positions offered chances to make personal gains, augmenting substantially what at first glance might seem a meagre wage. It remains the fact that social conventions required maintaining traditional differentials. In mid-2001, further wage increases, constantly needed to compensate for inflation, allowed for a 70 per cent rise to workers and 45 per cent to ITR. This should indicate that the newcomers in the mean time were committed to their observance.

The wage gap between workers was even more startling. The use of piece-rate and incentive pay, as we have seen, tended inevitably to generate differences among workers' wages even within the same occupational group. Yet the enormous gap between 'direct' workers and auxiliaries, and in particular between spinners and weavers on one side and other production departments, remains a striking feature of the pay scale.

The general understanding that sweeper or quality controller is a job with low professional content to be left to the less skilled, and often less motivated workers, makes common sense. Several managers and technicians, though, noted with regret that specific categories of auxiliary workers continued to be paid risible wages. They were alarmed that their poor performance might be extremely detrimental to production and economic results. A foreman assistant lamented:

> A lot of money is squandered here. Take this case. Machines sometimes break down because production waste has not been duly removed. What can you expect from cleaners? This is the lowest job, they earn 600 roubles, and they work as much as they are paid. Still, the machine has to be repaired and output is defective!
>
> (Interview with the mechanic-repairer of the combing–carding shop)

Production managers were left once again alone to work out how to get new recruits and stem the flood of cadres from their shop. Our key respondent, working from 1998 to 2000 as chief of the weaving department, referred, during our early interviews, to the fact that he adjusted upward the tariffs of the scarcest categories. As a senior manager he could plan his wage fund. Since part of the outflow of workers was due to temporary leave for more lucrative jobs in the capital-city surroundings, he sheltered his staffing levels from fluctuations by making seasonal adjustments to wages.

Most of the work, though, was made at the lower level where retaining and rewarding were indistinguishably tied to the continuous bargaining over pay between workers and their shop chief. Discussing discretionary forms of payment with a shop chief, the case of a fitter-mechanic emerged, whom he paid a higher wage under the table, admittedly to prevent him from quitting.

> This worker is really a special case . . . he does all the repair and looks after maintenance. In the past there was a special brigade for that but they have been dismissed. So I pay him thousands of roubles more. I managed to create a special fund for that with the wages destined by the administration for people who do not work here any more. The administration does not know about that and it would be very serious if they did. I do not pay him because I have to . . . It is to give him a certain status. Otherwise I suppose he might leave for a better-paid job.
>
> (Interview with the shop chief of the combing-carding shop, 2001)

As for the level of wages as compared with other enterprises in the local industry, the combine seemed to feature well for certain categories of workers while losing out for specialists. The average wage at the enterprise, as one worker noted at the trade union conference, was now only approaching the minimum subsistence level (see Smirnov, 2001a, p. 2). Still, the president of LTD, rejecting grievances over wages, noted that 'as for the level of wages the enterprise is rated 13th out of 43 textile enterprises in the region' (*Privolzhskyi Rabochij*, 2001d, p. 1). In fact the factory, while having problems with recruiting specialists, was doing quite well with worker recruitment. One respondent, a chief mechanic who had just moved to a new factory, referred to the fact that they had lost some weavers to his old employer. In that factory wages for main workers were apparently lower, staying at 1,300 roubles. The director of the factory complained that competing companies in the surrounding area were posing a serious threat to the stability of his collective by raising wages. He further explained that 'they are taking advantage of bankruptcy procedures. The state of bankruptcy permits them to get away with taxation and leave resources for paying better wages' (Interview with the director of factory n°. 2).

The outsiders, therefore, preferred to continue to favour traditional categories, upholding the customary differentials. They retreated over policies aimed at modifying the pay scale. They also froze plans to centralise and restructure offices dealing with wage and personnel management. Recruiting and retaining cadres was to remain a major task of production managers. The objective pursued with this policy was to consolidate the labour collective, restoring the administration's authority and avoiding generalised conflict. This comes with some specifications. The 'conservative' move has to be put into the larger perspective of the parent company, which was building modern managerial capabilities outside and above the enterprise and had therefore less need to restructure.

The crucial conflict with the workforce, and therefore with management, arose from the attempt to combine this policy of least resistance and concessions with the transmission of qualitatively and quantitatively different targets. To understand its nature and outcomes we have therefore to look at the reform of the wage system and its actual implementation by management. In a traditional Soviet policy, it is in fact the wage system that has to carry the modernisation drive through incentive schemes. Still, its manipulation is the essential device by which production management can achieve workers' consent.

Outsiders 2001: a new wage system

Between late December 2000 and May 2001, owing to developments in bankruptcy proceedings, the outsiders' role strengthened, permitting a greater involvement in the management of the enterprise. One of the most significant measures taken was the remaking of the payment and incentive system. Fulfilling the expectations of the union and experts, the flat-rate component of the basic wage, i.e. excluding bonus, was raised to around two-thirds of the wage. The new priorities of the administration led it instead to replace the traditional bonus tied to the fulfilment of plan targets in physical terms with coefficients depending on a combination of qualitative, quantitative and discipline-related targets. The reform involved both managers and workers and prescribed for each different goals, consistently with their role in production. In this section we concentrate on the changes to the salary of piece-rate workers. The new incentives were meant to modify the way workers made the plan and therefore also the job of the managers, who had to motivate and reward workers and make sure that the new targets were properly achieved. Differently from the brigade wage system, the reform extended to all production departments (spinning, weaving and finishing) with little variation. The main features of the new system can be summarised in the points given below:

(a) The hourly pay was raised to around 63 per cent of the basic wage, ranging from 62.9 per cent in weaving to 64.9 per cent in finishing. The wage of the piece-rate workers, we shall remember, consists of three main components, the tariff component, the piece-rate and the bonus. The two former considered together form the basic salary to which the bonus is added as a per cent coefficient. The manager could calculate the piece-rate in advance on the basis of production norms and piece-rate tariff, presupposing fulfilment and *prostoi* at given rates. The reform altered the structure of the basic wage, increasing the tariff or flat-rate component at the expense of the piece-rate. Considering the piece-rate component as given, the change consisted in raising the wage to the point at which the other component approached one-third of the total.

(b) The incentive mechanism was completely redesigned. A range of coefficients replaced the single bonus, related to the fulfilment of

production plans. Workers were to be assessed and rewarded mainly for achieving output quality standards and observing technological and labour discipline. Foremen and shop chiefs, who are stipend earners, had their bonus paid on condition of fulfilling both qualitative and quantitative targets.

(c) The mechanism of computation was also modified. In the previous system the bonuses were ideally added to the wage on condition of achieving certain targets. Now workers were entitled to a sum made up of all the wage components and had them deducted for failures to meet tasks. Managers talked now of a fine-based system replacing the previous bonus-based one.

Theoretically, the objectives of the new system were: to increase workers' motivation, achieved by offering higher and more stable salaries; to increase productivity and achieve greater accordance between results and reward, by means of using of targeted fines.

The first point was worked out with the participation of the trade union and appears formally as the implementation by the enterprise administration of the commitment to improve workers' remuneration. As reported in the factory paper:

> According to a tripartite agreement between the Ivanovo administration, industrialists of the Ivanovo region and the trade unions, it was established that the salary had to be taken to such a point that the tariff component would amount to almost 70 per cent. (Smirnov, 2001a)

The reform indubitably achieved an increase in nominal salaries, though workers and even the collaborative unions were unsatisfied with the actual figures. The stability of wages should have been another outcome of the reform, giving workers greater confidence over future earnings.

This goal seems also to match with the improved and more stable conditions of production produced by the takeover. In a highly unstable working environment, heavy reliance on the bonus was understandably the last resort for pressuring managers and workers to elicit any effort to keep production going. Now, when the outsiders had provided the financial and material resources to stabilise production and work at full capacity, the priority balance shifted in favour of productivity and quality targets. The reform moved in this direction by reducing the weight of the piece-rate in the basic salary and disentangling it from the calculation of bonuses. Workers were now asked to concentrate on improving their performance, while the achievement of output targets was the sole concern of the foremen and the managers, who had to organise and supervise the fulfilment of the plans.

It has already been observed how nobody among the managers was willing to dispose of the piece-rate despite concerns about its growing inadequacy. An interview with a top-brass representative of the textile industrialists' association confirms an identity of views with factory management in terms of finding a mid-way between the flat-rate pay prevalent in the West and the Russian appreciation for incentive schemes.

> I think that workers will remain essential to assuring quality in production. This means that we have to attract and motivate qualified workers. I admit that the critical point is to strike a balance between stimulation and stability. Yet the payment system has to reflect the importance of workers' qualification and dedication. This is why we have to maintain a piece-rate wage. Paternalism is necessary, despite all the criticism raised around the collusion between managers and workers. We could not cope otherwise with such low wages.
>
> (Interview: director, Regional Association of Textile Industrialists, 2001)

In any case, observation of its implementation indicates that the rationale of the new system, its motivating potential, is not univocal and should not be taken for granted. A satisfactory account of the impact of the reform cannot be made without reference to the actual experience of its implementation, carried out by workers and middle management, and the response it yielded from workers.

Work and wages after the reform: managerial implementation and workers' response

The reform was formally aimed at achieving higher and stable wages, redirecting workers' concerns from quantity to quality and easing the work of managers left in charge of plan fulfilment. Implementation on the shop floor demonstrates how its rationale turned out to be different from what was intended. Calculating the new wage, line managers showed that the stable component of the wage had been reduced and workers had to expect cuts in their upcoming pay. Managers and workers felt that the new focus on quality was nothing but an excuse to cut wages. The pressure to meet the plan was not reduced. Rather, targets were more ambitious and stringent than ever before, and the complication that came with it had changed little.

Workers rightly maintained that quality has to be a managerial concern, because it depends on the state of technology and cotton. They therefore responded to the reform by resorting to a combination of trickery and common understanding with managers. For their part, managers, while stamping out the most overt violations, have continued manipulating quality indicators and output reports, trying to favour the more reliable workers. Therefore informal practices continue with the consequence of continued conflicts and bargaining over pay, piece-rate prices and workloads. Workers show themselves to be even more divided as they compete for a shrinking wage fund.

Managers' understanding and implementation of the reform

We should now turn our attention to the shop floor, where I carried out participant observation, so as to verify the implementation of the reform and record people's reaction. As far as managers were concerned, I expected satisfaction with a reform that met in principle their expectation for a loosening of incentive pressure. It is certainly true that managers were going to lose a command lever, but since the old incentives had little motivational effect one might appreciate other, positive, outcomes of the reform. First, flat-rate pay would have lowered the conflict over pay and put an end to the juggling with norms and the fabrication of output reports aimed at 'saving' workers', and manager's own, bonuses. Second, it would have offered greater scope to plan production away from workers' individual struggle to meet their norms. If these were the wishes of, at least, the manager of this shop, they went unsatisfied.

A comparative analysis of the two payment systems from the point of view of those in charge of their implementation, i.e. transferring them into the real context of worker–management bargaining, will expose its drawbacks and the substantial lack of innovation. If we look at the figures of the old pay in percentages, we recall that the tariff, i.e. flat-rate pay, amounted to around 30 per cent, piece-rate to 70 per cent to which was added a bonus of 75 per cent. In practice, the manager[1] explains, the only variable was the piece-rate component. Informal arrangements between managers and workers, dating back to Soviet times, had led to the practice of considering both tariff and bonus pay a must: roughly calculating, 105 per cent of guaranteed pay. Now, applying the same logic to the new system, it turns out that the 63 per cent new tariff pay plus the 40 per cent coefficient gives a roughly similar figure of 103 per cent. More importantly, within this percentage has now been incorporated a 10 per cent bonus/fine for absence due to illness. Therefore, the manager concluded, it might well be said that the stable component of the wage has in fact been reduced and workers should expect cuts to the upcoming pay.

Managers, moreover, feel that the pressure to meet the plan, and the traditional complications that come with it, have changed little. So the piece-rate continues to operate as a contradictory mechanism spurring productivity at the expense of technological discipline. Evidence from various sources among senior managers of both the enterprise and outsiders' circles confirms that this is not a distorted perception of those in production. LTD managers at formal and informal meetings continued to stress the need to achieve higher production targets and heavily remarked failures. The official policy, maintained a well-informed representative of local industrialists in September 2001, is one of maximum utilisation of capacity. The chief engineer, a few months earlier, confirmed, not without a note of criticism, that quantity not quality remains the priority.

---

[1] This is Kolya, our main informant. In mid-2001 he was again working in the combing–carding shop as shop chief after losing his job as head of production owing to conflict with LTD.

What, then, of the new imperative for quality to which the bonus is now related? Several examples from everyday life in the shop reveal how the new element has in fact been incorporated into working arrangements and paid the necessary attention, but not without conflicts and contradictions – a reminder of *perestroika* when, it was said metaphorically, reform implementation implied changing the wheel without stopping the vehicle driving.

Technical and organisational constraints are a major obstacle to quality improvements, but since this is not the major point here we shall reserve discussion of it for elsewhere. It is sufficient to highlight that, in any case, managers did their best to overcome poor co-ordination and interdepartmental conflicts to keep quality of materials processed under constant check. Foremen and workers' co-operation remained a key question.

In one case a foreman complained at the loss of bonus, urging that having met her plan she felt there was no wrongdoing on her side, rejecting arguments about poor-quality output and poor discipline of her workers. The more so workers, both operators and mechanics, who rejected any remark on the achievement of higher quality claiming they only felt responsible for the quantity of work done while quality results were rather dependent on the materials and conditions provided by managers.

In another case, in the face of another apparent drop in quality, the manager convened the foremen and technicians of his shop to make clear the priority of quality and again explained its determinant weight in bonus payment. He then enumerated possible causes of failures, including technical and human errors. He clearly urged that workers had to put an end to violation of technical prescriptions to speed up or ease their work, but he consciously remarked that this had to be done 'at least on the line designated for export'. He was adamant that quality characteristics continued to be manipulated in order to meet formal standards. Therefore, the expected effect of the new coefficient in redressing management priorities, and therefore workers' behaviour, from quantity to quality was – at least, at this early stage – minimal.

For all the expectations and the determination to change, once again, a general assessment of the situation led him to conclude the conversation with the remark that little has changed in the way production in the shop is dealt with. This means that, as exemplified by the analysis of wage computation earlier in this chapter, informal determination of wages remains a consolidated practice.

The key question is therefore the effective discretion of middle management in the use of incentives in their struggle with both administration above and workers in the shops. Recalling the many examples provided above we can already assume that individual bargaining over wages was present and its intensity had not decreased. It remains to expand on its evolution within the new framework established by the reform, looking again at evidence of bargaining practices observed in the shops.

During observation of managerial work in the factory – at least, until autumn 2001 – it was common to hear about *kompensatsiya* (compensation or indemnity). Workers requested or were granted compensation under very different circumstances. Nevertheless, these cases seem unified by the consideration that an adjustment is possible when the 'expected' or 'deserved' wage differs from the one that workers would be paid if their job was to be computed according to statistics.

A typical case is when workers fail to fulfil the plan or incidents occur which prevent them from satisfying all the conditions settled to achieve a higher wage, like output quality, number of hours worked, machines operated et cetera. Here the question arises whether the worker should be paid in full – that is, to receive compensation approaching or equalling the expected wage.

After privatisation the unevenness of production had, as we have seen, multiplied grievances and related payments. In any case, until a couple of years ago the payment of *prostoi* made it possible to compensate almost automatically at least for losses due to machine idleness. Now these institutions had been obliterated, but the pressure was kept high for managers to intervene. As a foreman assistant noted: 'when problems arise the women [i.e., machine operators, CM] go and cry to the manager and sort it out "somehow". Basically, everyone tries to sort it out by himself' (Interview with assistant foreman, combing–carding shop, 2001).

It is a quite different case when the worker claims a higher wage from their foreman or shop chief, on the grounds that his/her work is not adequately rewarded. These are the cases commonly observed in shop chiefs' offices. Workers require higher wages irrespective of the number of hours worked, output quality, professional eligibility to higher pay rates et cetera, because they are in need, they did unrecorded work or simply are used to receiving such pay. In these cases the manager has first to decide whether the claim is justified. Our key respondent, working in summer 2001 as chief of the combing–carding shop, grumbles: 'There are too many workers turning to the managers after a chat with fellows pretending that they work better and they should get more'. Then the manager is presented with different options: he can use the incentive funds available, of which presently a dramatic shortage is felt, or apply for individual compensation – with no guarantees of approval, as workers complained.

Interviews with the most valuable cadres[1] in the shop tell of the expectation of some sort of supplementary payments for extra work and more or less explicitly confirm the manager's continued willingness to compromise: '. . . with the shop chief we can come to an agreement on these matters'.[2] Their discontent with the

---

[1] These are two assistant foremen and a fitter-toolmaker. The assistant foreman is a key figure within the shops. This is a male-only profession. It requires technical knowledge and a high level of practical skills. The post is usually granted after an exam requiring technical-school attendance. The assistant foreman works in constant touch with line managers and enjoys their trust and support. As reminded by the combine director himself, he is a natural leader in the shop. The assistant foreman is in charge of fitting looms, replacing spare parts and performing emergency repairs (*avariinyi remont*), as opposed to scheduled overhaul and major repairs (*kapital'nyi remont*), which is the job of a separate sub-unit, the RMO.

[2] Workers and managers referred to informal practices of bargaining and mutual understanding with the well-known saying: 'kak platyat tak i rabotaem' (we work as much as they pay us).

situation also made clear that the manager now had in fact less room to secure resources for compensating their services:

> 'They do not pay me any more what they should. I get only 10 per cent more than those who drink the entire shift around', says the fitter[1] and 'they do not pay us as we deserve . . . but he [the shop chief, CM] himself does not have the power to change the situation', adds the foreman assistant.

A last resort, the shop chief confessed, is to make an arrangement outside the official channels, offering as a reference the above case of the mechanic. In order to reward a mechanic for his essential contribution to machinery maintenance and repair, he diverted funds of the enterprise constituting a shadow fund made up of the wages of 'dead souls', i.e. workers made redundant and no longer working at the enterprise.

The shop chief makes me notice how this is a slippery ground for analysis, where different phenomena can be observed and changes have occurred over time. We have to distinguish the institutionalised practices which descend from the then (i.e. under 'red' directors) approved policy of 'stick and carrot' from those that managers arranged autonomously to favour their cadres.

The whole case about compensation boils down to the need to use funds in a discretionary manner at shop level so as to guarantee workers' loyalty. But we are inclined to think that, while in the past this was a widely accepted policy, now it seems to have become the sole concern of the line manager struggling with the administration to achieve the necessary funds. Managers have approved the gradual elimination of the institutionalised forms of compensation, like *prostoi*, but only in so as far as these are replaced by other mechanisms under their direct control. The shop chief suggests, for example, that the 200 per cent increase of the bonus under the brigade system worked to this purpose. Yet, now that the administration pursues a stricter financial policy, the system has become more rigid, and this is felt to be detrimental to managerial authority and to the manageability of the labour force. On this ground the historical loss of the plethoric incentive apparatus offered by the socialist system continues to be felt negatively and the grip of outsiders on the concession and use of compensation is interpreted as a further limitation. A tentative conclusion should therefore concentrate on the following points:

Objective constraints, technological as well as organisational, still force managers to engage in individual bargaining;

---

[1] The repairer or fitter (*slesar'*), like the assistant foreman, is a highly skilled mechanic. He enjoyed the status and the privileges attached to skilled manual professions. This job in particular requires higher skills and experience than that of the assistant foreman as he decides on the restoration and reconstruction of looms. For this reason he has his own engineering shops. He works in tandem with the shop chief, with whom he exchanges information and decides about major technological problems. Here there is an overlap with other auxiliary repair services. This can be partly explained by the Soviet practice of breaking down tasks and partly by the tendency to autarky, which dominated at every level of the production organisation.

Manipulation of targets and incentives continues, but the scarcity of resources has seriously undermined the scope of managerial action;

The conclusive outcome, as commonly reported by respondents, is the transition from a system based on incentives to one managed through fines.

For a general appraisal of these aspects it would be useful to explore workers' opinions and reaction. Not simply because they are the other party upon whose co-operation the system relies. Workers, despite having little say in decision-making, are still recognised at every level of the managerial hierarchy as a pillar of work organisation. Managers, as emerges clearly from the previous account, have to come to terms with the limits and opportunities offered by their co-operation. Second, poorly paid and evidently mistreated, workers can offer an entirely different perspective on how their work is paid for and why it is not sufficiently stimulated. Third, any change should inevitably be understood, at least partly, in the forms and within the limits it effectively influences their work.

Low wages, little incentive: workers talk

There is very little at the factory that workers could be satisfied with; and wages are, as universally in Russia, a major ground for complaint. Here will be reported those causes of discontent directly related to the working of the wage system and its effect on work organisation and practices.

A methodological observation is also due. Workers' opinion has been collected, as for managers, in semi-structured interviews, generally with key informants, with questionnaires completed collectively by two shifts of the combing–carding shops, and more generally in discussions, often prompted by workers themselves. In any of these cases workers' responses were more fragmented, less 'reasoned', than those offered by managers and also more reticent. Workers know little about the way they are paid, though more than they would like us to believe. They stressed in interviews that they are hardly informed about the functioning and changes of the payment system. Looking at their pay slip, we are forced to believe them: a badly printed piece of paper, the size of a memo, with no explanation or notes, just a few figures and the corresponding bureaucratic voices.

Workers, like any employee, are in the first place concerned with the total amount of their take-home pay rather than with the way this is structured internally. This does not mean that they ignore completely the functioning of the incentive mechanism – at least, in terms of the priority managers attach to the accomplishment of certain targets and tasks. Again, workers pay attention to differentials both within the shop and among categories within the enterprise. Those who show a higher mobility, men more than women, the younger and skilled more than others, always have an eye on the local labour market. Third, there is a marked gender divide not only in the amount but also in the form of pay, strengthened by informal practices.

The overwhelming concern of workers, always lying at the top of their grievances, is the abysmally low level of wages. This is obviously a feature of the country as a whole and particularly in this region and sector. Is there therefore any specific significance or consideration to attach to this claim? The average wage, according to data provided by the chief engineer at the union conference in May 2001, amounted to less than 1,000 roubles in the previous year and was approaching 1,300 Rb – the subsistence minimum – at the end of the year. But manager-respondents tended to give figures higher by at least one-third, probably having in mind the well-paid professions, operators and mechanics, which make up the bulk of workers in the shops.

Wages, in any case, vary greatly among categories and within shops: just to give examples, from the average wage of weaving and spinning operators around 1,700 roubles, to the three, even four thousand paid to a mechanic, the best-paid manual profession so far. At the bottom, we find the six hundred roubles for cleaners, internal transport workers and the bulk of the finishing department – considered the workers' graveyard – mostly unskilled. Clearly, for the latter, a low wage means that they cannot hope to sustain themselves on their wage only; for the better-paid it is to renounce the pattern of consumption they had got used to since the mid-seventies. Irrespective of differentials, they all feel their work is not adequately rewarded. The reference is both to their particular job in the enterprise but also to the industry or manufacturing in general. Some respondents also pointed at growing disparities with lower managers' pay and to the fact that managerial clout let them get away with failures, unlike workers. This should not, however, bring us to the immediate conclusion that any sort of collective consciousness exists, let alone grounds for collective action, beyond the boundaries of a shift or shop collective.

In fact, workers' claims for fairness steer away from any idea of equality we might be used to from traditional European working-class discourse. Both men and women, operators and mechanics, complained at the fact that differentials were minimal and pay seemed to be calculated irrespective of individual performance. This is what the workers of the carding shop said about their salary:

> Furthermore they calculate us [wages, CM] all the same. For example, it can happen that we work all month and make the plan or take half of it off, and still the wage will be the same.
>
> (Interview with shift n°. 1 of the carding shop)

A typical argument was to throw any responsibility on 'dropouts', the alcoholic journeymen who had little to lose and drove down productivity. This was to disguise a ferocious competition, primarily among shifts, which were 'stealing' from each other cotton threads, tools, spare parts et cetera: a practice, managers commented, coming as a result of the piece-rate, bonus-driven mentality.

Seemingly, complaints about the existence of 'unfair' differentials continued to poison the atmosphere of the working places. Workers seem to pay enormous attention to even the slightest difference in the level of payments within the factory, especially when it comes to the same profession. In one case, reported below, the complaint concerns differentials between spinners working on the same type of machinery and allegedly producing the same articles. The fact seemed to be so serious that complaints were published in the factory paper and managers felt compelled to intervene with an explanation.

The workers' letter was published in the factory paper in February 2001, and a sequel of managers' replies and workers' counter-accusations followed in the next two editions (see Ivanova, 2001; Taranova, 2001). According to the workers in one shop, the others are paid an unjustifiably higher rate. They also maintain that they had their piece-rate price cut from 27 to 23 kopecks and accused the deputy head of production of favouring 'the spinners of the 4th floor'.

The reply was provided by the head of the department, followed by an article from the chief engineer for norm-setting in the spinning shops. The former presents itself as an attempt to clear up what seemed to be a misunderstanding: she explains how the tariffs were in reality much lower and only lately raised, to 23 kopecks for the 3rd floor and 27 for the 4th. Then she goes on to explain the reason for this difference in pricing (Ivanova, 2001). The point made here is that, given the use of piece-rate and the intricacies of norm-setting, one should not expect any easy grasp of the matter or a straightforward solution. More explicative but also more paternalistic was the second article. First, the engineer explains the details of norm setting in the case in question.

> On the 4th floor, [she says], the norm consists of 6.11 kg of yarn an hour, on the 3rd floor this amounts to 7.4 kg an hour. Why do norms differ? This is because they are affected by the spins. On the 3rd floor, it amounts to 1330 spins a meter; on the 4th it is 1370. (Taranova., 2001)

At first sight, it appears that price-setting was intended to equalise wages by conceding the shop with the lower production capacity a more favourable price. Not surprisingly, though, the manager does not make this point in her argument. She concludes provocatively: 'so, my dears . . . if you want to work with higher prices let's ask a favour. The others [on the 4th floor, CM] will take your place with pleasure' (ibid.).

Workers did not seem fully satisfied with this. To the contrary, they raised doubts about the truthfulness of the engineer's account – 'we dare say that this difference [in spins, C. M.] has arisen only recently' – and urged more serious accounting: 'It is obvious that an account about differences in production norms should not be given in simple words' (*Privolzhskii Rabochij*, 2001f).[1]

What emerges here is, in the first place, an enormous gap in knowledge, made more difficult by lack of information. Yet communication proves difficult, given the high level of distrust and resentfulness on both sides. Workers might be badly informed; still, they feel quite safe in talking about their job and do not appear to accept being contradicted.

The use of piece-rates, as the managers themselves suggest, is certainly an objective cause of these conflicts. In so far as it naturally produces differentials

---

[1] Open letter sent to the enterprise weekly paper by 'The spinners of the 3rd floor'.

it results in a source of jealousy. What workers claimed, in the end, was higher prices to compensate for increased efforts and greater planned output, but the only form in which they felt it appropriate to formulate their request was to take it out on other workers rather than raising an open claim with the administration.

Consequently these workers, while claiming equal prices, do not seem to show any solidarity with their colleagues. For all the criticism spelled out against managers, workers still make them their only and immediate reference; neither other workers nor the trade unions are called into the question. Though at a price, we suspect that this might rather reinforce than undermine the managers' authority.

A separate case should be made for cadre workers, essential figures like fitters, repairers and mechanics who suffered particularly from the lack of ad-hoc measures to compensate for overtime. These workers are in charge of repair and maintenance, and their work has immediate effects on the good state of technology. Their activity, given the poor state of technology and the lack of planning, is difficult to measure but at the same time extremely valuable. No wonder it is subject to individual bargaining with managers, always in search of a means of channelling extra money to them. The fitter in the combing–carding shop reported that his work includes partial machine redesign and reconstruction, for which he used to be paid by a special department existing during Soviet times. The department had been closed, and now he had to 'bag' every time to get this kind of work paid somehow. Another mechanic, an assistant foreman, complained how his overtime repair work was agreed upon with the manager but then remained unpaid as 'up there' rejected the manager's applications.

These accounts stand for the continued dominance of the piece-rate and the goal of making the individual norm. Again, the existence of differentials and conflicts between workers reproduces a situation in which the manager–worker relationship is highly individualised to the advantage of managerial authority.

Workers, as we saw, also stressed their annoyance and disbelief in a policy aimed at stimulating them but closing room for sustaining differentials. What, therefore, about the new incentive mechanism, the coefficients?

Workers' criticism was pointed at both the quality and illness bonuses. During the previous months these had been the cause of partial bonus losses, and this was clearly felt as an unjustified and punitive intervention. Workers maintained in conversations that they could do little to increase productivity and quality standards. In particular, they stressed the contradiction between the two goals. Female operators and mechanics referred to the long night shifts and weekends, when auxiliary services are unavailable and managers are away at home, as the time when quality suffers the most. They concluded that this was simply a mechanism to reduce wages. The loss of bonus for sick leave was particularly stigmatised. The shop fitter commented angrily:

> What I found really offensive is the fine for sick leave. In the past, we were paid a lower wage but the rate was made dependent on grade and seniority. Now workers only [the ITR are excluded from this measure, CM] are subject

to an outright 10 per cent wage cut. Furthermore, those who will suffer most are the women, who fall sick quite often because of the bad working conditions. (Interview with the fitter of the combing–carding shop)

This was clearly a disciplinary measure aimed at discouraging 'self-reduction' of working time. High in the complaints of many managers was in fact the unjustifiably high level of absences due to illness.[1] Workers, though, felt this was fully in their rights, given the low level of wages.

Problems and conflicts also arose along the gender line, represented, in the shop under my observation, by the professional divide between female operators and male mechanics. The female collective of the shop reported that men and women had their own professions, which were therefore paid differently. Gendered pay discrimination was not felt as such primarily because women workers intended their factory job as something alien to their life. 'We consider that there are no professions adequate to women in this enterprise,' they reasoned; an argument which reappears constantly in the answers of female cadres and managers to this question. (Interview with shift n°. 1 of the carding shop, 2001)

What they complained about, as far as wages are concerned, was that women were forced to take up men's tasks: 'if there is no *vozchik* (male carrier) or *ugarshchik* (male machine cleaner), then they can even put in a woman and, we think, this is not fair' (ibid.).

Another shift of women operators openly voiced at the manager their complaint about the continuous absence of auxiliary males. More and more often they were forced to take up 'male' tasks in order to keep the machines going in their absence. The issue was becoming critical because of serious lack of technical male personnel and growing workloads for those remaining owing to deteriorated technology. Women pointed out that they received no compensation for that – unlike, it might be added, skilled male workers.

On their side, mechanics, whose bonus was calculated according to results of the brigade, felt particularly penalised by the new system. They openly stated that they did not like to see their pay depending on someone else's performance. One of them complained how, in case of failure, 'women' went to the managers and solved the problem 'crying and shouting', while he suggested that he had to find the way 'to make it up', on his own 'somehow' (*koe-kak*), referring to the informal bargaining with the manager. (Interview with assistant foreman, combing–carding shop, 2001)

Workers' general dissatisfaction could be moderated by the observation, with which they closed interviews to justify their patience and resignation, that even this was better than the terrible years of non-payment of wages and there was not anything better out there. Women in particular with their family responsibilities felt little room for escaping what is still the only job in town.

---

[1] This and other issues of workers' 'indiscipline' and defiance, and policies aimed at achieving greater control over workers, will be discussed in detail in the next chapter.

Men, especially skilled, were more flexible, making the life of managers harder with their constant threat to leave.

Summary and conclusions

In summary, we can see that technological and organisational constraints still force managers to engage in individual bargaining. The new wage system has failed to put an end to these practices and reorient manager–worker relations to the achievement of quality or efficiency targets. The only significant change, the transition from a system based on incentives to one managed through fines, indicates that workers (female more than male, unskilled rather than skilled) are paying the price of adjustment. By sustaining differentials and keeping wages low the system tries to foster atomisation, defuse conflict and promote enterprise survival despite numerous inefficiencies.

The point of sufferance was therefore discipline in its various aspects. Not surprisingly this issue became another crucial goal in the struggle of the administration to strengthen the effectiveness of the production process. It is clear in fact that incentives could work only in a normalised environment – that is, where workers had no choice but to adhere to the prescribed path. Moreover, discipline violations are another major element of departure from the experience of capitalist industrialised countries. They therefore deserve a specific analysis, which will be carried out in the next chapter.

8   Labour and technological discipline

Do not pay attention to what workers say; they are just a bunch of alcoholics!

Chief engineer, Upper Volga Textile Combine, 2000

Personally, I do not understand what we need all these managers for. The manager's job should be one of co-ordinating and supporting production, but this is what foremen do.

Vitya, senior foreman, shop chief, self-employed bed linen maker

This chapter presents an analysis of cases of discipline violations and disruptions of the production process, in an attempt to trace the ultimate causes of their endurance at the enterprise and the implications it bears for restructuring. These phenomena may vary greatly as to their immediate causes and consequences, and it could be questioned whether they should indeed be grouped and analysed under a single heading. Still, they seem to find a common root in the traditionally limited form of managerial control over the production process. Their combined effect, reinforced by the material and psychological consequences of transition at the enterprise, provide a direct and visible representation of the state of production management at the factory and the reasons why half-hearted reforms, including the wage reform seen in the previous chapter, are not succeeding. In fact, they account for, and are strictly interrelated with, the chaotic state of production, its inefficient and irregular operation, and represent a formidable obstacle to the assertion of managerial control.

Loss of working time, absenteeism and other discipline violations (theft, alcoholism, slack and careless work, output restrictions) were a persistent feature of the labour process in Soviet factories from Stalin onward (Arnot, 1988; Filtzer, 1986). They deepened in the 1970s and 1980s and escalated out of control in the final years of *perestroika* owing to labour shortage and the aggravation of supply problems (Filtzer, 1992, 1994). The situation was such that it is impossible to distinguish between objective and subjective causes, i.e.

173

the system both compelled and allowed workers to commit such violations. Immediate causes were the most diverse (lack of co-ordination, poor pay and motivation, bad working conditions). There is an active component in these events, which expresses the conflictual character of manager–worker relations (attempts by workers to free time for themselves, access scarce goods and exercise control over the production process). The sheer size of the phenomena is due to the fact that managers *and* workers alike violated procedures to protect their earnings and meet the plan. Their ultimate causes lay in the social relations on the shop floor, which resulted in workers' atomisation and managerial leniency.

The case-study enterprise presents a record of these phenomena before privatisation, which have been growing into a problem of major importance lately, as appears from the outcomes of observation and interviews presented hereafter. Discipline violations and the more general effects they cast on work organisation and the structuring of social relations will be taken into account for each of the most recurrent forms of violation. Two categories of violation have been identified, namely those of labour discipline and technological discipline: the former comprising loss of labour time, theft and alcoholism, the latter referring to workers' circumvention of work instructions aimed at easing work or simply making the plan.

The focus in this chapter is on the labour process and managerial strategies. However, professional identities, gender issues, and forms of authority will also be covered to ascertain the intricacies of conflict and consent on the shop floor (Collison, 1992). This chapter consists of two sections. In the first section I analyse different types of discipline violation. In the second section I provide an account of the disciplinary campaigns assumed by the enterprise administration and present an account of shop-floor practices that shed light on the contradictions of the production process and explain the continued failure of these initiatives.

Transition to increased indiscipline

Since the second half of the 1990s, discipline violations in the factory have increased, undermining an already deteriorating economic climate and further poisoning manager–worker relations. At the factory, there are problems of absenteeism, on-the-job time losses, theft, and alcoholism. Staffing levels are plagued by high levels of sick leave and other kinds of administratively authorised absences, and by workers simply not coming to work. Idle time, especially during shifts, is due to repairs and due to conscious violations, such as extending the break period. Theft has raised as much concern among management as has absenteeism, and it causes security problems. Alcoholism affects almost all cases of discipline infraction. I review below these phenomena, presenting the findings of interviews and observation in order to identify their causes and the extent of managerial involvement.

Absenteeism

Truancy problems were first brought to my attention while studying the official factory diary at the office of the head of production. The book contained a record of the staffing level and absences in the shops, arranged in three columns. The first column presented the level of staffing minimally needed relative to the production capacity installed in the shops (*po spisku*). The second indicated the maximum staff number allowed to insure managers against absences and unusual production peaks (a 10 per cent addition to the first figure). Last, there was the actual figure of those at work (*po yavke*) reported on a daily basis. As far as one could see, that figure, though fluctuating, was always below the required staffing minimum. The manager commented that there were invariably too many people off work with some excuse or another – especially sickness – and that he had to struggle to keep them at work.

Workers had two legitimate ways to stay out of work for one or more days. They could do so either by obtaining a medical certificate or by asking for days off 'on their own account' (*za svoi schet*). In the eyes of the administration these allowances were being abused by managers and workers to justify truancy. Detailing the daily bargaining between managers and workers helps to illuminate this issue.

In the case of medical leave, a certificate has to be sought from medical services either at the factory infirmary or at the hospital.[1] The procedure is bureaucratic and cumbersome, and the quality of healthcare services inadequate. It does not come as a surprise, therefore, that doctors tend to be permissive and, especially after their wages declined, amenable to bribes.

During my fieldwork in 2001, a friend of mine working at the factory had a bad accident which required my help.[2] Since we had neither a car nor a telephone, I had to rush to our neighbours asking them to make a report to the foreman (he had to arrange for a replacement). Second, we had to go to the hospital so that the injured friend would be granted her medical certificate. Thanks to my personal connections, I managed to obtain the help of the deputy director's driver and, since his wife served as a nurse, we received preferential treatment at the hospital.

This case suggests that personal connections are essential to overcome inefficiencies in the provision of services. It must be remembered, however, that informal relations, just as formal ones, have their own rules that impose constraints and opportunities. On many other occasions, it proved much harder

---

[1] Under socialism, workers were entitled to paid leave on medical grounds for as long as medically needed. The only significant exceptions were cases of accidents when it could be proved that the injured had been acting recklessly (usually in a state of intoxication). This general rule was continued for a period of time after privatisation. The new owners have recently decided that each absentee case will be judged individually.

[2] The economy of personal favours, known as *blat*, was an important feature of Soviet society (Ledeneva, 1998). Here I turn to a case of absenteeism on medical grounds to illustrate its operation under current conditions.

for me to seek or offer favours, for the following reasons. First, becoming a factory insider meant that I entered a network based on mutual obligations. This implied, among other things, that relations with non-members, who enjoyed different status and resources, were discouraged or precluded. Second, the very same trend of pauperisation and loss in security that resulted in close-knit groups led others to break up, making traditional informal social means unavailable. Workers, oriented to survival, tended to follow the former path; managers, more concerned with career and under greater competitive pressure, reacted in the latter way. This indicates that personal networks are playing multiple roles in shaping social relations during the transition. On the one hand, such networks, while working as a safety net, reflect a social system based on inequality and fragmentation. On the other hand, in relation to corporate interests, they also have a dual character – as an autonomous source of obligations they are an obstacle to the extension of formal, centralised management of personnel; by the same token, they help to buffer the inefficiencies of management and the State, thereby providing some social stability.

Pressure from senior management to restrain these permissive attitudes was already mounting in 2000, before the newcomers required more stringent action, as illustrated by the following occurrence at the office of a weaving shop manager. Quoting from my fieldnotes,

> A male worker comes into the office asking for a day off on medical grounds because he has to take a relative to the hospital. The shop chief inquires whether he has obtained a medical certificate, to which the man replies that they have so far rejected his request; he carries on trying to push his case with the manager. At this point, the shop chief cuts short the discussion, making clear that things have changed. There are orders from above, and he [the chief] is certainly not going to expose himself without the infirmary giving its consent.

The pressure from below is equally strong. Two factors lead to the inflation of sick leave. First, there is an increase in cases of illness directly related to the worsening working conditions.[1] This emerges clearly from the speeches of the delegates at a factory trade union committee meeting, held at the end of February 2001.

---

[1] There is plenty of evidence that the sanitary situation in the town has deteriorated in recent years. Reversing this trend, as managers and workers unanimously reported, has been postponed owing to production requirements and lack of funding – and this in a polluting industry with many dangerous processes. The ventilation system in the shops, for example, works at 50 per cent below standard, working premises are literally falling apart, cleaning is carried out superficially, and canteens have no washing machines. The situation is more serious in bleaching and dyeing shops where aggressive chemicals are handled without precautions, prompting one foreign consultant to suggest its closure. Consequently, high levels of respiratory diseases, infections, and cases of gangrene exist.

No less emotionally, the issues of working conditions and the situation of drinking water were discussed, which are directly related to workers' morbidity. Information on this matter was provided by the chairman of the commission for production standards . . . Leaking roofs, leaks in the water pipes, messy and dirty toilets and showers . . . these facts appeared again and again [in his report]. Basically, all living spaces on the production premises call for desperate attention . . . The issue of living standards was taken further by the deputy chief of the town's state hospital . . . He remarked that unhygienic and unpleasant working conditions in several shops constitute one of the causes for the rising incidence of diseases among workers . . . This at a time when hepatitis and tuberculosis are 'running' in the town and at the enterprise: their incidence has grown already tenfold! (Smirnov, 2001b)

This was stated without considering that faulty equipment may also result in disasters such as fires and explosions. The chief state inspector, visiting the factory after a serious incident, had to declare that:

The investigation has found out that people in your production work with malfunctioning equipment. Such a [slovenly] attitude of factory technicians towards labour protection not only meets my disbelief, but outrages me deeply.

(Svetlakov, 2001)

Another factor causing absenteeism and bringing havoc to work scheduling is the presence of working mothers in the workforce, especially single mothers. In fact, they are entitled to a permit to look after their children. Managers, not surprisingly, are not particularly fond of single mothers and consider them the worst category of workers in terms of performance. This issue has grown into a problem of its own after the transition started. First, the relative proportion of working mothers in the workforce has increased, as they are the least likely to leave and the most unsuccessful in finding better-paid jobs. Second, during the transition period their specific needs have grown, leading to more absences.

Workers are also entitled to request days off without pay for personal reasons. Though costly, this is a common solution for workers who want to manage family businesses and see to bureaucratic obligations in a town where services are either unavailable or flawed by access barriers. Absenteeism worsens during summer time when workers and managers alike spend most of their time on the family plot, and when some workers leave for seasonal jobs in major cities.[1]

[1] For the majority of employees, leaving permanently for a new job/location is impossible. Most workers are unskilled or trained only in the textile line. There are few attractive jobs outside this industry in the region, and the high cost of living in the cities prevents even versatile professionals from abandoning their local dacha or flat for good. Services, such as housing and schooling, help retain married or single mothers. In addition, the company town, with its close network of kin and comrades, represents an essential safety net against economic disruptions and social dislocation.

Difficulties managers encountered in handling this issue are exemplified by the following case taken from my field notes.

> An argument in the office of Kolya (shop chief). Women who work on the cotton supply unit complain about the continuous absences of the mechanics, without whom it is difficult to repair the machinery. Kolya replies that it is difficult to impose tight discipline and that, in the end, things have always been going this way, the more so when there is the risk of walkouts whenever people are put under even the slightest pressure. 'What about higher wages?' [I later suggested.] The reply was that 'people are working in the fields, you have to understand, and this is the only way they could prepare for the winter'.

Absenteeism appears to be well rooted in the social and economic upheaval of the transitional experience at the factory. Evidence indicates that managers show compliance with workers' claims and leniency towards cases of truancy. Yet workers do not benefit equally from managers' understanding. Greater pressure is imposed on the more vulnerable workers, the young, the unskilled and working mothers. This seems to breed overall absenteeism by creating a mismatch in time management between workers' needs and managerial concessions. The general attitude is to let the issue slip down the hierarchy, leaving the problem to the foremen and other workers' 'leaders'. Ultimately, it is up to the workers themselves to avoid visible holes in staffing and to ensure that essential duties are covered.

Time losses at work

Another form of discipline violation that has increased during the 1990s is the practice of arriving late at work and leaving before the end of the shift. While discussing discipline violations, one key informant maintained that

> Arriving late at work has become common practice. People do not even bother to seek justification for it – they simply said they overslept (*ya prospal*). It is not like in Stalin's times when, as I was told, you could walk a long way through the snow to the combine and still you could get imprisoned for several days for a five minutes delay.

Managers consider late arrivals especially pernicious as they create delays and bottlenecks in the production flow when the work has to be passed on from one shift to another. One cause of this type of indiscipline is dissatisfaction of women workers with a new timetable. Replying to my questionnaire, women operators of the carding shop wrote:

> The change in the shift system has cast a significant influence on our work. [The old system entailed a night shift only twice a month; now it has increased to twice a week, CM] We believe that it is very difficult for women

to work on a night shift, both physically and psychologically. Night shifts are particularly tiring, but for women there is no chance to rest afterwards as they still have a family, a home, and a plot of land [to manage]. Vacation days are no longer felt as such.

(Interview with the shift n°. 1 of the carding shop, 2001)

The most typical forms of time loss are those taking place during the production process itself. Textile production is characterised by relatively simple and repetitive production tasks; in fact, female workers did complain that their job was as tiring as it was monotonous. Therefore, despite the lack of processing material, faulty machinery and so on, the working life of women machine operators was, and still is, very much confined to the supervision of looms.

Matters are different for ancillary and auxiliary jobs staffed mostly by men. They enjoy greater autonomy in their work than others do. While regularly inspecting factory premises, it was possible for me to spot loaders, cleaners[1] as well as repairers and mechanics wandering around apparently with purpose. Often it was difficult to determine whether the workers' behaviour was related to a production task or was mere loafing. Loaders and shop cleaners, usually young unskilled males, are notorious for their indiscipline. Still, if these show so little motivation in carrying out their duties, it is also true that their working conditions provide a good excuse for such behaviour. As managers complained, loading and unloading devices are primitive or non-existent, shipments from the preparation shop are irregular, and the shop chief often fights with the manager of the neighbouring spinning shop for the use of trolleys. Equally, cleaners, who were often criticised for their poor work, could be granted some excuse. With no proper clothing and appropriate tools, they have to deal with polluting material scattered all over the shop with a faulty ventilation system. In general, the problem for ancillary mechanics is that most of their work is left to their own judgement and resourcefulness, and to their ability to bargain with the managers. As one assistant foreman put it,

Of course our work is scheduled; but, then, again, problems begin: no parts, no personnel to help out, and no co-operation. We have to do everything in a rush because managers want as many machines as possible at work, so we simply make them up and so we keep going!

(Interview with assistant foreman of the carding shop, May 2001)

Whether failure to meet job specifications was the immediate result of higher plan targets or workers' attempts to skip them, it is clear that managers found it difficult to judge on the matter. Therefore those who were controlled less and/or had greater bargaining powers could more easily get away with discipline violations.

[1] Here we refer to the *ugarshchik*, usually a male worker taking care of industrial waste removal and cleaning of looms. The cleaning of offices and other living premises is another profession (*uborshchitsa*), generally carried out by women.

Soaring theft: misappropriation or reappropriation?

The outbreak of large-scale theft in 1996–7 and its continuation over time tells us much about the nature of the enterprise as a social organisation, and it indicates the state of crisis in which management–employee relationships exist. Moreover, it is an indication of the inability of management to enforce property rights, a serious matter for an enterprise in transition to capitalism.

By 1997, the second year of shortages of supplies and non-payment of wages, senior managers were denouncing the outbreak of thefts in the factory paper.

> The epidemic of thefts continues to be equally worrying among our miseries. This is one reason why our production shows worse conditions. All measures taken by the administration have turned out to be ineffective. We have installed alarm systems in all warehouses. They obviously give results, but until people understand that they are robbing themselves – until they stand up to preserve enterprise assets – there will be no change. (Svetlakov, 1997)

The factory paper started a regular a section about *zaderzhany c pokhischennym* (detained with stolen property), reporting full details about employees stopped and charged with theft. These notes read as follows:

> 6th of February, K. Vladimir V., loader of the packaging shop, [found in possession of] 6.9 m. of bleached calico.
> 14th of February, K. Galina V., machine operator of the combing–carding shop, [. . .] 850 gr. of copper.
> 19th of February, Sh. Konstantin V., assistant foreman of the weaving section, [. . .] 860 gr. of aluminium parts of ATPR looms. (*Privolzhskii Rabochij*, 2001a)
> 16th of May, L. Ljubov' V., [female] accountant of the catering shop, [. . .] 4.4 m. of bleached calico. (*Privolzhskii Rabochij*, 2001b)

Managers lamented that all were involved, though men were more likely to steal than women, because their profession as auxiliaries gave them easier access to goods and greater freedom to move; by contrast, workers (mostly female) stole more than ITR because of their greater need. The fact that employees continued to plunder the enterprise property, irrespective of the controls and punishments administered, reveals that senior management was not equipped to control such an outbreak of insubordination.

The long-term causes of this situation can be traced to the approach in allocating the means of production. The fact that there was no identifiable owner to assume its proper use is usually blamed for the large-scale misuse of state property. That said, the situation on the ground seems to point to a more complex set of causes. State ownership and a planned economy meant that the state enterprise owned everything and the people nothing; shops were empty, and most essential goods and services were unavailable for individual purchase. The illegal private use of enterprise property was an unavoidable consequence of this situation. Yet, under the Soviets, misappropriation of enterprise property did not mean generalised and unregulated plundering. In contrast to the later transition period, there were strict, even if informal, rules about who could have what. Under the Soviets, at the core of this mechanism were not property or money but status and authority. This enabled managers to retain customary income and wealth differentials between themselves and workers.

With most goods and services nowadays available only at unaffordable prices in private establishments, the temptation has increased to use illegitimate means to get resources. Moreover, workers have felt justified in pilfering when noticing the blatant escalation of money squandering and misappropriation displayed by senior management of the enterprise in the early 1990s. At that time, while the enterprise was obtaining high-interest credits, the director and his deputy did not deny themselves the construction of villas worth tens of thousands of US dollars, and management took business trips, thereby depleting valuable hard currency. Evidence suggests that privatisation itself could neither prevent the misappropriation of collective property, nor turn it into the efficient allocation of resources.

The factory and the bottle: alcoholism and discipline

The abuse of alcohol consumption has long been a distinctive characteristic of Russian society. In an encompassing study of the anti-alcohol campaign launched by Soviet authorities in the second half of the 1980s, it is reported that, already 'in the 1970s, alcohol was not simply "Commodity number 1" but also "Calamity number 1" ' (White, 1996, p. 41) in the Slavic parts of the Soviet Union. Soviet economists in the 1980s were alarmed about how 'violations of labour discipline . . . were nearly always associated with alcohol' (White, 1996, p. 49). This was the one issue on which the CPSU and the Soviet state fought and lost its last battle for social control and cultural hegemony. More specifically, it tried to fight the issue in the workplace with the prohibitionist policies initiated under Gorbachev in 1985 (White, 1996).

The company town – with its exiguous social life, its empty shops, and a factory that combined hard work and low pay – offered a climate conducive to high rates of alcoholism. This is probably the reason why the anti-alcohol campaign was implemented here in its most vehement form:

> First of all that year [in 1985], and this cannot be overlooked as it is our history, we all tried to struggle for a sober way of life. The town was declared an area of absolute sobriety by the city council. [After its demise the campaign attracted such comments:] What a pity it is, said the retired worker Elena G., as we, women, had all to gain from this campaign. At home things were easier, without that poison, men (*muzhiki*) began to come back home sober and, on the job, to work. (Schelkov and Antonov, 1998, p. 41)

The failure of the 1980s national campaign gave way to an increasingly gloomy picture (Schelkov and Antonov, 1998, p. 41). In 1997, during my first stay in the town, I observed how drinking of spirits was common among the workforce and that it reached inside the factory walls. Security guards were at times too 'happy' to operate gates, or a brigade leader on a repair job could handle a bottle and the direction of the works at the same time. Vodka would flow during convivial occasions, trade talks, and even during electoral ballot counting. In 2000–2 the situation appears to have turned even worse, as suggested by my experience. To quote from my field notes:

> Returning to the research site after several years, I looked forward to seeing those I had dealt with on my first visit, among them a security guard. Enquiring of a friend about his whereabouts, I was informed that he had died, stabbed by his wife at a time they were both drunk. The fate of the surviving partner was no less surprising. She escaped punishment by bribing the judges, I heard in bewilderment, and was now back at work in her shop. Still shaken, I enquired as to why no one had reported such a shocking event to me. The reply was that 'something like that happens every day'.

Less dramatic cases leading to divorces, domestic violence, infidelity, and so on are more common and are responsible for contaminating interpersonal relations *and* broader social networks. Drinking has not simply continued to be a main ingredient in an increasing number of domestic tragedies; it has become also a major problem in the factory. Shop-floor leaders presented the shop chief with a constant flow of reports about cases of on-the-job alcoholism. The chief's desk was never short of fresh handwritten slips reading: 'I have to inform You [the chief] that [this worker] has been found in a state of intoxication and has been expelled from work.'

The perception and the level of tolerance by senior management had also changed by the second visit in 2000–2. If they could pretend that in the early 1990s troublemakers were a minority that could be easily dealt with, now top managers could not refrain themselves from bitterly remarking that their workers were 'a bunch of untrustworthy alcoholics'. Punishments include demotion and relocation, and increasingly firing workers, especially when, as it is often the case, drunkenness is the cause of discipline violations. In this, as in other instances, line managers demonstrate a reluctance to intervene, fearing unpopularity, but also out of awareness that better workers are not available. Part of the explanation for the lack of action in this area is provided by the failure of the Soviet anti-alcohol campaign, and rests on the commonsensical understanding that the pervasiveness of the phenomenon would not be solved by half-hearted interventions.

As a result one could have the perception that the problem is not dealt with seriously but at the level of conversation. In fact, during the fieldwork period it was clear that drinking in itself was not a problem even when taking place on the factory premises, except when it became excessive and harmed someone's status as a reliable and respectable cadre. Second, I observed that, while drinking appeared to be a pervasive practice, its impact on factory life followed the economic and social dislocation of the enterprise. This 'anti-social behaviour' seemed in many cases to combine defiance and despair among workers in the face of an unbearable material and psychological situation. Managers, therefore, can do little to reverse such trends and do not want to risk open confrontation with the workforce by addressing alcoholism and its consequences openly. Whatever the economic costs related to alcohol abuse, it is easier to let it serve as a coping strategy for the harshness and sheer lowliness of everyday life.

From Soviet populism to managerial authoritarianism?

In this section I shall analyse the policies introduced by the administration to deal with discipline violations. The first part of this section will review the Soviet attitude as it was retained by the enterprise management during the early transition. This will be followed by a review of the measures introduced after privatisation. Finally, in the third part the more recent decisive actions brought forward by the new owners will be considered.

Disciplinary problems and solutions in the Soviet context

During the last decade of Soviet rule, discipline in the workplace became a major target of Party policy in an attempt to revive a stagnating economy. Several campaigns were launched to raise awareness of the damage produced by violations and to mobilise labour collectives 'in the struggle for strong discipline'. The case enterprise has records of participating in these initiatives as well as of experiencing their long-term failure.

> In the mid 1980s, strengthening of labour discipline became an acute problem at the combine. During a single year more than seven hundred cases of unjustified absenteeism (*progul'*) were reported. That's no good at all! How many moral and economic losses have such violations of labour discipline brought about! Could textile workers further accommodate these losses? No! Therefore, in 1996 . . . brigades . . . began to work under the motto 'Labour discipline – pledge of the collective'. The moral factor was placed highest as a resource of the labour collective in the struggle for strong discipline. Brigades wrote it down in their work instructions and from that moment began to operate the lever of material incentives.
>
> (Schelkov and Antonov, 1998, p. 40)

This campaign was combined with the equally extensive and no more successful anti-alcohol campaign (ibid., p. 41).

Ten years afterward the situation was further aggravated by the consequences of transition. We have already reported, in the previous chapter, the alarm raised by senior production managers on theft and demoralisation; years later the chief engineer, reporting publicly on the state of affairs at the enterprise, still remarked the seriousness of the issue.

As in the past, the level of labour discipline is low. As a whole, in the past year, four hundred sixty eight people were involved in discipline violations, which is one hundred seventy eight more than in 1999. Among them four hundred fifty six were cases of absenteeism, of which one hundred nineteen were related to alcoholism. One hundred fifty three people have been fired for absenteeism. The number of thefts amounted to two hundred twenty eight, or twenty-one cases fewer relative to 1999, but this negative tendency has not been eliminated and the combine continues to suffer serious losses because of theft. (Smirnov, 2001c, p. 1)

These reports speak for themselves as for the seriousness and continuity of the phenomenon. They also suggest that, if only figures could be comparable, the absolute decline of cases, seen in perspective with the fall in staffing levels, which affected the less productive and certainly the persistent offenders, corresponded to a relative increase. The managers' opinion was confirmed by even the most superficial observation that these phenomena had become generalised among the workforce. It now involved more than the usual suspects (the working-class underdogs, the alcoholics et cetera), following the deterioration of living standards and the growing cynicism surrounding the state of the enterprise and the managers' ability to handle it. The persistence and the scale of the disruptions meant that these phenomena could not be simply treated as individual cases and referred to the correct administration of the disciplinary procedures but called for a wider policy aimed at the strengthening of managerial control and workers' consent. Soviet and enterprise leaders were, despite all, well aware of that, and the campaigns mentioned above embraced these objectives.

The two strategies behind most of these initiatives were, first, to attempt to raise managerial status and organisational capabilities and, second, to appeal to workers, specifically the cadre elite, to address these problems themselves through a combination of material rewards and political pressures. The approach senior management of the combine tended to embrace was the bonus-driven populist appeal to workers. This approach involved persuading without open confrontation in accordance with the way social relations in the shops were traditionally constructed. Well into the 1990s, enterprise administrators continued to rely on this strategy, maintaining that the 'principal means to ensure the respect of discipline is the personal interest (*zainteresovannost'*) of the worker in the results of work' (Enterprise Code of Conduct, 1998, p. 13). 'The check over workers' discipline, including the right to initiate hiring and firing procedures and impose reprimands and fines' was formally accorded to shop chiefs, with personnel officers relegated to the traditional rubber-stamp role (Interview with the shop chief of the weaving shop, 2000).

The official position of senior management on the issue is offered by a formal interview with the director, reported in a commemorative publication. The interviewee praises the leading role of cadre workers in labour organisation and suggests the kind of behaviour expected in the management of critical situations.

In his shop he [the assistant foreman, CM] revealed his talent as organiser and educator. He works with people individually, always aware of their problems, personal as well as professional. He helps as he can. In his shift are employed six youngsters – two of them are 'difficult'. Still he can find a common language with all of them. (Schelkov and Antonov, 1998, p. 62)

This meant that the management of punishments and rewards was left in the hands of line and production managers, and was handled in the customary Soviet manner.

Managerial tactics on the shop floor

Lower managers and workers' leaders are therefore those who normally deal with disciplinary problems. In the context produced by privatisation and crisis at the factory, line management found itself confronted with the need to tighten discipline if it wanted to achieve higher productivity in the face of decaying technology and a reduced and less skilled workforce. Workers, though, were less committed to their factory work owing to decreasing pay, declining social services, and the physical and moral deterioration of the social environment in which they worked and lived. In the face of the central office's tightening bureaucratic and physical control, line managers seemed caught between Soviet-style compliance and a new and more authoritarian approach.

Managerial response during transition can be understood within the framework of the Soviet-type relationship on the shop floor. In Soviet times, managers exercised authority over workers by entering into individual bargaining and by using their powers in a discretionary manner. In this context, managers were expected to consider workers' needs on an individual basis, taking into account the different status of categories and even of individual workers. Therefore, entering the transition, managerial attitudes towards discipline violations were neither consistent (with new tougher policies) nor based on (increasingly pressing) workers' needs. It tended, instead, to favour previously privileged categories, penalising instead the most vulnerable and less combative among workers, such as the unskilled, the young trainees and women, especially single mothers.

Furthermore, their tactic – again in line with the Soviet informal rules concerning the exercise of authority – was one of avoidance of conflicts and responsibility. Managers would routinely allow exit or leave permits if foremen had done so and reject them if no other authority supported the requests. They would not start a disciplinary procedure unless forced to do so, such as if the case had been made known to senior management. They took care to make their intervention appear as resulting from the specific circumstances of the individual case, rather than stemming from the imposition of an impersonal law. In this way, line managers were able to turn workers' solidarity in their favour and encourage workers to isolate wrongdoers singled out by managers.

The likelihood that the discipline problems could be reduced in this manner was dim. As for the rewards, they were too limited and were unequally distributed. Already thriving cadres were more likely to be rewarded than low-earning and under-achieving workers. As for the punishments, there were limits to their use. This was the case especially concerning dismissal. As my key respondent, the head of the weaving department, remarked, in the late Soviet period the policy was to educate rather than to expel offenders. The labour collective was a community that had to take care of all of its members. The Soviet disciplinary system worked as a complement to the incentive system to marginalise wrongdoers, not dismiss them.

Tackling discipline? Crisis of authority in the newly privatised enterprise

From the mid-1990s, discipline violations became one of the major issues in the enterprise and a key ingredient in the polemics between the administration and employees. Now the enterprise could no longer afford the amount of waste this entailed. Therefore, while still pledging allegiance to the voluntaristic and paternalistic approach of Soviet times, senior management began to introduce measures aimed at strengthening control over workers. One of the first signs of this was the installation at the factory's main gates of barriers with magnetic cards in 1999, shortly before LTD took over the enterprise. Security staff were also instructed to strengthen their vigilance over movements of people and goods. Soon after, CCTV cameras appeared on the factory premises, and tools were locked up in warehouses and safes. It seemed that, years after privatisation, management was finally displaying the will to transform the 'old socialist enterprise' into a modern private firm, and to assert its control in an impersonal and orderly fashion. Yet, the eventual failure of these measures showed the limits and contradictions of these actions.

In the first place, security personnel were limited in number and notoriously unreliable. Retaining the Soviet arrangements, the factory continued to employ recruits from the local police (*militsia*), who colluded with the workforce and tended to ignore infractions. Moreover, workers, seemingly so deferential and apparently incapable of asserting even their most basic rights, reacted angrily at any attempt to be physically controlled. Guards complained that they were subjected to physical and verbal abuse by workers while carrying out their search duties.

More importantly, even the new ability to monitor the movement of employees through the gates electronically did not alleviate the problem of truancies. Because production managers, down to the level of shop chief, retained the right to admit people into the factory whenever they wanted, it was up to them to keep latecomers out. However, they frequently failed to do so. As one manager commented during an informal conversation with me, 'the data are there but no one from the shops cares to use them'. Instructions were also issued to put an end to absenteeism. In any case, truancy, like other forms of discipline violation, continued to proliferate.

The second phase in privatisation and the new owner's struggle for control: Restoring (what) order?

When, in the year 2000, LTD prepared to takeover the enterprise, its incoming management strongly criticised the inaction and ambivalence of the former administration towards discipline violations. It made it abundantly clear that it was going to take decisive action to restore order in the factory.

In a long interview with the factory paper, the leader of LTD, Anatolij Zaryanovich, after accusing the old management of continuing to 'work under socialism', presented the action plan of the new administration by arguing that,

> it is also essential that we, all together and each of us on his own, will join in the struggle against theft. In the end, is it not true that they [the workers] are stealing from themselves and those closest to them? For this reason, in the case of theft-related charges we will punish harshly whomever, from the worker to the manager. We will not allow anyone to work 'staying aside, working for himself'; similar attitudes will translate into instant dismissal and full repayment of the material damages incurred. Having said that, we will also offer everyone the opportunity to earn on the basis of real work performance, high quality of output, efficient use of resources, and strong discipline. (Smirnov, 2000)

Between mid-2000 and the end of 2001 the new owners made discipline one of the key goals, in order to achieve greater productivity at lower costs. Managers were now targeted no less than workers as part of the wider bid for control over the enterprise, and were subject to constant pressure and deprived of some prerogatives.

Security issues were to be dealt with centrally by a restructured security department, whose chief was now a man installed by LTD and made accountable only to it. Security personnel, both at the gates and elsewhere, were selected by him. These personnel were given greater powers to check the movements of people and goods, and they received the right to inspect any freight or employee by means of personal searches. Managers were also given greater responsibilities. The enterprise territory was divided into sectors, and heads of production were made responsible for any accident occurring in their area. Controls extended into the shop with LTD dispatchers who assessed the progress in production, and who frequently appeared in offices of the shop chiefs to verify that they were carrying out their duties.

Administrative controls consisted of requiring managers to record their own activities. For any spare parts, wage money, or other activities involving extra expenses or use of materials, a request had to be filed and submitted to senior management. To make this control system more effective, the security department was entrusted with inspection powers to verify the observance of these internal procedures. This caused some problems. In the shop I studied, the shop chief maintained that requests were usually agreed to by upper management. This was in the autumn of 2000. A year later, after the new rules had been implemented, the situation had changed. When another shop chief was carrying out repair work after an accidental explosion, he encountered resistance by the financial department for a consignment of fabrics. As recorded in my field notes,

> A bureaucratic nightmare: Kolya has signed an order to obtain fabrics. A lot of confirmations are required, but the whole procedure is stopped by the accountants. They are afraid to attract the attention of security because to the latter asking for fabrics automatically means theft.

An effective, though quite crude, way to achieve savings in the use of resources (such as spare parts) consists in limiting the flow of material into the shops; in fact, shortages were already acute since the onset of privatisation owing to mismanagement of supplies and lack of funds. Currently, however, with the new owner stocking the warehouses, shortages are the result of a conscious decision, as confirmed by one of the assistant foremen: 'There is a severe shortage of spare parts. Foremen seem to care little and the procurement service is uncooperative. Those in the warehouses refuse to hand out spare parts because they have been ordered to economise' (Interview with assistant foreman, combing–carding shop, May 2001). As a result, the shop chiefs now have to arrange for worn-out pieces of equipment to be repaired, and mechanics and workers alike have to seek 'easy fixes' to keep machinery going.

Restrictive measures were accompanied, as promised, by interventions in the area of incentives, with the reform of the wage system. In this way, the newcomer's strategy seemed to revamp, ideally, the traditional Soviet campaigns, which matched appeals and initiatives in favour of stronger discipline with a renewed set of incentives. The administration of bonuses is now guided by the new philosophy of making the 'rouble' the new 'criterion of work assessment'. This takes the form of fines for failures, rather than of bonuses for improvements (as said in the previous chapter). To tackle truancy disguised as sick leave, a fine amounting to 10% of the incentive pay has been introduced for any such case, causing outrage among employees. Already in May, a few months after its introduction, the management staged a retreat, agreeing minor corrections presented by the trade union in the resolution approved at their annual conference:

> The Administration should also . . . amend the Regulations on work remuneration in the following points:
> – if sick leave extends from one month into another, then the loss of bonus will apply to the first month only.
> – Working mothers, with children up to three years of age, will have their bonus paid in full, in case of child's sickness. (Smirnov, 2001c, p. 3)

Even like this, there were plenty of workers losing their bonuses, as exemplified by countless grievances against the new wage system. Workers feel that they are being cheated, and managers tend to agree that workers could not be expected to do better in the present precarious conditions.

By May 2001, discipline violations did not show any signs of decline despite the many dismissals (Smirnov, 2001c). An important test lay ahead during the forthcoming summer. As I previously noted, the summer is a time of large seasonal outflow of workers and managers into private enterprise and agricultural work, against which now stood the determination of the new administration to keep production going – business as usual even during the summer.[1]

At the end of August 2001, in answer to the workers' claims for higher wages, Anatolij Zaryanovich presented a very gloomy picture of the performance of the enterprise in the previous summer months – discipline violations were again singled out as the main reason.

> Since April, labour productivity has sharply declined, the amount of defects [in products] has increased and labour discipline has fallen . . . Inexplicably, the number of truancies went up. For instance, in one shift the staffing records count 126 employees, and out of this figure 40 are off on medical grounds. Who is going to benefit from this? We planned an output of 650 tons of yarn and we got 550. Late arrivals and early exits at work are proliferating. Assistant foremen hand over a shift without seeing each other, not reporting what went on during the shift and what problems are left to be sorted out. All this impacts seriously on the quality of work.
>
> (*Privolzhskii Rabochij*, 2001d)

A further tightening of the grip on labour organisation was eventually introduced in January 2002, after disappointment had already emerged from the results of the first wave of interventions. This time, production managers were instructed to file cards reporting any movement of workers within the factory, but outside their usual workplace, explaining the purpose of these 'business trips'. Quite commonsensically, this initiative in particular, but in general any bureaucratically informed measure, was taken by most production managers, at best, as a *boutade* or at worst as a nonsensical act of coercion. In order to understand why, we can report an excerpt from a workers' letter that exemplifies how difficult it is for managers no less than for workers to plan time and conditions of work and how workers' autonomous decision-making is the rule in overcoming his/her daily amount of uproars:

---

[1] The interest of LTD management in putting an end to this practice requires explanation. While in the early years of the transition the market cycle had affected businesses in this summer season with low prices and a scarcity of raw materials, eventually local manufacturers had managed to stabilise both sales and supplies. This good news came from an interview with the director of the local textile industrialists' association, chaired at that time by the ubiquitous Anatolij Zaryanovich. He was convinced that his own factories could now make the most of the market innovation he himself had fostered.

At the beginning of their workday (*razvod*), brigade leaders receive their daily tasks for their brigade. Yet quite often these tasks have to be put aside and we are all sent to the loading/unloading job. Here they come, trolleys, ropes, panels, crowbars. What bright minds have not invented; but then again these bare hands remain the most reliable 'mechanism' in Russia. After heavy work, as a rule there'll be some smoking where everyone joins in, including the non-smokers. We just lighted up when the foreman rushes in 'with fire on his tail' (*nastegannyi*): here we got another disaster (*avral*). Cigarettes fly into the dustbin and once again to work. Obviously, it is not like that every day, but it does happen . . . Still, time passes and the daily plan must be fulfilled, especially since shift workers press us. Here, there is no need for managerial control. Everyone can understand that the faster machinery is repaired the fewer problems we have, the fewer stoppages. True, our equipment is astonishingly die-hard. Our belts and conveyors, pulleys and reducers, which become 'a century old every year', keep working fine, till they eventually disintegrate. How could this super-new computerised machinery ever compete with them! Here will come welding tools, milling machines, or sometimes just a bit of a worker's wit.

(Suvorov, 2002)

This account shows that the production process has maintained its traditional – that is, Soviet – disorganised elements and that, consequently, cadre workers continue to be relied upon for their skills and flexibility 'to keep things going somehow'. Their autonomy remains unchallenged and their daily movements difficult to restrain in practice. A closer look into the production process will unveil much of the rationale for managerial compliance with discipline violations.

Workers' autonomy and the production process

In this section I shall analyse a case of technological discipline violation to show how the production process relates to manager–worker relationships that result in continuing breaches of discipline. In this case, the problem of improving product quality among female machine operators is considered. It is acknowledged that quality standards of textile goods in the Ivanovo region are low (Okhotnikova, 2001), and that they have continued to deteriorate since privatisation. There are several external factors involved in this decline that range from the disruption of the supply chain to low cotton quality. However, factors internal to the factory are also important. With managerial consent, workers tamper with goods and machinery in order to achieve more output, and they do so mainly because of the piece-rate payment system. The new owners have made upgrading of quality a strategic aim and have reformed the wage system accordingly, making bonus payable on quality and discipline performances.

With the co-operation of the shop chief,[1] I recorded an account of the production process for the carding–combing shop, detailing workers' infringements of technological discipline, which lowers product quality. The following summarises the manager's argument and technical observations.

In order to make the plan, workers have developed a series of practices which violate technological discipline. Some of them are detrimental to the quality of output. A detailed description of the production process and of some characteristics of cotton processing reveals the causes of these practices. Unlike synthetics, natural fibres, such as cotton, present the disadvantage that their physical characteristics cannot be easily predetermined. Maintaining quality requires strict adherence to certain procedures and constant control over standards. The lack of sophisticated testing and control equipment installed on machinery and in laboratories at the factory makes workers' skills and dedication essential to maintaining high quality standards. One of the important properties to determine the quality of cotton in carding and combing processes is the weight of threads, which should be kept constant at 4 kilotex. Obviously, if we measure this value over time, figures tend to oscillate around this standard. The quality indicator considered in the field is the coefficient of variation of this measure, CV. After the preparation process, consisting of cleaning and opening of cotton bales, carding and combing are the first phases of the production process. A conveyor leads the raw cotton to the carding machine, where it is transformed into threads (the card slivers) which are wound up into drums placed below each carding head. The machine lies longitudinally to the conveyor, and has ten carding heads which are fed in succession. The cotton tends to be deposited according to its weight, so we will find that the weight of the threads has descending values, moving from the first drum onward. The second phase of the process consists in the combing of slivers. The same drums are now laid out in two layers of six on each side of the combing machine, which feed the slivers into two main heads. After combing, the threads end up in two larger drums. This phase is important because it allows the mixing of the cotton threads to achieve the 4-kilotex standard, while sharply reducing the CV. The crucial task in this process is the dislocation of drums between the two machines. The drums, which carry slivers with different kilotex values, have to be placed in a certain order so as to achieve a proper mix in the combing process. Care has to be taken in the preparation of the two extra drums required by the combing machines, but which were not filled automatically by the carding machine. Workers, however, are mainly concerned with

---

[1] The following notes were collected when the struggle for quality was first implemented on the shop floor. The shop chief agreed to explain how it came about that workers were disrupting the production process. Interviews with the chief engineer, the chief of the quality department, and quality controllers confirmed that similar practices were common elsewhere in the enterprise, and in fact also in other factories of the region.

having a constant supply of slivers to feed into the combing machines because this output represents their plan. For several reasons – including problems with carding, competition between shifts, and delays in shipments – it regularly happens that workers are short of slivers. The solution is simply to run the combing with fewer drums or to fill the empty drums with slivers picked up from the others. Sometimes – due to lack of time, inaccuracy, sloppiness, or irresponsibility – workers simply ignore the rules about the deployment of drums. In other cases, workers run the very same slivers more than once through the combing machine. Since there is a counting device installed on this machine from which metres produced are counted and the piece-rate quota fulfilment calculated, this is an easy way to meet the production plan in case of shortages of cotton threads. In all these cases quality is compromised. To make matters worse, because of the complexity of testing, it is difficult to determine the causes. The low quality of the raw cotton and the machines is also responsible for the poor quality and the chaotic state of production. Therefore, to determine responsibility is always discretionary. Managers, admittedly, know about these practices but feel unable to put an end to them. Foremen and workers are determined to meet their plan at any cost. Managers themselves are convinced that until the administration provides better working conditions and greater powers to managers, there is no reason to modify their behaviour.

This case suggests that what seems to be discipline violation represents in fact the form in which the production process itself takes place. The technical shortcomings, as well as the lack of effective organisation, which appear to cause these disruptions, and are usually blamed on the failures of managers and workers, are themselves the product of the labour process. In other countries the relative simplicity of the technical processes involved in textile production resulted in strict supervision and managerial planning a long time ago. In the present case, management still seems far from achieving these goals. There seem to be two key problems. First, there is the continued reliance on the commitment of individual workers in determining the actual form of his/her activity in production. This dilutes control mechanisms to nothing more than a retrospective assessment of the worker's performance. Second, there is the corresponding disengagement of line managers from intervening in the production process.

What went wrong? Managerial discipline and workers' control

In order to strengthen discipline, senior management wanted to impose accountability while trying to promote initiative. In practice, though, the measures adopted introduced greater individual responsibility, which fosters parochialism and narrow-mindedness in low-ranking managerial decision-making.

In the Soviet system shortcomings were overcome by informal, and often wasteful, initiatives which bridged the gaps between complementary services.

The new measures, however, while addressing gross mismanagement and inefficient use of resources, endanger co-operation. Senior management has been increasingly conscious of this issue and has, in fact, taken counter-measures. Usually this consists of tying specific monetary incentives to collective targets in order to prevent individual self-interest from undermining these targets. For instance, collective payments – the brigade system – were introduced in weaving in 1998 by the previous administration. More recently, repairers in the spinning department have been promised a bonus payable if the women in their shifts operate a greater number of looms (*Privolzhskii Rabochij*, 2001c). The returns, though, are disappointing because the relationship between managers and workers has remained dominated by the traditional motivations of individual achievements and accountability.

The other major obstacle to stronger discipline is the weak position of the enterprise as an employer in the job market. It is not enough to have regained the full right to hire and fire if, owing to the low ability of the enterprise to pay decent wages, the best workers are leaving and the unskilled are the most likely to be hired. Disciplinary measures, including firing, do not work as a deterrent because, as many workers pointed out, 'the "truant" (*gulyaka*) or the "idler" (*bezdel'nik*) does not fear dismissal because he knows that the shortage of personnel will drive him back to the factory' (Interview with shift n°. 1 of the combing–carding shop, 2001).

To sum up, organisational and job-market conditions tend to reproduce a peculiar relationship between managers and workers that permits the latter to violate discipline and encourages the former to tolerate it. This form of relationship on the shop floor prevents the establishment of discipline from above.

Discipline violations as a form of sabotage?

A vast literature suggests that the violation of discipline in the workplace, whatever the immediate form it assumes or the reasons adduced, contains an element of intentionality. It is, in other words, a way to manifest dissatisfaction with the condition of alienated and dominated work in an exploitative and hierarchical system (see Sprouse, 1992). Here we briefly consider how this argument applies to the Soviet economy and what implications it might have for explaining discipline violations at the enterprise after transition.

In the Soviet Union the large-scale occurrence of discipline violations has been explained as, among other things, a form of individualised resistance of the atomised workers. In fact, since the 1930s the banning of strikes and the transformation of the trade unions into a satellite of the Party-State, channelling and enforcing its targets from above, left workers with no means to further their grievances and engage in collective action. Therefore, 'denied any means of collective organisation and opposition, Soviet workers, at least until recently, have adopted essentially defensive and generally individualised, responses towards both management and the regime' (Filtzer, 1992, p. 41).

The disappearance of the Party-State and the transition to liberalism, both in the political and the economic spheres, has not meant an automatic resurgence of the workers' movement. Despite the fact that *perestroika* ignited mass protests and strikes, which were repeated in the mid-1990s, neither new independent organisations nor the old trade unions emerged to foster the democratisation of industrial relations (see Filtzer, 1994; Clarke, 1993, 1996, 2002).

If collective action or trade union activism should be taken as an indicator of change on these grounds, the enterprise shows a high level of continuity with the past. Workers staged only one strike during the entire decade, in 1998, when non-payment of wages had thrown the majority of employees into misery. For the rest of the time both the old and the new administrations successfully adopted a paternalistic approach, leaving to line managers the handling of day-to-day individual bargaining. As for trade unions, they survived by perpetuating their role of welfare administrators and management aides as indicated by the following passage in the factory paper:

> In all productions and departments of the combine, the primary Trade Union cells play, indeed, a noticeable role in the life of labour collectives . . . Today I would like to remind the administration, and in the first place the foremen, that primary cells are their first assistant in their job. By making the proper arrangements with these organisations . . . you can overcome mountains. Their influence on the climate in the labour collective, on productivity, quality of production and labour discipline should be reappraised. One of the main tasks of the cells consists in co-operating with the administration to constitute the adequate conditions for the achievement of plan targets, to conduct educational work with workers and so forth . . . Where the tandem 'foreman–TU cell' works in harmony, as a single bundle, things proceed significantly better. The primary cells in conjunction with other Trade Union activists, especially with insurance delegates, provide, let us say, sick workers with visits at home. This has not only a great moral and psychological effect but also reinforces discipline . . . The trade union is now a school of life and survival and we should remember that. (Sloveva, 2001)

This does not mean that unions are as respected and influential as their leaders believe them to be. In private, managers, clerks and workers alike would all play down their effective ability to operate. In the opinion of managers, these organisations are powerless and inefficient; for workers, they are nothing more than corrupted individuals manoeuvred by the administration. Still, in the eyes of the administration, they serve as a formal counterpart in industrial relations; and, for workers, as providers of what is left of the enterprise welfare. More importantly, such an organisation is something of a hindrance to the emergence of any alternative to individual action.

Managerial power on the shop floor is in any case a more immediate and certain obstacle to any attempt by workers to challenge the administration in direct fashion on fundamental issues. Workers themselves depicted in this way the situation of industrial relations and the actual causes of their apparent resilience:

> They [the workers] fear managerial authority. If a worker receives a reprimand the others would rather line up behind the management throwing the blame at him/her. If I acted as a trade union leader they would find a way to kick me out. The trade unions are totally on the side of management; the enterprise pays each and every of them. (Interview with spinner, 2001)

Others signalled that their condition, in terms of bargaining power and status *vis-à-vis* their superiors, had deteriorated significantly after the end of *perestroika*. Enterprise employees, therefore, had only as much scope, if not less, to make their voice heard and achieve improvements as they had in the socialist past.

The moral and material aggravation that transition had brought in terms of material deterioration of living conditions and growing divide of status and consumption levels with the few at the top provides the fuel for cynicism and social hatred. Under these circumstances, workers' demands and expectations rather tend to surface in the form of individual destructive actions. Short of collective action and outright defiance, everyday forms of resistance may take the form of 'foot-dragging', 'dissimulation', 'false compliance', pilfering' et cetera (see Scott, 1985, pp. 29–34). They are 'covert', 'anonymous', 'concerned largely with immediate de facto gains' (ibid., p. 33) so as to avoid exposing the perpetrator to the risk of retaliation. 'Resistance is influenced by the existing forms of labour control and probability and severity of retaliation' (ibid., p. 34). Where piece-rate prevails, resistance is likely to find expression in 'the shortweighting of finished cloth, defective workmanship and the purloining of materials' (Wright, 1978, in ibid.) rather than in slow-down. Many cases already described in the chapter fit well in this categorisation and the ensuing analytical argument.

An extreme case was, for example, reported in factory n°. 2. Here a worker was electrocuted by accidentally touching an unprotected wire. The investigation concluded that a section of it had been chopped with the intention to steal (Interview with the chief of labour protection and safety standards, 2001). Less dramatic cases, such as stealing vital tools, processing materials or spare parts, or concealing their whereabouts, may have serious consequences for plan fulfilment, the state of technology et cetera. This is, bearing in mind the distinction drawn between female and male jobs, very much the product of male, especially mechanics', activity. Most of the time, 'minimal or reluctant compliance' is sufficient to wreck managerial plans. Loom operators could simply fail to report machinery faults, resulting in defective output or protracted idleness. Again, these actions, while lacking the intentionality of sabotage, certainly imply the awareness of producing disruptions. When workers have no immediate interest in it, they justify such behaviour by saying that working more or better is not worth the pay and the treatment they receive.

Finally, it is also important to consider that 'forms of resistance are also intended to . . . deny claims made by superordinate classes' (Scott, 1985., p. 32). There is an argument between a fitter and a shop chief that well exemplifies this. Kolya reproaches a repairer for not having completed his work on time, the mechanic replies that it is not his fault if spare parts do not fit and have to be replaced or rectified. Listening to him, Kolya clarifies that those parts were of the needed specification and turns it into a matter of principle. He asks: 'If you dismantle a machine and replace all of its parts with new ones, will it not be the same again?' The worker rejecting the point discloses his thoughts: 'This is what you read in books but it is not the same in practice!' – as if to remind us that resistance is also a symbolic struggle concerning thoughts and ideas that define roles regulating everyday activities.

Managers, especially those on the front line in the shops, can merely accept it as a safety valve, as they have to face a very tense situation augmented by the personalised nature of intra-employee relationships. As they often put it, they could not ask more from workers, because, very much like the latter, line managers also feel themselves cheated by the Administration.

Summary and conclusions

Delays, idleness, misappropriation of employer's property, and outright sabotage occur in the world of production wherever domination and alienation exist as structural features of the production process. The experience of the Soviet economy[1] is nevertheless unusual, for discipline violations proved to be exceptionally widespread and pernicious, enjoying silent support or at least tolerance by production managers. This is because Soviet management and their present-time successors – contrary to the widespread assumption of a converging path of the major industrialising countries – have transferred the responsibility of everyday production management to workers, and to their cadres and supervisors.

The cases of discipline violations presented in this study highlight how far post-Soviet managers are from achieving control over the place, the time and the methods in which production takes place. This failure not only allows considerable room for infractions to go undetected but, more importantly, also contributes to a type of management–worker relationship in which the former has no interest in preventing discipline violations, and in some cases instigates them. Discipline violations, in fact, are not only a safety valve – the only form

[1] The history of Western management is interwoven with the struggle to achieve full control over the production process. Though this goal could hardly be fully achieved and is constantly put into question by workers' individual and collective action, the historical changes usually associated with the names of Taylor and Ford have marked a turning point in this direction. The standardisation of social practices, at work and beyond, and the diffusion of ever more sophisticated mechanisms of supervision to achieve their implementation, have all meant that discipline violations are aimed against this pervasive control and limited to the grey area outside it.

workers have been left with through which to express their mistrust and dissatisfaction – but also are a means to solve personal and production problems.

Still, infractions do not pass without consequences. Even if they are not prevented and harshly sanctioned, they are still punished by the social stigma and loss of status that allows management to reinforce its upper hand over the workforce. Therefore, discipline violations represent an organic part of the mechanism of social control and work organisation at the enterprise. This explains the caution with which line managers have handled the latest disciplinary campaigns by the new owners and brings to light the contradictions of the newcomer's policies.

We can now return to the debate about manager–worker relations, and the nature of workers' control and resistance in Soviet and post-Soviet Russia. Our findings suggest that: (1) the persistence of discipline violations indicates a continuity with the Soviet past in manager–worker relations; (2) yet discipline violations do not represent organised protests against the steady deterioration of working and living conditions and/or the acceleration of production. Therefore, they do not qualify as conscious resistance. Instead, discipline violations by workers are a last resort, since the means of collective bargaining and open conflict are denied to them (cf., Scott, 1985). This supports Clarke's thesis that considers workers' autonomy as a consequence of managerial strategy. To put it in terms of Di Leo's (1973) idea of the Soviet social order as a political accommodation, with privatisation the existing compromise between upper enterprise administration and workers has been breached unilaterally from above, without workers being able to renegotiate this process. Once again, this confirms the intrinsic weakness of the workers' position. Discipline violations, and the underlying model of work organisation, are another obstacle to the introduction of best-practice Western factory systems. Yet present management does not seem ready to reject the past Soviet order in the factory; instead, it is adjusting incrementally to the new constraints imposed by the commercialisation of the economy.

9 Conclusions

In the previous chapters we have seen how the story of enterprise restructuring has been characterised by a striking continuity in Soviet management practices. The findings from our case-study make clear that social and organisational change, and resistance to it, can only be explained and understood in the context of the struggle for survival engaged by the enterprise and the conflicts it generated. Social relations in production represent the framework within which they develop and the particular form of labour process existing in these factories the main obstacle to their modification.

In the conclusions we would like, on the basis of such arguments, to readdress our initial question about the rationality of managerial practices. To this end, the account of restructuring at our company-town enterprise is followed by, and contrasted with, a second case-study of a fully restructured urban enterprise. Third, we consider the state of restructuring in holding companies. The striking similarities in terms of the limits and contradictions of change in production in these different settings suggest that the failure of restructuring has less to do with forms of property, managerial strategies or enterprise-specific circumstances than with deeper social structures. And that owners and managers alike, for different but converging reasons, tend to reproduce rather than modify them.

This conclusion has led us to switch the focus from the worker–manager to the owner–manager relationship and consider another set of questions concerning the nature of management in post-Soviet enterprises and the role of managers in the development of capitalism in Russia. Namely, how can this relationship in post-Soviet Russia be conceptualised, as opposed to its capitalist equivalent, and under what conditions can it be modified in order to overcome its existing contradictions? It has been observed that the emergence of holdings has created the conditions for the development of capitalism in Russia but also that capitalist relations and ideology have so far not spread below the level of corporate top executives (Clarke, 2004, 2007).

It is difficult to establish at this stage whether this process will follow a path similar to that of Western capitalist economies and in particular whether it will rely on imitation and adaptation of Western managerial practices. Analysing examples of transformative agency by Russian managers can give an indication as to *how* this transformation might happen.

Mainstream arguments about restructuring have either ignored or diminished the role of the external environment on enterprise development. As we saw, the role of private and public institutions operating 'out there' has had a significant impact on managerial strategies and outcomes. It is therefore important in these conclusions to broaden our focus to consider the restructuring of textile enterprises as mutually dependent on the socio-economic fate of the Ivanovo region. The relationship between state and local officials and industrialists has been changing rapidly in recent years while losing nothing of its complex ambiguity, but there is no doubt among managers and owners as to the importance of state intervention for the further development of the industry.

Social relations in production and the fate of enterprise restructuring in Russia

A central argument of this study is that the dismantling of the institutional framework of the Soviet economy would have delivered neither free-market nor enterprise restructuring. Liberalisation, rather than freeing enterprises and imposing the more rational control of hard budget constraints, has seen the reaffirmation of stifling political tutelage and economic control by outside agents such as banks, trading companies and industrial groups. The newest industrial–financial groups have proved no more capable of fostering change than earlier formations based on Soviet ties and are certainly better-equipped to turn autarchy into solid monopoly. If hard budget constraints and greater trade volatility have continued to lower enterprise revenues and decision-making, exacerbating the problems enterprises suffered under planning, the contradictions of the system at this level had more chances to worsen than to be overcome.

The fundamental task of management, I contended, was to regain control over the production process so as to regularise production and increase productivity as the only way to generate profits. I maintained that managers in Soviet times had to rely on workers' co-operation, therefore tolerating low productivity and high indiscipline. This system of social relations allowed management in turn to atomise workers and defuse conflict, allowing for labour-force flexibility against a picture of scarce resources and uneven supplies. The current lack of resources, the decline in technology and the unfavourable job markets have all played in favour of strengthening the need for workers' co-operation as other options seem barred by lack of serious investments.

Why, more specifically, could not marketisation, hard budget constraints and even outside ownership achieve this goal, and what does it mean for the enterprise to reproduce these practices in an entirely new economic and institutional context? The findings of the case-study, within its own limits, show what the intrinsic rationale of retaining the Soviet form of management is.

In the fourth chapter I observed that management was both conscious and willing to carry out reforms. However, the external environment in which they operated left them with neither resources nor opportunities to turn a production unit into a market-oriented firm. Given the evident dysfunctions of Soviet management in planning, accounting and marketing goods, one would have expected greater determination by outsiders to achieve these goals once their involvement in enterprise management had increased. They tried to make managers more responsible and production management more efficient by strengthening control, streamlining decision-making without granting autonomy or conceding anything to requests for investments. Over the two following years of outside ownership I experienced the growing frustration of the new owners' attempts to get results because of managerial resistance, amidst claims from management that they were unable to bring order in the shops. I set out to understand better the substance of these arguments by looking into the situation of production units.

In the sixth chapter I consider to this purpose the functioning of the wage and incentive system. Managers had been used to manipulating the existing Soviet system so as to achieve workers' loyalty and overcome production bottlenecks. They maintained that the piece-rate and a large array of bonuses were an essential tool to elicit workers' efforts. The deterioration of material and economic conditions during the 1990s has deprived the system of much of its potential. The reforms introduced by the new owners, though, have not met with either workers' or managers' favour. The findings of my investigation show that, in fact, reform, rather than altering the system, has more simply reduced the scope of managerial discretion and lowered the resources available for the wage fund. Since low wages and poor technical conditions have not changed the conditions in which production takes place, managers are still forced to enter into informal bargaining with workers. Evidently the new owners were content with the system, being rather oriented to intensification than to rationalisation.

One of the prices that management had to pay for renouncing control over the production process, apart from low productivity and higher costs, was the high level of workers' indiscipline. Violations of labour discipline have been growing in the 1990s at the enterprise and have not shown signs of decline following the apparently tougher stance assumed by new owners towards them. In the last chapter of the case-study I try to understand these phenomena that puzzled me, no less than worrying senior and line managers. Findings suggest that workers find indiscipline to be the only way to express their discontent at the deterioration of living and working conditions, given the impossibility of overt and organised conflict. Managers' tolerance, though, was the result of a peculiar situation which saw them allowing those practices in so far as they helped achieve production targets. They exploited workers' failures to diminish their social standing *vis-à-vis* their fellows, while also appreciating the relief of tension they produced.

What I found at the factory was therefore not simply the chaotic state of production and the stubborn reliance on old Soviet practices denounced by reformers, but a system that, despite its inefficiencies, manages production within the constraints of scarcity and lack of technological and economic means for controlling workers. Soviet informal practices still prove a formidable social control tool. Despite the abysmally low level of wages and the steady deterioration of working conditions, the new owners have managed to intensify work, contributing to the evident redistribution of resources in their favour without entering into open conflict with employees.

Managers know that a different strategy is possible and so do the outsiders, but they are also aware of the costs. So far, despite much waiting for financial–industrial groups to enter into direct control of enterprises, in our case they have shown neither a different approach to organisational change nor a commitment to restructuring.

What are the conclusions regarding the nature, progress and determinants of transition at the level of the enterprise which emerge from these cases? In trying to answer this question we confine ourselves to the results of our case studies. At the same time, while recognising the importance of restricting our conclusions, it is equally essential to point out that the cases presented here are not isolated. Indeed, evidence suggests that enterprises across regions and branches of the economy display similar features (Clarke, 2007).[1] The significance of the pervasiveness of similarity compels us to make some basic claims about the nature of the social organisation of production in present-day Russia.

The conditions in which managers operate in the realm of production have not significantly changed, while the contradictions of the Soviet production process, which justified many managerial practices in the past, have become more acute.

In such conditions, any alteration of informal Soviet practices, such as individual bargaining over wages, tolerance towards indiscipline and so on, will immediately translate into open conflict with the workforce. Low wages, wage arrears and non-payments mean that managers are constantly required to defuse conflict over these issues, which is chiefly achieved by dividing and fragmenting workers.

Enterprise management can hope to challenge the limitations imposed by the current form of organisation of production by thorough restructuring on the basis of large-scale investment. However, economic instability hampers such a radical transformation of production management, generating low morale and poor productivity which constitute the major obstacle to attracting the badly needed private investment.

---

[1] There appears to be a considerable degree of commonality between a vast number of Russian industrial enterprises in the area of wages and management, as confirmed by the results of collaborative research projects between the Centre for Comparative Labour Studies, University of Warwick, and the Institute for Comparative Labour Relations Research, Moscow, which have involved longitudinal and survey-based studies in Moscow, Kemerovo, Samara, Syktyvkar, Perm', Yekaterinburg, St Petersburg, Ul'yanovsk and Minsk. Fieldwork reports and statistical sources can be obtained from the project website, http://go.warwick.ac.uk/russia/.

Restructuring at a second textile factory: a different model?

Every enterprise is a unique combination of general, country- and sector-specific features and the individual factors provided by the interaction between managerial strategies and environmental conditions. In the Russian case, as pointed out throughout this work, both the constraints of the Soviet legacy and the limiting circumstances of transition left very limited scope for strategising. Then, again, the situation and path of development of each enterprise is not identical, depending on a plurality of factors such as its ability to export, its role in the local economy, its ties with local authorities and Soviet networks (Clarke, 1994, pp. 12–14). From this perspective, the position of our case-study enterprise was defined by its status of company-town, or city-making enterprise (*gradoobrazuyuschoe predpriyatie*) as the Russian term literally translates. This condition imposed a specific set of constraints and opportunities.

The enterprise capitalised on strong political ties and on its preferential treatment in resource allocation because it was the sole employer in the locality. It also bore the weight of its social responsibilities. Its isolation also influenced local labour-market conditions, making it difficult to recruit specialists but easier to retain the bulk of the city workforce. The combination of these elements weighed heavily on management strategies, in the sense of preventing restructuring, even when the outsiders took over. Even though company towns abounded in the USSR and were the model-type for planners, it was felt that conclusions drawn from this case should rather be tested on a second unit that primarily for its urban location might show a different set of strategies and outcome.

A second enterprise was therefore identified in the neighbouring province capital city, which presented very different characteristics indeed and proved an interesting case for comparison. The enterprise was a cotton spinning and weaving textile manufacturer. Like our main case-study it was quite a large enterprise by output, capacity and staffing levels, which amounted to above 5,000 just before privatisation, and size of the social sphere. This enterprise, too, was a historical establishment, founded in the late nineteenth century, with most of its infrastructure dating back to the immediately pre- and post-revolution years. Privatisation was carried out along the same lines, though with quite different outcomes.

Visits were paid regularly to the enterprise during May 2002. Interviews were carried out with all key managers in the main offices and in production. Gatekeepers again were fundamental in the task of identifying and then securing contacts and access as well as providing vital background information. These were namely the chief mechanic, previously working at the combine, and the former combine legal assistant. As a private consultant the latter had assisted the management of the second factory in piloting the bankruptcy of the enterprise. The process concluded with its purchase by outsiders, making it a profitable deal for both parties, apart from the workforce, dismissed *en masse* without compensation and deprived of its ownership rights.

I would like to highlight that what attracted me when I was first presented with this opportunity was the fact that a summary description of the enterprise affairs seemed to respond to the ideals of restructuring as advocated by Western consultants. In fact, the enterprise was already solidly under outside ownership and had severed all ties with its Soviet past. The labour collective had been disbanded, with old and new staff alike recruited according to market conditions. Wage differentials were much higher in favour of management, as the more dynamic urban market would have suggested. More importantly, staffing levels had dwindled to a mere 500, so that most of the cumbersome managerial and auxiliary apparatus of its Soviet predecessor had been dismissed. It was equally the case with the social sphere, which had been turned over for a profit to building developers. But production and marketing also looked promising. Capacity was retained only in profitable export areas and was planned according to market demand; finishing and maintenance were outsourced. If analysis had stayed at this level, this enterprise would represent, as has been said, a restructuring ideal and would certainly occupy the opposite side, relative to the combine, in an ideal spectrum measuring managerial attitudes to restructuring. Then, again, both the history of privatisation, managerial practices and the state of production make this success story a bit more complicated.

The enterprises presented very similar initial conditions in terms of economic and organisational structure, but the way managers dealt with transition made all the difference. This second enterprise had suffered since the late Soviet period from poor leadership and was subject to high top-management turnover. This prevented the establishment of a network of connections, which proved vital to the initial survival of the Combine. To make things worse, from the start, alleged cases of embezzlement of funds by the director jeopardised key procurement deals and seriously undermined his authority among lower managers and workers.

Since the early 1990s the enterprise had struggled to keep production going, and already key shops destined for export production were rented out to outside businessmen. The 1998 crisis brought the final blow, and the enterprise came to a standstill, with its entire workforce sent on administrative leave indefinitely. The enterprise stayed idle for two years, during which time top management designed the most profitable way out of the crisis. The enterprise was split into two legal entities; in the words of the lawyer who actually designed it, 'we left the liabilities in the old company, including the labour collective, and we transferred all assets, estates, machinery and equipment to a new one'. Stocks were purchased from workers for pennies as they put up little resistance after two years of unpaid leave, one of them regretfully admitted.

But it was the way in which personnel were managed that betrayed greater similarities with our original case than might have been expected. The managerial structure had been highly simplified, in particular by cutting the shop-chief layer, whose tasks had been transferred to the head of production on the one side and the foremen on the other.[1] It was apparently aimed at streamlining decision-making and, we suspect, at eliminating a main point of resistance (and bargaining). Then, again, it did not seem that the head of production, foremen or brigade leaders were in any way satisfied with it. They reported very much the same complaints that shop chiefs had filed at the combine, such as shortages of personnel and materials, unrealistic production plans, conflicts with other departments and main offices, and so on. They also engaged in informal adjustments with workers. Here the difference was, while the wage system had been left unaltered, wages were very low and differentiation minimal. The result was that managers had to tolerate high levels of indiscipline and turnover because, as they said, 'with such wages it was impossible to recruit better workers' (Interview with the head of weaving production). The same problems arose with outside maintenance contractors, as the chief mechanic pointed out. As a result, working conditions were, if possible, even worse than those at the combine, and this despite the fact that operating premises were only one tenth of those at the latter. Accidents, some fatal, were one of the tragic consequences of this situation (Interview with the head of the safety department).

As for relations along the managerial hierarchy, greater interaction between the director, the chief engineer and the marketing director, on the one side, and top production managers, on the other, had brought neither greater inter-personal understanding nor better planning. On the contrary, the objective proximity of a much smaller enterprise meant that pressure was exerted for results on a daily basis, and failures and successes were personally reviewed, and rewarded accordingly, by the director. In short, smaller size and more favourable market conditions did not mean that production managers had greater control over production nor that top managers were very concerned with this, continuing to act towards production as an outside entity.

Other than just similarities in specific areas, therefore, I felt that the policies towards production, as well as the way in which relationships with subordinates were managed, remained very much the same as in the previous case. This case also conveyed the solid conviction that, whatever changes had occurred, this was in the sense of making old Soviet practices more acute and their effect more pernicious descending along the hierarchical line.

Restructuring in holding companies: trends and tasks

Technological modernisation and the introduction of modern management techniques figure highest in the holdings' agendas. While the need to intervene in these areas might attract little disagreement, it is the complexity and the scale of these issues, and the awareness of managers and owners to solve them, that is questionable. As noted above, still in 2005 most industry equipment was

---

[1] Interestingly, such an innovation was introduced a year later at a combine restructured under LTD control and experimented with at our combine.

obsolete, and few businesses have so far implemented serious modernisation plans.

According to production managers, in any case, the purchase of new looms or the installation of new production lines is insufficient evidence of innovation. First, the mere replacement of depleted capital stocks offers no guarantees of efficiency gains or market success. Second, the state of depletion of both civil and industrial infrastructures, grossly overlooked, also represents a serious obstacle to achieving quality and efficiency gains. What industry needs is comprehensive modernisation plans, with up-to-date production facilities leading to a re-engineering of the workplace.

Technological reconstruction is essential to change the behaviour of workers and line managers but requires equally wholesale changes in management. Experiments in this area have been conducted since the late 1990s but have really stepped up with outside ownership, without so far achieving substantial change. Managers involved in implementing these reforms over many years talk of little awareness at the top and hostility to change at the bottom. The major problem lies in the way holdings are structured and the particular relations between ownership and management. The picture is one of over-centralisation with little managerial autonomy; rigid planning but lack of procedures and monitoring. Holdings are still very loose organisations pursuing short-term profits with little expertise in capitalist manufacturing. Their reorganisation as efficient capitalist enterprises is emerging as a complex process dependent on competitive pressures, technical change and growth in managerial autonomy and responsibility.

Current research reveals that continued reliance or even restoration of Soviet practices is a general trend in manufacturing under the influence of holding companies. Yet some interpret this as a temporary solution rather than a case of adaptation of Soviet institutions to a 'market' environment (Clarke, 2004). The main point in favour of this argument lies in its historical perspective, identifying the present situation as a stage in the gradual 'penetration' of capital into the enterprise. This research provides a partial confirmation of this interpretative line, while also highlighting the obstacles and possible gateways to the present stalemate.

Summarising our findings, it can be observed that: *(a)* holding companies have initially shown both reluctance and inability to be directly involved in the management of production units and have consequently relied on the traditional Soviet handling of trust–factory relations; *(b)* once holdings have been driven into enterprise management and restructuring, particularly considering the higher level of obsolescence inherited by this sector, the outcomes have been partial and unsatisfactory in the absence of large-scale investments; *(c)* at the same time owners' determination and top management commitment to restructuring is unquestionable, and setbacks in individual instances seem rather to sharpen them by contributing to a learning curve.

The major problem lies in that: *(a)* management at company level, i.e. above the individual manufacturing unit, remained a missing link in Soviet planning, and in any case previous experience can tell little about the co-ordination of manufacturing under profit-driven organisations such as the merchant houses; therefore *(b)* the merger between new private businesses and former Soviet enterprises calls into question the formation of a unitary managerial stratum amid the bitterness, conflicts and distrust following takeovers. This poses a number of new analytical and theoretical problems concerning the function of management and the circumstances of its developments in Russia; which will be dealt with extensively in the next section.

Post-Soviet management and the future of Russian capitalism

Continuity with the Soviet past seems to predominate at the point of production: whether in the form of subtle and involuntary reproduction of managerial practices and workers' resistance tactics or as the outcome of deliberate policies from owners. Changes in ownership and governance structure seem to have produced little effect, despite the relentless effort to redirect work organisation or incentive systems towards the new goals of financial efficiency and product quality. The findings of this research highlight how this is the product of a specific system of social relations, inducing co-operation of line managers and cadre workers to control labour but also to resist the scrutiny and the demands of owners.

The research also bears witness to the dissatisfaction of both owners and top managers with the current situation in the shops, and their growing awareness of the need for change in production and employment policies, yet also of the limited means for achieving it. The most advanced figures representing the local elite, owners, top managers and politicians, have firmly put on the agenda the need for substantial private investments and reorganisation of management aimed at achieving world standards in product quality. There are a number of objective external conditions that militate in this direction, such as foreign competition, the obsolescence of Soviet production outlets as well as the feared narrowing of the grey areas for speculation and tax evasion, owing to what respondents referred to as the 'awakening of the State'. The urgency of these challenges and the appetite of owners and their agents for change do not yet prefigure in itself an analytically or practically sound response to the strategic objectives of restructuring.

The current struggle over restructuring between owners and managers, including top management, highlights in fact the profound gulf existing between them while, most obviously, any change in production presupposes an alignment of interests between owners and managers over the pursuit of controlling labour, ultimately achieving 'the real subsumption of labour under capital' (Clarke, 2007, p. 241). Problematising the management–ownership relationship, understanding its features and contradictions, becomes a fundamental task to clarify the undertaking of restructuring and, at the theoretical as well as the practical level, the current state of capitalist development in Russia.

In this perspective, one can observe how owners are trapped in an apparent vicious circle. They have acquired manufacturing enterprises and expect them to become profitable but have very limited control over the way they are managed. So they have come to accept managers' reliance on Soviet practices, which is what the latter are constantly blamed for, if they want production to carry on and businesses to stay afloat. Why, therefore, do owners not carry out the necessary investments providing their businesses with the opportunity for a fresh start? Because, I suspect, they find it difficult to entrust managers with substantial powers and resources at a time when the latter are engaged in a form of management that is definitely inefficient (from the point of view of a capitalist owner). The answer emerging from the accounts of respondents points to the absence of trust as a primary determinant of this impasse. Owners quite reasonably expect managers to deliver in terms of cutting costs, raising quality and reducing the workforce's indiscipline to acceptable levels. Managers at almost all levels feel deprived of the autonomy, the material resources and the rewards which they deem essential for achieving these goals. A crucial argument by the latter consists in the observation that owners expect individual managers to make the difference while organisational changes are just being started, which in their view equates to asking them 'to build the castle in one day' and 'to fight windmills'.

The conflict between managers and owners escalated at the combine following the appearance of outside owners with mutual manifestation of distrust and reciprocal accusations of betraying legitimate expectations. As we saw, initially the matter at issue was dependent on the contingencies of the takeover and revolved around stereotypical (yet bearing much truth) views of outsiders as robber barons and managers as incompetent socialist bureaucrats.

The path of reconciliation and co-operation drawn by the career of our key respondents indicates the potential but also the structural limits of sound management development policies in which both sides engaged in the early 2000s. Under no illusions about the immediate intentions of the owners to commit to investment and managerial autonomy, which disgruntled most middle management, Kolya adopted a tactic of positive engagement, depicting himself as a committed collaborator and enlightened reformer. But, when presented with the task of carrying out restructuring in the combine, he became victim to the direct confrontation between holding management on the one side and factory line management on the other.

If trust implies the granting of autonomy and responsibility to delegated agents, its absence generates the need for direct control. At the combine this acquired escalating proportions, at the same time reproducing and expanding pre-existing Soviet practices, such as administrative control over the use of physical *and* financial resources, minute planning of production, duplication of managerial positions and so forth. Most disruptive of all, in terms of undermining factory top-management authority, is the practice of divisional managers directly scrutinising the activity of key production shops, bypassing the factory director of production, something that had a devastating impact on

Kolya's authority over his closest subordinates and aides and his credibility as a leader invested with real powers.[1] This is to confirm that distrust is not dependent on the contingencies of the outsider–insider confrontation, instead presenting the structural features of a permanent distortion in the mode of administration of the enterprise. If distrust can be seen as a structural feature, related to the problems and contradictions of a Soviet-type organisation, the question arises whether its continued existence at the combine and the Trading House holding as a whole might not be the result of a deliberate policy – in such a case the company-specific strategy aimed at retaining aspects of the system as long as investment is held back and profits made out of the best use of available human and capital stocks – representing therefore just an exceptionally backward case. Looking elsewhere, to more 'mature' cases of restructuring, provides further evidence to the contrary.

The Holding Company has already been introduced in Chapter 5 as an example of a 'fast-moving' business in contrast to the combine's owner, the Trading House. This company represents a case in which, by all standards, restructuring is well under way, approximating the state of such domestic consumer-goods manufacturers as food and drink, long pointed at by foreign analysts as models. In the language of business, the owners have pursued a strategy of technological modernisation oriented towards branded finished goods, consciously seeking to adjust production capacity to market niches. Awareness rather than fear of competition and growing ability to engage with foreign partners are indications of greater confidence and business skills. This was an ideal place for managerial cadres, like our respondents, to find new stimuli and develop professionally.

Kolya has no illusion that his employer might be either fully aware or committed to putting the management of his company into firm managerial hands. His only hopes, he confided in 2006, hinged on the activities of Gregory Moiseev, a top manager who had lobbied the owners to support the introduction of Western managerial systems in the company. Kolya was impressed by his rigorous analysis of managerial problems and his severe assessment of existing practices. At one of the training seminars he organised, Moiseev made the following points: *(a)* the enterprise has grown, acquiring new production facilities, but for the time being production is planned on the basis of forecasts rather than being driven by sales; *(b)* this has put pressure on warehouses and the distribution network; *(c)* the need has therefore arisen for the creation of a proper logistics service for the efficient management of stocks. This area is presently in tatters; it seems the perfect combination of the wrong people in the

---

[1] It is quite remarkable that a practice which scholars of the Soviet economy report appearing as early as the first five-year plan in the 1930s – one of the consequences of forced industrialisation – was still observable in the year 2005. Historically such a practice is seen as one of the symptoms of the then incipient demise of managerial powers under the command economy. This is not to say that adherence to rigid hierarchical command lines should be taken as an invariable feature of modern economic organisations; rather, the problem with this practice is precisely that it was not envisaged in an otherwise extremely hierarchical organisational setup.

wrong places, collecting complaints from all sides. But the response from the holding leadership, i.e. introducing modern information systems and cutting staff, is not the definitive answer; according to Moiseev, it has nothing to do with management.

The real problem is the flow of information and ultimately the definition of the sphere of autonomy and responsibility among various layers of management and different departments. At present, he argues, regional distribution managers have no real instructions or clear guidelines for their activity. Production plans and marketing forecasts decide what they get and what they should sell: but what happens when distribution returns unwanted items or suffers shortages? They can simply do nothing, putting pressure on salesmen to turn things around; but, if the problem persists and bosses are alerted, they can always play each department against the other, planning, marketing, production, all giving different instructions.

Managers' amateurism and inaction is blamed on the individual and normally leads to replacement but actually it is a systemic problem. Paradoxically success is not less damaging than failure since a good performance will yield the junior manager a promotion, once again leaving its department in the dark about how to continue working.

His plans for reform were centred on the introduction of the IDEF technology.[1] This methodology originally applied to software development, but it is understood to be a relevant technology to analyse, assess and restructure organisational routines and information flows. In this case, its appeal derived from the possibility to make managerial activities transparent and therefore liable to rationalisation with a view to the elimination of the 'human factor', i.e. managerial discretion. Its implementation features a regulation of information flows, establishing clear mechanisms and responsibilities for problem-solving and decision-making. Crucial steps include the definition of routines and standards by assessing and formalising managerial activities.

Kolya was extremely enthusiastic and supportive of the introduction of the new technology. In particular he stressed the need to reduce the 'human factor' in decision-making failures that he claimed was the main cause of mismanagement in Russia as opposed to a mere 10 per cent in Western companies. The demotion of Moiseev, entangled in a power struggle with the old but still powerful company vice-director, in late 2006 and the difficulties he himself encountered in introducing rationalisation in the shops made him more cautious about the short-term viability of these technologies. He now believes that the main reason for Moiseev's failure lies in the particular forms of control on which the top manager's authority ultimately rests, and to which his ideas represented a threat. These are, in the first place, the old Soviet favourites – conformism and *stukachestvo* (control by fear of arrest or demotion) – then personal loyalty, acquired via secret funds and under-the-table payments.

---

[1] IDEF stands for Integrated Definition methodology; in practice it is a 'tool that supports the application of methods and methodologies to business needs' analysis' (Hanrahan, 2007).

The problems highlighted by the failure to introduce quality management in logistics and production as well as the continued reliance of top management and owners on loyalty (rather than on trust) and individual initiative (and the fear of demotion or worse in case of failure) rather than 'Western-like' standardised procedures indicate the extent to which enterprise power relations remain deeply rooted in the Soviet tradition.[1] Specifically, this case-study reveals that: *(a)* technological innovation and appointment of qualified managers, the policy followed by the company leaders, can temporarily raise the market leverage of the enterprise leaving managerial problems unaltered; *(b)* it can ease the situation in production but actually increases tensions in other areas, such as marketing and logistics. This also leads us to conclude that the burden of the Soviet legacy is not confined to production and therefore the identification and solution of such problems cannot be reduced to competition between managerial competences and areas but call into question the relationship between ownership and management as a systemic whole.[2]

Theoretically what these findings suggest rather strongly is that the management–ownership relationship is itself contradictory. And trust – or, rather, the lack of it – is a fundamental aspect and manifestation of such a contradiction.

At this point it is important to return to one of the central theoretical tenets of this book, i.e. that the peculiarity of the Soviet economic system rests on the limited control of the elites over the labour process, which translates into a conflictual and distrustful relationship among the agents distributed along the hierarchy of its centralised command structure and particularly between enterprise managers and overarching bodies. In fact managers had to be relied upon to generate and execute plan orders; but, to the extent that such tasks implied managers' mobilisation of labour collectives, they also forced them constantly to distort and falsify plan targets. The use of tight planning and the recurrent innovation campaigns launched by the leadership to enforce productivity growth and innovation countervailed by managers, bargaining for easier plans and resisting modernisation, represent the conflictual (and in the long run paralysing) dynamics generated by this contradiction. From the point of view of each participant in such bargaining the problem consisted in the expected inability of the system to provide sufficient resources to meet the expectations of the leadership.

---

[1] Here it might be worth recalling the considerations made by the manager in charge of overseeing Total Quality Management in the Corporation's top production facility: 'New shops have sprung up in the streets, quality housing is being built, and even factories have seen up-to-date equipment being installed but the command system (*sistema upravleniya*) has remained substantially unchanged' (Interview with Kolya, 2007).

[2] While this case-study also presents important elements pointing towards capitalist development, the point made here serves to identify the key elements characterising the relationship between managerial problems and fundamental contradictions in managerial relations at this stage.

The best way to clarify such a contradictory relation in terms of trust is offered again by Kolya, commenting right after the takeover, on the conflicts with outside owners: he described their relationship as the 'Great Deceit' or *Bolshoj Obman*, meaning that higher-standing bodies would consciously assign tasks which they knew to be unrealistic in order to achieve the maximum possible result from subordinates, while at the same time keeping managers, failing by design, under constant check. This is consistent with a situation in which the dominant group, lacking control over the labour process, also lacked the means, informational and operative, necessary to quantify and implement realistic targets and relied ultimately on individual responsibility, manifested in the form of administrative control and direct interference, as the real incentive to counterbalance centripetal tendencies. From such a perspective the political economy of such a system can be defined as an 'economy of distrust'.

Loyalty, as we have argued consistently throughout the book, was in Soviet times, and to an extent still is, an essential ingredient of the social texture within managerial circles. 'Interpersonal trust', though, cannot be equated with 'trustworthiness as an agent' (Armstrong, 1991, p. 14). Interpersonal relations rather work as a bridge in a context characterised by relative distrust and provide evidence for the absence of mechanisms securing, formalising and reproducing trust between agents. Observation of individual career paths of managers-respondents provides strong anecdotal evidence of the use of informal networking but also bears witness to its crisis (Ledeneva, 1998) due to the increasing difficulty of reconciling mutual commitments with personal interests in a corporate environment shaken by changes in ownership, lay-offs and so forth. Networks do not simply disappear, though; rather, they seem to reorganise along new social lines – a process far from consolidation as it necessarily depends on, and interacts with, the settlement of managerial status at a formal level.

The temporary composition of interests in Soviet management rested on the fact that managerial practices represent ultimately an effective form of social control consistent with the then primary objective of eliciting workers' efforts towards the fulfilment of planned physical output. The problem arises when, with privatisation and then with the appearance of outside ownership, demands from above gradually shift towards the achievement of financial and quality objectives, i.e. from product to commodity, introducing a new set of contradictions, namely between the production of things and the generation of profit, familiar to the management of the capitalist enterprise but alien to Soviet management and the system of social relations upon which it relies. Before exploring the consequences and possible outcomes of such a change, it is necessary to consider the form in which the ownership–management relationship exists in the capitalist system and explore how trust and control function within it.

Theoretically this work is founded on the presupposition that the enterprise, and management structures within it, should be understood as a social construct shaped by power relations and characterised by crisis and contradictions. To analyse it requires a comparative and historical perspective which recognises that managerial issues differ substantially depending on the environment in which they develop.

As we have seen in the case of the Italian consultants and more generally in relation to mainstream transition theories, mainstream managerial approaches provide little help in this respect as they fail to recognise: *(a)* the specificity of the British and American conception of management, which conveys the notion of a function in its own right, 'exclusively identified with planning the profitable deployment of capital . . . and with the . . . control of subordinates to that end' (Armstrong, 1989, p. 310); *(b)* the identification of management with capital functions. This second point in turn poses further questions; on the one side, stands the risk of reducing management to a mere control function, ultimately identifying managers with capitalists, i.e. owners, which reduces managerial work itself to a 'black box'; on the other side, the issue has been raised, specifically within the labour process debate in relation to the emergence of critical management, to avoid the 'depressing prospect' of falling into theoretical speculations generating 'venerable pseudo-problems concerned with the mismanagement of management' (Armstrong, 1989, pp. 310–12).

The possibility of problematising managerial issues of control and decision-making without losing sight of the fact that real managerial work occurs in the circuit of capital is best dealt with in the context of a 'critical agency theory' (Armstrong, 1991). Its main assumptions are that managerial tasks cannot be separated from 'managerial social relationships' and, therefore, 'the managerial problem', from the point of view of ownership, 'is not one of expertise but of agency' (ibid., 1989, pp. 311–12). Only that classical agency theory is based on a paradigm of individual utility maximisation and it is mainly concerned with the design of appropriate incentive and monitoring systems aimed at aligning managerial interests with that of the owners in order to fight opportunism, identified with an undetermined concept of moral hazard.

A critical approach, instead, moves from the idea that principals have to trust someone and in the context of complex capitalist organisations owners have to trust managers since they cannot trust workers! Monitoring and incentives do not eliminate the need for trust, which becomes the term on which this contradictory relationship hinges. Yet the social construction of trust, its commodification, is expensive, and employers are tempted to dispense with it on economic grounds. The history of capitalist organisations is characterised by the dynamics of control and trust.

The development of management can be understood in terms of attempts to solve the agency problem, driven by competition between agents interested in securing 'the loyalty dividends' attached to high trust positions. The main function of new managerial professions is to provide principals with economies, derived from replacing trust with control of existing agents and delegating routine elements of managerial work to subordinates, ultimately achieving greater control over labour.

The major point of this conception contributing to a comparative perspective consists in highlighting the agency role played by managers themselves in designing control strategies; second, that such strategies succeeded in winning employers' support because they responded to the need of capital to increase control and profit extraction from enterprises. From this vantage point, the managerial problem in Russia can be looked upon from a new perspective.

First of all, it becomes clear that management in Russia exists as such only in name. The formation of a managerial stratum acting in the interest of capitalist employers is certainly in the making but it is a historical process to be ascertained rather than assumed. This task cannot be reduced to change in corporate culture (production collectivism versus market individualism),[1] a shift in professions (finance and marketing rather than engineering) or generational turnover (young business graduates replacing Soviet-era executives).

What qualifies management is less expertise than the ability to make decisions in the interest of employers, in particular regarding the control of subordinates. It is the active contribution of managers to their novel design or implementation – to the extent that existing organisational technologies might be imported and adapted to the Russian context – that characterises capitalist development in the Russian enterprise.

Historically, scientific management first appeared in Western capitalist countries as the strategy of a specific profession, the engineers, to break up workers' control of the labour process. Despite many claims to the contrary, the Soviet enterprise was not organised along Fordist and Taylorist principles and resembled a nineteenth-century workshop dominated by several layers of cadre workers. It is likely that capitalist development in Russian manufacturing should see substantial changes in this area. This is not to suggest that Russian line managers might follow an identical path or in fact reach the same conclusions as early US managers but to recognise what is at stake in the conflict clearly observable in the case-study enterprises.

If we look at the Russian managerial problem in terms of the trust and control dynamic at a very general level, we can say that, whereas the capitalist ownership-management relationship is built on trust, or aims at its achievement, in the Russian case, to the extent that it retains its Soviet features, it is instead focused on control. It was the cadre workers, including in some cases shop chiefs, that were entrusted with the control of the production process in the Stalinist model of work organisation. A restructuring of management can not but put into question such an arrangement, leading to a break-up of this structure, the subordination of these agents, with all the consequences in terms of possible conflict with the workforce.

A dominant theme in management restructuring in Russia is represented by the idea of integration of line management into the managerial structure. It is evident from the aforementioned considerations that such an approach fails to

---

[1] Clarke (2004) correctly relates the problem to the fundamental contradiction between capitalist ownership and Soviet production with management caught in the middle. Here we want to emphasise the processual character of management restructuring driven by the conflict over decision-making powers, trust and commitment among different groups of management and between them and the owners.

capture the contradictory and potentially conflictual nature of the process of change. In a way, line managers are already integrated, only in a distrustful relationship, within enterprise administration. Second, if integration means subordination to capitalist management to the extent that this implies not overcoming but replacing one contradictory relationship with another, it is inevitably going to produce resistance, especially from all those cadres who are bound to lose from this new deal.

Russian employers have initially attempted to reinforce control, on both workers *and* managers, pursuing a quite indiscriminate strategy – most likely, it can be said, in order to avoid direct confrontation with any specific group. It is now clear why this has generated resistance on the side of both lower ranks in production, who have seen their customary sphere of influence curtailed, but also of top enterprise executives who have been given greater responsibilities without powers. The break-up of vertical solidarities under such pressures has produced the need and the room but not yet the answer to such problems. The work of managers like Kolya and Moiseev shows how managers with a background in production are shifting their allegiances, prefiguring a new alliance between owners and enterprise executives.

The role of the 'public hand': industry perspectives and policy options

The main thrust that sustained transition ideologically has been the idea that the State is a bad decision-maker in the economic realm and the running of the economy should be placed in private hands. Neoliberal reforms have formally put the economic apparatus of the country in private hands or otherwise subjected it to the rules of the 'market', but large-scale privatisation and liberal legislation have not solved by themselves the question as to what role the State should play in the new economy. On these grounds, once again, liberal economists have insisted on the assumption that public intervention is universally harmful and ineffective, blaming drawbacks in the expected progress of the reform programme on the failure to achieve the full operation of private initiative *vis-à-vis* continued state interference in the economy.

In the aftermath of the 1998 crisis, economic recovery and political stabilisation – with a marked authoritarian character – have once again raised fears that the state might regain a strong economic role with the alleged effect of further hindering enterprise restructuring. In synthetic terms the impact of public intervention on enterprise restructuring – whether by regulation or by direct management – is reduced to a strictly dualistic model in which, on the one side, stands the sequence state intervention, protectionism and continuity of Soviet legacies and, on the other, liberalisation, competition and restructuring. In this final section we would like to focus on this question within the limits of our regional and sectoral settings, proposing a different approach.

In previous chapters, it has become apparent how the separation of functions between state bureaucracy and privatised enterprises was very much in the making with a quite substantial confusion of roles. This was very much the case because in the Soviet Union, unlike in the Eastern European popular democracies, economic structures had been erected contextually to the party-state apparatus and their management represented its core function. As well observed by Granick, enterprise top managers and party-state bureaucrats were very much one and the same breed.

More than privatisation, it was the severance of informal networks in the state-party hierarchy that set them adrift. The development of this relationship has since been characterised by ambiguous and contradictory movements rather than by a linear and clear-cut process of differentiation of interests and definition of roles. Federal and local authorities had subscribed to the liberal manifesto in view to regaining control over the economy via economic mechanisms rather than administrative ones, yet individual officials always felt entitled to intervene whenever personal or political interests dictated.

Red directors and, more obviously, new owners pursued privatisation in order to free themselves from the tutelage of administrative bodies but had difficulties in reconciling this with the fact that ultimately they relied on the complicity of the authorities to legitimise their ownership rights as well as to provide the regulatory and fiscal environment essential to the survival of the industry. In a striking analogy with what some historians observe to be the situation of the incipient capitalism of czarist Russia, it can be said that state authorities are at one time liberal and interventionist while industrialists show growing discomfort at state interference while constantly seeking protections and favours from the authorities. The challenge consists in moving from petty tutelage towards effective regulation, including a consistent industrial and social policy.

The textile industry both owes and requires public support for a number of reasons: *(a)* It has been badly discriminated against throughout the entire Soviet period; *(b)* it suffered a major blow from ill-conceived liberalisation; *(c)* both its Eastern and Western competitors have received state support of some kind. The crucial question revolves around the role that federal and regional authorities should play at a time when the availability of large budget surpluses allows public intervention but also heightens the risks of mismanagement and misappropriation by local elites. The recent debate around the agenda for the Ivanovo industrial region provides a good example of such entanglements.

At the end of 2004 the Ivanovo representatives in the Russian Federal Council began a lobbying campaign to achieve public support in the form of subsidies, tax relief and the like in favour of the textile industry (Preobrazhenskaya, 2005). They expressed a firm conviction that the industry still had a role to play in the regional economy and that local businesses were committed to doing their part; yet, they argued, the State has to intervene to create a level playing-field in competitive conditions *vis-à-vis* foreign competitors. On the other side, evidence from a wide range of sources questions the actual willingness of textile oligarchs to cope with these challenges and the desirability of public support for the industry.

A good starting point is the agenda set by the lobbyists themselves. After admitting that 'enterprises are mostly private and therefore it is not to the state that we should look for solutions, in the first instance', it is suggested that 'issues concerning the sector should be divided into three categories: (1) those pertaining to the owners; (2) those concerning the regional administration; and (3) those requiring state intervention' (Preobrazhenskaya, 2005).

As for the first point, the priorities are, in their view, technological modernisation, the introduction of modern management techniques and ISO-based quality systems. While the need to intervene in all these areas might attract little disagreement, it is the complexity and the scale of these issues and the awareness of managers and owners to solve them that is questionable. As previously mentioned, in 2005 most industry equipment was still obsolete, and few businesses have so far implemented serious modernisation plans.

Technological reconstruction is essential, but changing the behaviour of workers and line managers requires equally wholesale changes in management. In this area, as we saw, experiments have been conducted since the late 1990s, so far without achieving substantial change. Managers involved over many years in implementing these reforms talk of little awareness at the top and of hostility to change at the bottom. The picture is one of over-centralisation with little managerial autonomy; rigid planning but lack of procedures and monitoring. Holdings are still very loose organisations pursuing short-term profits. Their reorganisation as efficient capitalist enterprises is a complex process dependent on competitive pressures, technical change and growth in managerial autonomy and responsibility.

Yet public regulation and institutional pressure for greater responsibility and transparency in corporate matters is essential to facilitate this process.

In order to sustain restructuring in terms outlined above, the lobbyists suggest measures such as fiscal allowances and financial support towards the purchase of key imports, including raw materials and foreign equipment, stricter regulation of imports and actions against counterfeiting and local support to innovative enterprises on a non-preferential basis. While these measures are all legitimate and useful, they are also clearly insufficient.

The monoindustrial character of the region suggests that its crisis be better understood as part of a more general decline similar to the experience of other 'old industrial regions' in Europe (Treivish, 2004). Public intervention should learn from these cases in that it should design a comprehensive set of measures aimed at revitalising the social and economic environment in the region. This implies the need to overcome what has been so far the dominant ideological frame in which local discussions about the industry have developed, i.e. the idea of Ivanovo as a Textile District (*Tekstil'nyj Raion*). Identifying the region with the industry and its inhabitants, including workers, managers and owners, with an unspecified category of stakeholders (*Tekstilschiki*) has in fact: *(a)* contributed to reinforcing the acquiescence of workers, trade unions and authorities towards the virtual monopoly over economic activities by textile oligarchs; *(b)* justified enormous sacrifices in the name of 'saving the industry'; while actually *(c)* preventing enterprises from carrying out restructuring.

In reality it is hard to believe that existing enterprises might retain current levels of employment if restructuring is carried out. Under present circumstances the effect would be to depress employment and wage levels further, contributing little to the welfare of most employees and the general population. Only the creation of alternative sources of employment can stem the demographic crisis which has made Ivanovo a 'shrinking city' and put pressure on the labour market for the industry to raise its job and pay profiles. This can hardly be achieved in the short term without regional authorities supporting 'true' entrepreneurial activities and sectoral diversification by investing in education, retraining and infrastructures.

What has made it possible for the industry to decline in such a fashion is, among other things, the qualification of the industry as a 'women's sector' (*Zhenskaya Otrasl'*) which combines gender segregation with the dis qualification of women's work (Filtzer, 1992). It would there fore be essential for the trade unions and public authorities alike to engage critically with such issues, putting into question institutions that perpetuate women's marginality such as the separation of educational and work career paths between sexes, the absence or disappearance of public services relieving women from the family burden, and the systematic exclusion of women from decision-making bodies.

A major obstacle to such initiatives being adopted and correctly implemented is the almost non-existence of popular participation in decision-making, the weakness of the trade unions and the strong links between business and political leaders. The Ivanovo region is renowned for high levels of corruption, exemplified by scandals involving major figures in the governor's administration and bitter confrontation between the then governor and textile oligarchs over alleged tax evasion (Interview with political consultant, 2005).

The present social and political climate makes a shift in policies of the kind referred to above unlikely to happen in the short term. In the absence of change, the most likely scenario is regrettably one of slow and partial change in the industry accompanied by uneven regional development marked by outward migration, growth in the informal economy and low-profile service activities and persistence of poverty and decay. The policy conclusions outlined above are primarily aimed at highlighting that it will take more than the simple operation of market forces or traditional pro-industry policies to reverse the decline of this industrial region and to improve substantially the working and living conditions of its inhabitants.

Final considerations

As the research process unfolded, thematic areas began to take shape and analysis develop along a clearer track; it also became evident that a good deal of material had been collected for which no sufficient commentary had been produced and, by the same token, significant leads from fieldwork, however promising and relevant, had not been pursued.

For example, the largest factories in the region, despite bankruptcies and lay-offs, still sported staffing levels up to and above three thousand workers, representing a clear sign of continuity. Yet observation and reports indicate that these were far from being the labour collectives of the Soviet time and the 1990s transition. The outflow of qualified cadres and low-profile recruitment among the urban unemployed and unskilled youth means that the 'class composition' is changing. More importantly, the close-knit set of personal ties that regulated informal relations and made it possible, with the smooth generational turnover, to sustain and reproduce informal managerial practices has been severely damaged by these labour-market shocks. In the short term this increases difficulties for management on the shop floor but can represent a powerful spur in favour of greater managerial regulation and ultimately control over the workplace.

The break-up of enterprise networks is equally important for changes in social relations outside production. It has already been pointed out how the dismantling of enterprise-centred networks should shift attention towards other types of linkage and related survival strategies. Further research should point to the opening up and restructuring of existing ties which seems influenced by geographically specific patterns of employment as well as by the deepening of the social divide. For many of our key respondents, both male and female, the option pursued was self-employment or semi-autonomous activities, including production or sale of goods outside their living area. In these cases factory links weakened substantially while family links were reinforced and new business ties developed. For those who stayed in manufacturing, informal ties lost the character of stability and universality enjoyed in the past to become weaker in the sense employed by Granovetter (1973). The effect of these dynamics both on the workplace and on the wider social context might be significant.

Throughout the book we have stressed the crucial role of the gender division of labour and of gendered patterns of bargaining and resistance as well as of gendered stereotyping and ideologies. In an industry largely staffed by women but dominated by men in a 'male economy' it is evident that social relations in production are structured by gender no less than by class; or, to be more precise, one cannot be conceived without the other. Yet it was not possible to follow such a research lead further in order to establish stronger and more general hypotheses on the position of women workers and the reciprocal interaction of gendered workplaces and the overall gender order in the Soviet and post-Soviet society (Ashwin, 2000, 2006).

The question at stake is the persistence of gender discrimination at work in the face of the apparent adherence of women workers to traditional gender roles and quiescence to continued discrimination and increased exploitation. Our main argument is that women are subjected *as workers* to the form of atomisation that affects workers in general; this in turn prevents them *as women* from perceiving the discriminatory character of gendered employment patterns relegating them to industries and professions with lower pay, skills and job-market appeal.

The gendered segmentation that exists in the internal job market and the feminisation of professions allow for continued discrimination against women at work. This rigid gendered pattern results in a profound gulf between men and women in terms of their experience and understanding of work, reinforcing the ideological construct of an alleged natural gender order. Nevertheless, in my view, the persistence of gender segregation in the workplace cannot be simply ascribed to the efficacy of managerial control or patriarchal ideology but rather must be interpreted as resulting from a specific patriarchal system, which calls for considering the position of women in society. While the literature so far seems to have considered the two issues separately, it is only by combining them that a plausible explanation can be brought forward.

In particular, the dominant trend has been to focus on individualised dimensions such as labour-market strategies, survival strategies or business endeavours, while such a 'liberal' approach to gender has left aside its social content, paying little attention to the collective experience of the majority of Russian women.

Such limitations, as is often the case, are very much the results of the many practical and intellectual turns that over time the research, and the researcher, have gone through, but ultimately respond to the simple need to keep a publication plan within reasonable limits of time and space. While committing to strive for completion and continuous improvement of this research, I would like to invite the community of those committed to the object of our research to build further on these findings.

References

Adams, D. and Vassilieva, Y. (2003a) 'Global Agriculture Information Network Report: Russian Federation Cotton and Products' (Report #RS3002), United States Department for Agriculture: Foreign Agricultural Service: http://www.fas.usda.gov.

Adams, D. and Vassilieva, Y. (2003b) 'Global Agriculture Information Network Report: Russian Federation Cotton and Products' (Report #RS3015), United States Department for Agriculture: Foreign Agricultural Service: http://www.fas.usda.gov.

Adams, D. and Vassilieva, Y. (2004) 'Global Agriculture Information Network Report: Russian Federation Cotton and Products Report' (#RS4012), United States Department for Agriculture: Foreign Agricultural Service: http://www.fas.usda.gov.

Adams, D. and Vassilieva, Y. (2005) 'Global Agriculture Information Network Report: Russian Federation Cotton and Products' (Report #RS5015), United States Department for Agriculture: Foreign Agricultural Service: http://www.fas.usda.gov.

Amodio, N. (1993) 'From Ministries to Corporations', *Journal of Communist Studies,* 9, 1, 227–39.

Armstrong, P. (1984) 'Competition between the Organisational Professions and the Evolution of Management Control Strategies', in *Work, Employment & Unemployment* (Ed. Thompson, K.), Open University Press: Milton Keynes, pp. 97–120.

Armstrong, P. (1989) 'Management, Labour Process and Agency', *Work, Employment & Society,* 3, 3, 307–22.

Armstrong, P. (1991) 'Contradictions and Social Dynamics in the Capitalist Agency Relationship', *Accounting, Organisations and Society,* 16, 1, 1–25.

Arnot, B. (1988) *Controlling Soviet Labour,* Macmillan: Basingstoke.

Ashwin, S. (Ed.) (2000) *Gender, State, and Society in Soviet and post-Soviet Russia*, Routledge: London/NY.

Ashwin, S. (Ed.) (2006) *Adapting to Russia's New Labour Market: Gender and Employment Behaviour*, Routledge: London/NY.

Aslund, A. (1995) *How Russia Became a Market Economy,* Brookings Institution: Washington, DC.

Bailes, K. E. (1978) *Technology and Society under Lenin and Stalin,* Princeton University Press: Princeton, NY.

Bell, C. and Newby, H. (Eds) (1977) *Doing Sociological Research,* Allen & Unwin: London.

Berliner, J. (1957) *Factory and Manager in the USSR,* Harvard University Press: Cambridge, Mass.

Berliner, J. (1988) *Soviet industry from Stalin to Gorbachev: Essays on Management and Innovation,* Elgar: Aldershot.

Bertolissi, S. (1978) 'L' organizzazione scientifica del lavoro nella Russia degli anni '20', in *Studi di Storia Sovietica* (Eds Benvenuti, F., Bertolissi, S., di Biagio, A. and Sestan, L.), Editori Riuniti: Roma.

Blasi, J. R., Kroumova, M. and Kruse, D. (1997) *Kremlin Capitalism: Privatising the Russian Economy,* ILR Press: Ithaca, NY.

Bowers, E. (1996) 'Gender Stereotyping and the Gender Division of Labour in Russia', in *Conflict and Change in the Russia Industrial Enterprise* (Ed. Clarke, S.), pp. 191–209.

Burowoy, M. (2001) 'Transition without Transformation: Russia's Involutionary Road to Capitalism', *East European Politics and Societies,* 15, 2, 269–90.

Clark, E. (2004) 'Power, Action and Constraint in Strategic Management: Explaining Enterprise Restructuring in Czech Republic', *Organization Studies,* 25, 4, 607–27.

Clark, R. (1979) *The Japanese Company,* Yale University Press: New Haven, Conn./London.

Clarke, S. (1993) 'The Contradictions of "State Socialism" ', in *What About the Workers: Workers and the Transition to Capitalism in Russia* (Eds Clarke, S., Fairbrother, P., Burawoy, M. and Krotov, P.), Verso: London.

Clarke, S. and Kabalina, V. (1994) 'Privatisation and the Struggle for Control of the Enterprise in Russia', *Conference on Russia in Transition*, Unpublished paper: Cambridge.

Clarke, S. (Ed.) (1996) *The Russian Enterprise in Transition: Case Studies,* Edward Elgar: Cheltenham.

Clarke, S. (2002) 'What Do Enterprise Trade Unions Do', *BASEES 2002,* Unpublished paper: Cambridge.

Clarke, S. (2004) 'A Very Soviet Form of Capitalism? The Management of Holding Companies in Russia', *Post-Communist Economies,* 16, 4, 405–22.

Clarke, S. (2007) *The Development of Capitalism in Russia,* Routledge: Abingdon/New York.

Clarke, S. and Kabalina, V. (1994) 'Privatisation and the Struggle for Control of the Enterprise in Russia', *Conference on Russia in Transition,* Unpublished: Cambridge.

Collison, D. L. (1992) *Managing the Shop Floor: Subjectivity, Masculinity and Workplace Culture,* de Gruyter: Berlin/New York.

Cowley, A. (1995) 'A silent revolution', *Economist*, Vol. 335, 3–5.

Dakli, A. (2000) 'Chi Comanda nelle Fabbriche Russe', *Il Manifesto.*

Di Leo, R. (1973) *Operai e fabbrica in Unione Sovietica nelle lettere alla 'Pravda' e al 'Trud',* De Donato: Bari.

Di Leo, R. (1980) *Occupazione e Salari nell' URSS, 1950–1977,* Etas Libri: Milano.

Di Leo, R. (1983) *L' Economia Sovietica tra Crisi e Riforme (1965–1982),* Liguori: Napoli.

Di Leo, R. (1985) 'La gestione populista delle relazioni industriali nell' URSS degli anni '80', *Giornale di Diritto del Lavoro e di Relazioni Industriali,* n. 26.

Di Leo, R. (1993) 'The Former USSR in Search of New Rules', in *The Soviet Transition: From Gorbachev to Yeltsin* (Eds White, S., Di Leo, R. and Cappelli, O.), Frank Cass: London.

Dore, R. (1973) *British Factory–Japanese Factory: The Origins of National Diversity in Industrial Relations,* Allen & Unwin: London.

Ericson, R. E. (1998) 'Economics and the Russian Transition', *Slavic Review,* 57, 3, 609–25.

Federal Service of State Statistics (2004) *The Ivanovo Region in 2003*, Ivanovo Region Branch of the Federal Statistical Service: Ivanovo.

Filtzer, D. (1986) *Soviet Workers and Stalinist Industrialization: The Formation of Modern Soviet Production Relations, 1928–1941,* Pluto Press: London.

Filtzer, D. (1992) *Soviet Workers and De-Stalinization: The Consolidation of the Modern System of Soviet Production Relations, 1953–1964,* Cambridge University Press: Cambridge.

Filtzer, D. (1994) *Soviet Workers and the Collapse of Perestroika: The Soviet Labour Process and Gorbachev's Reforms, 1985–1991,* Cambridge University Press: Cambridge.

Fligstein, N. (1990) *The Transformation of Corporate Control*, Harvard University Press: Cambridge, Mass./London.

Frydman, R., Pistor, K. and Rapaczynski, A. (1996) 'Investing in Insider-dominated Firms: A Study of Russian Vaucher Privatization Funds', in *Corporate Governance in Central Europe and Russia: Insiders and the State*, Vol. 2 (Eds Frydman, R., Gray, C. W. and Rapaczynski, A.), Central European University Press: Budapest/London, pp. 187–241.

Glickman, R. L. (1984) *Russian Factory Women,* University of California Press: Berkeley, Calif..

Goble, P. (1997) 'Russia: Analysis from Washingon – The Paradoxes of Privatisation', *RFE/EL.*

Grabher, G. and Stark, D. (1998) 'Organising Diversity: Evolutionary Theory, Network Analysis and Post-socialism', in *Theorising Transition: The Political Economy of Post-communist Transformations* (Eds Pickles, J. and Smith, A.), Routledge: London, pp. 54–75.

Grancelli, B. (1995) 'Il Management Post-Sovietico', *Sviluppo e Organizzazione,* 149, 24–42.

Granick, D. (1954) *Management of the Industrial Firm in the USSR,* Columbia University Press: New York.

Granick, D. (1960) *The Red Executive,* Macmillan: London.

Granovetter, M. (1973). 'The Strength of Weak Ties', *American Journal of Sociology*, 78, 6, 1360–80.

Gregory, P. R. (1989) 'Soviet Bureaucratic Behaviour: Khozyaistvenniki and Apparatchiki', *Soviet Studies, 41*, 4, 511–25.

Grimond, J. (1997) 'From Marx, Maybe to Market', *Economist*, 344, 11–13.

Gurkov, I. (1998) 'Ownership and Control in Russian Privatized Companies: New Evidence from a Repeated Survey', *Communist Economies and Economic Transformation, 10*, 2, 259–70.

Hanrahan, R. P. (2007) 'The IDEF Process Modeling Methodology', http://www.stsc.hill.af.mil/crosstalk/1995/06/IDEF.asp: Software Technology Support Center.

Hanzl, D. and Havlik, P. (2003) 'Textiles in Central Eastern Europe and Russia: A Comparative Analysis in the European Context', *East–West Journal of Economics and Business, 6*, 2, 63–88.

Hendley, K. (1998) 'Struggling to Survive: A Case-study of Adjustment at a Russian Enterprise', *Europe–Asia Studies, 50*, 1, 91–119.

ILO (1995) 'The Effects of Technological Changes in the Clothing Industry', *Recent Developments in the Clothing Industry, Reports for the Tripartite Meeting*, ILO: Geneva.

ILO (1996) 'Effects on employment and working conditions', *Globalisation of the footwear, textiles and clothing industries, Report for the Tripartite Meeting*, ILO: Geneve.

Ivanov, I. (2005) 'V Sostave Kholdinga <<Yakovlevskij>> Tekstil'nye Predpriyatiya Stabil'no Dvizhutsya Vpered' (Once they have joined the Yakovlevskij Holding Company textile enterprises develop steadily), *Tekstil'nyj Kraj,* 31, 67, 1.

Ivanov, S. (2001) 'Light Industry 1991–2000', *Kommersant – Russia's Daily Online*, http: //www.kommersant.com.

Ivanova, N. (2001) 'Poshchitaem Kopeechki' (Let's count the pennies), *Privolzhskij Rabochij*, 1.

Johnson, J. (1997) 'Russian Emerging Financial–Industrial Groups', *Post-Soviet Affairs, 13*, 4, 333–65.

Kabalina, V. (2005) 'The Management of Enterprises in Holding Companies', *Management Structures, Employment Relations and Class Formation in Russia Project Seminar*, unpublished: Sharm-el-Sheik.

Kapushinski, R. (1994) *Imperium*, Feltrinelli: Milano.

Keune, M. (1996) *Economic Restructuring and Employment Promotion in a Russian Crisis Region: The Case of Ivanovo*, ILO Central and Eastern European Team: Budapest.

Kirsch, L. J. (1972) *Soviet Wages: Changes in Structure and Administration since 1956,* MIT Press: Cambridge, Mass.

Kouznetsov, A. (2004a) 'Russian Old-Industry Regions in the Transformation Process', in *Ivanovo – Eine Stadt in Postsozialistishcher Transformation*, Vol. 1, http: //www.shrinkingcities.com, pp. 28–30.

Kouznetsov, A. (2004b) 'Ivanovo Region (Ivanovskaya Oblast')', in *Ivanovo – Eine Stadt in Postsozialistishcher Transformation*, Vol. 1, http://www.shrinkingcities.com, pp. 31–40.

Kreuger, G. (2004) *Enterprise Restructuring and the Role of Managers in Russia*, Sharpe: New York/London.

Lazonick, W. (1991) *Business Organization and the Myth of the Market Economy*, Cambridge University Press: Cambridge.

Ledeneva, A. V. (1998) *Russia's Economy of Favours: Blat, Networking and Informal Exchange*, Cambridge University Press: Cambridge.

Lester, J. (1995) *Modern Tsars and Princes: The Struggle for Hegemony in Russia*, Verso: London.

Linz, S. (1988) 'Managerial Autonomy in Soviet Firms', *Soviet Studies, 49*, 2, 175–195.

Linz, S. and Moskoff, W. (Eds) (1989) *Reorganization and Reform in the Soviet Economy*, M. E. Sharpe: Armonk, NY.

Lipsic', I. V. (Ed.) (2000) *Monoprofil'nye Goroda i Gradoobrazujuschie Predprijatija* (Company Towns and City-making Enterprises), Ekspertnyj Institut: Moscow.

Littler, C. (1984) 'Soviet-type Societies and the Labour Process', in *Work, Employment and Unemployment* (Ed. Thompson, K.), Open University Press: Milton Keynes/Philadelphia, Pa.

Monousova, G. (1996) 'Gender Differentiation and Industrial Relations', in *Conflict and change in the Russia Industrial Enterprise* (Ed. Clarke, S.), pp. 162–90.

Morrison, C. and Schwartz, G. (2003) 'Managing the Labour Collective: The Wage Systems in Russian Industrial Enterprises', *Europe–Asia Studies, 55*, 4, 553–74.

Naishul', V. A. (1991) *The Supreme and Last Stage of Socialism*, The Centre for Research into Communist Economies: London.

OETH (1999) *The EU Textile and Clothing Sector*, OETH: Brussels.

Okhotnikova, V. R. (2001) 'Ivanovskie Stradanja', *Rynok Legkoj Promyshlennosti*, 13, 9–11.

Okhotnikova, V. (2006) 'Andrej Smirnov: <<Nam Nuzhny usloviya . . .>>' (Andrej Smirnov: 'We have to be provided with an enviroment where textile manufacturing is no less profitable than in China or Pakistan'), *Chastnik.ru*, http: //www.chastnik.ru.

Parker, A. (1998) 'Staying On-side on the Inside: Problems and Dilemmas in Ethnography', *Sociology Review, 7*, 3, 10-13.

Polonsky, G. and Edwards, V. (1998) 'Transformation in Russia: insights from the Russian Province', *Leadership & Organisation, 19*, 1, 332-339.

Preobrazhenskaya, T. (2005) 'Tekstil' s Vysoty <<Federal'nogo Poleta>>' (Textiles from the Heights of Federal Authorities), *Chastnik.ru*, http: //www.chastnik.ru.

Privolzhskij Rabochij (2000) 'Prikaz o naznacheniyakh' (Instructions about appointments), p. 2.

Privolzhskij Rabochij (2001a) 'Zaderzhany c Pokhischennym' (Detained with stolen goods), p. 4.

Privolzhskij Rabochij (2001b) 'Zaderzhana c Pokhischennym' (Detained with stolen goods), p. 4.

Privolzhskij Rabochij (2001c) 'Ot chego v Prjadenii Veselej gudenie?' (What spinners are so happy about), p. 2.

Privolzhskij Rabochij (2001d) 'A Otdacha Slabovata' (Yet performance is still weak), p. 1.

Privolzhskij Rabochij (2001f) 'Davajte Razberemsya do Kontsa' (Let's have a better look into it), 2.

Rossman, J. (1997a) 'The Teikovo Cotton Workers' Strike of April 1932: Class, Gender and Identity Politics in Stalin's Russia', *Russian Review,* 56, 1, 44–69.

Rossman, J. (1997b) *Worker Resistance under Stalin: Class and Gender in the Textile Mills of the Ivanovo Industrial Region, 1928–1932,* UMI: University of California: Berkeley, Calif..

Rossman, J. (2005) *Worker Resistance under Stalin,* Harvard University Press: Cambridge, Mass./London.

Sachs, J. (1993) *Poland's Jump to the Market Economy,* MIT Press: Cambridge, Mass./London.

Sapelli, G. (1990) *L' Impresa come Problema Storiografico,* Il Saggiatore: Milano.

Scheffer, M. (1994) 'The Changing Map of European Textiles: Production and Sourcing Strategies of Textile and Clothing Firms', OETH: Brussels.

Schelkov, A. and Antonov, I. (1998) *Navoloki,* Ivanovskaja Gazeta: Ivanovo.

Schroeder, G. (1989) 'Soviet Economic Reform 'Decrees': More Steps on the Treadmill', in *Soviet Economy in the 1980's: Problems and Prospects* (Ed. US Congress Joint Economic Committee), US GPO: Washington, pp. 65–88.

Scott, J. C. (1985) *Weapons of the Weak: Everyday Forms of Peasant Resistance,* Yale University Press: New Haven/London.

Siegelbaum, L. H. (1988) *Stakhanovism and the Politics of Productivity in the USSR, 1935–1941,* Cambridge University Press: Cambridge.

Singleton, J. (1997) *The World Textile Industry,* Routledge: London.

Sloveva, E. (2001) 'Profgruporg – Figura Ser'eznaya' (The importance of Trade Union cells), *Privolzhskij Rabochij*, p. 2.

Smirnov, E. (2000) 'Kombinat Mozhet i Budet Rabotat' (The combine can and will continue working), *Privolzhskij Rabochij*, pp. 1–3.

Smirnov, E. (2001a) 'Menya Bespokoit Ravnodushie Ljudej . . .' (I am concerned with people's well-being), *Privolzhskij Rabochij*, pp. 1–2.

Smirnov, E. (2001b) 'V Profkome OAO' (At the Trade Union Committee of the enterprise), *Privolzhskij Rabochij*, pp. 1–2.

Smirnov, E. (2001c) 'Znajte: Vas Nikto ne Brosit' (Reporting from the Trade Unions conference), *Privolzhskij Rabochij*, pp. 1–3.

Spinanger, D. (1995) 'Textiles Beyond the MFA Phase-out', in *Beyond the Multifibre Arrangement: Third World Competition and Restructuring Europe's Textile Industry* (Eds. Navaretti, G. B., Faini, R. and Silberston, A.), OECD.

Sprouse, M. (Ed.) (1992) *Sabotage in the American Workplace: Anecdotes of Dissatisfaction, Mischief and Revenge,* Pressure Drop Press: San Francisco, Calif.

Sutton, A. C. (1968) *Western Technology and Soviet Economic Development,* Hoover Institution Publications: Stanford, Calif.

Suvorov, L. (2002) 'Khronika Odnogo Dnja' (A one day chronicle), *Privolzhskij Rabochij*, p. 2.

Svetlakov, L. (1997) 'Kadry Vse Reshajut' (Cadres decide everything), *Privolzhskij Rabochij*, p. 2.

Svetlakov, L. (2001) 'Poka Grom ne Grjanet' (As long as you can get off scot-free), *Privolzhskij Rabochij*, p. 1.

Taranova, V. (2001) 'Radi Yasnosti, v Dukhe Glasnosti' (Clarification about the norms in spinning), *Privolzhskij Rabochij*, p. 1.

Ticktin, H. (1992) *Origins of the Crisis in the USSR: Essays on the Political Economy of a Disintegrating System,* M. E. Sharpe: Armonk, NY/London.

Treivish, A. (2004) 'Ivanovo Long-term Socio-economic and Urban Development', in *Ivanovo – Eine Stadt in Postsozialistishcher Transformation*, Vol. 1, http: //www.shrinkingcities.com, pp. 11–27.

Upper Volga Textile Combine (1998) *Pravila Vnutrennogo Trudovogo Rasporjadka* (Enterprise Code of Conduct): Ivanovo.

Vassileva, Y. and Hager, R. (2002) 'Global Agriculture Information Network Report: Russian Federation Cotton and Products' (Report #RS2013), United States Department for Agriculture: Foreign Agricultural Service: http: //www.fas.usda.gov.

Vassileva, Y. and Trachtenberg, E. (1998) 'Global Agriculture Information Network Report: Russian Federation Cotton' (Report #RS8075), United States Department for Agriculture: Foreign Agricultural Service: http: //www.fas.usda.gov.

Vassileva, Y. and Trachtenberg, E. (1999a) 'Global Agriculture Information Network Report: Russian Federation Cotton and Products' (Report #RS9064), United States Department for Agriculture: Foreign Agricultural Service: http: //www.fas.usda.gov.

Vassileva, Y. and Trachtenberg, E. (1999b) 'Global Agriculture Information Network Report: Russian Federation Cotton' (Report #RS9035), United States Department for Agriculture: Foreign Agricultural Service: http: //www.fas.usda.gov.

Vassileva, Y. and Trachtenberg, E. (1999c) 'Global Agriculture Information Network Report: Russian Federation Cotton' (Report #RS9012), United States Department for Agriculture: Foreign Agricultural Service: http: //www.fas.usda.gov.

Vassileva, Y. and Trachtenberg, E. (2000) 'Global Agriculture Information Network Report: Russian Federation Cotton and Products' (Report

#RS0026), United States Department for Agriculture: Foreign Agricultural Service: http: //www.fas.usda.gov.

Vassileva, Y. and Trachtenberg, E. (2001) 'Global Agriculture Information Network Report: Russian Federation Cotton and Products' (Report #RS1016), United States Department for Agriculture: Foreign Agricultural Service: http: //www.fas.usda.gov.

White, S. (1996) *Russia Goes Dry,* Cambridge University Press: Cambridge.

Willmott, H. (1997) 'Rethinking Management and Managerial Work: Capitalism, Control and Subjectivity', *Human Relations,* 50, 11, 1329–59.

Index

228

For Product Safety Concerns and Information please contact our EU
representative GPSR@taylorandfrancis.com Taylor & Francis Verlag GmbH,
Kaufingerstraße 24, 80331 München, Germany

Batch number: 08153780

Printed by Printforce, the Netherlands